WAR DIARY OF AN AIRMAN

FOSS

VOLUNTEER FOR FLYING DUTIES

You can be accepted

NOW

For the **R.A.F.** as a

PILOT (AGE 17¼ TO 30)

AIR OBSERVER (AGE 17¼ TO 32)

WIRELESS OPERATOR/ AIR GUNNER (AGE 17¼ TO 32)

APPLY

R.A.F. SECTION COMBINED RECRUITING CENTRE

WAR DIARY OF AN AIRMAN

Guiding the Planes that Defeated Rommel

Vivian Ridler

WITH EXTRACTS FROM THE WAR DIARY OF VIOLET BRADBY
WRITTEN ON THE HOME FRONT

EDITED AND INTRODUCED BY
Colin Ridler

THE PERPETUA PRESS
OXFORD

HALF-TITLE AND FRONTISPIECE
RAF recruitment posters produced by the Ministry of Information during World War II.

EDITOR'S NOTE

War Diary of an Airman focuses on my father Vivian Ridler's experience in the RAF during World War II, particularly the year he spent as a young man in Nigeria in 1943, during which he kept a brief daily record in a small diary. This record has been transcribed, lightly edited and annotated, and forms the major part of the text that follows. An extensive Epilogue tells the story of what befell him and other family members in the British Armed Forces during the closing years of the war: it comprises extracts from the vivid war diary of Violet Bradby, herself a novelist and the mother of Vivian's wife Anne. To set both diaries in the wider context of the war I have added a substantial Introduction and Chronology, both of which highlight the importance of the so-called Takoradi Route – the aircraft supply route for the British fighting Rommel in North Africa, which passed through Nigeria where Vivian was stationed at two of its staging-post airfields.

Vivian had grown up in Bristol, where he became close friends with David Bland. David too joined the RAF during the war: Appendix 1 consists of short extracts from some of his letters, recounting his hair-raising experiences as a navigator in Halifax bombers. I am immensely grateful to David's son, Roger Bland, for kindly supplying and allowing us to publish these previously unseen letters. Sincere thanks too are extended to Edward Wates, who has charge of the Perpetua Press imprint, for allowing its use for this publication. My cousins Diana Marchant and Hugh Bradby have been unfailingly helpful, providing key information about their respective parents, Matt Bradby and Edward Bradby. Without the support of my siblings Ben Ridler, Jane Scott and Kate Wilson, this project would never have seen the light of day. My daughter Isobel Ridler gave the invaluable perspective of a member of the younger generation to the Diary, which informed the final editing process. Hilary Bird expertly produced the index. Tracey Salt kindly transcribed and typed Violet Bradby's diary. Sally Nicholls, picture researcher, and Karin Fremer, designer, have brought their imaginative flair to the book's creation.

A CIP catalogue record for this book is available from the British Library

978-1-870882-26-2

Further copies of this book may be obtained by contacting
Ben Ridler: b.ridler@talktalk.net or
Colin Ridler: colin.ridler@gmail.com

Designed and typeset in Adobe Caslon and MT Gill Sans by Karin Fremer

Printed in Great Britain by Gomer Press Ltd, Llandysul, Ceredigion, Wales

CONTENTS

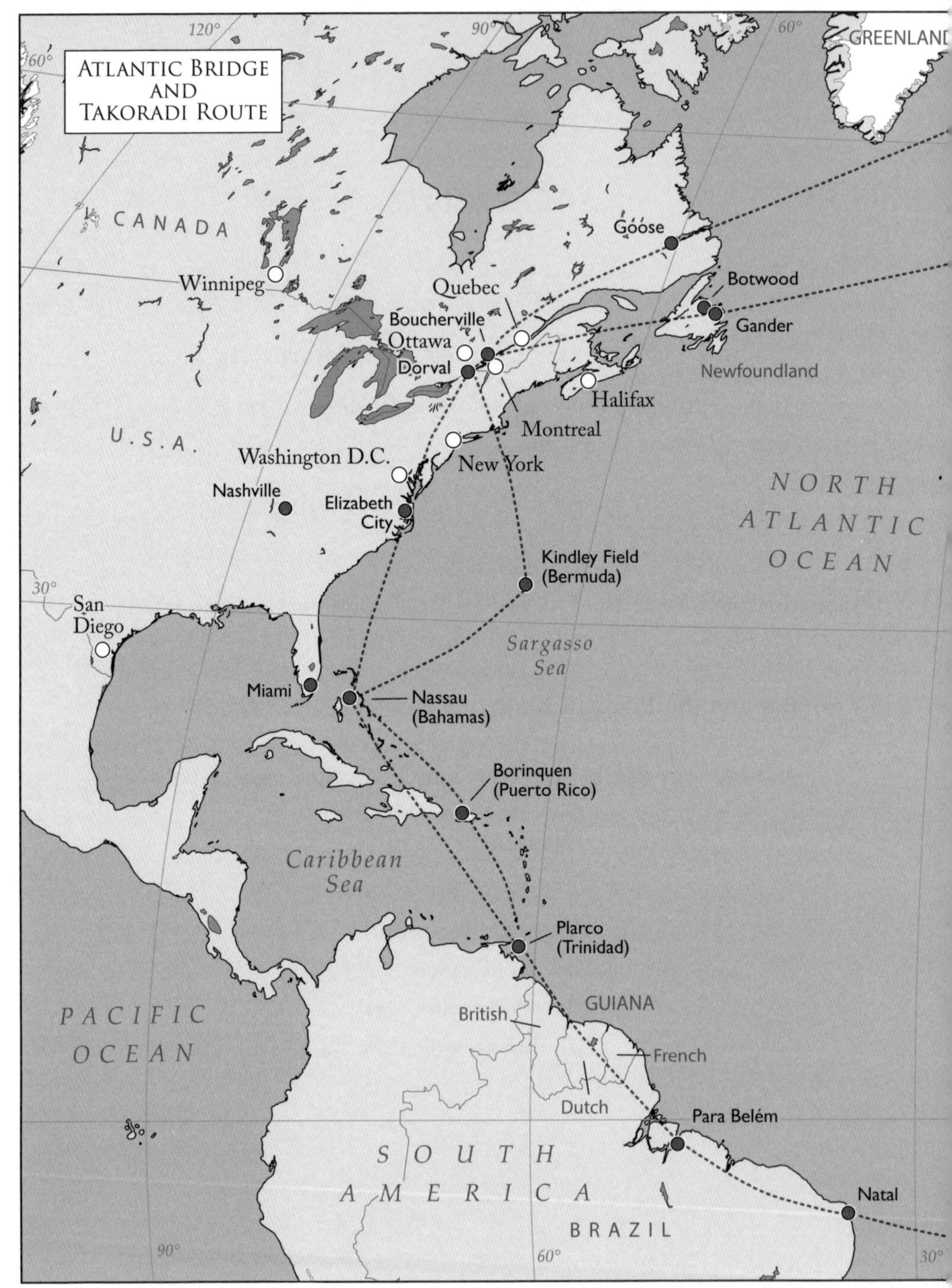

Simplified map showing the flight routes that brought thousands of vital US-made bombers and fighters across the Atlantic once America entered the war in late 1941. The North Atlantic Bridge supplied Britain itself. This book focuses on the South Atlantic Bridge, and most importantly the route from Takoradi to Cairo in Egypt where the Allies confronted Rommel. Vivian Ridler was stationed at Ikeja and Kano on this route. In Africa, only British-controlled territories are marked.

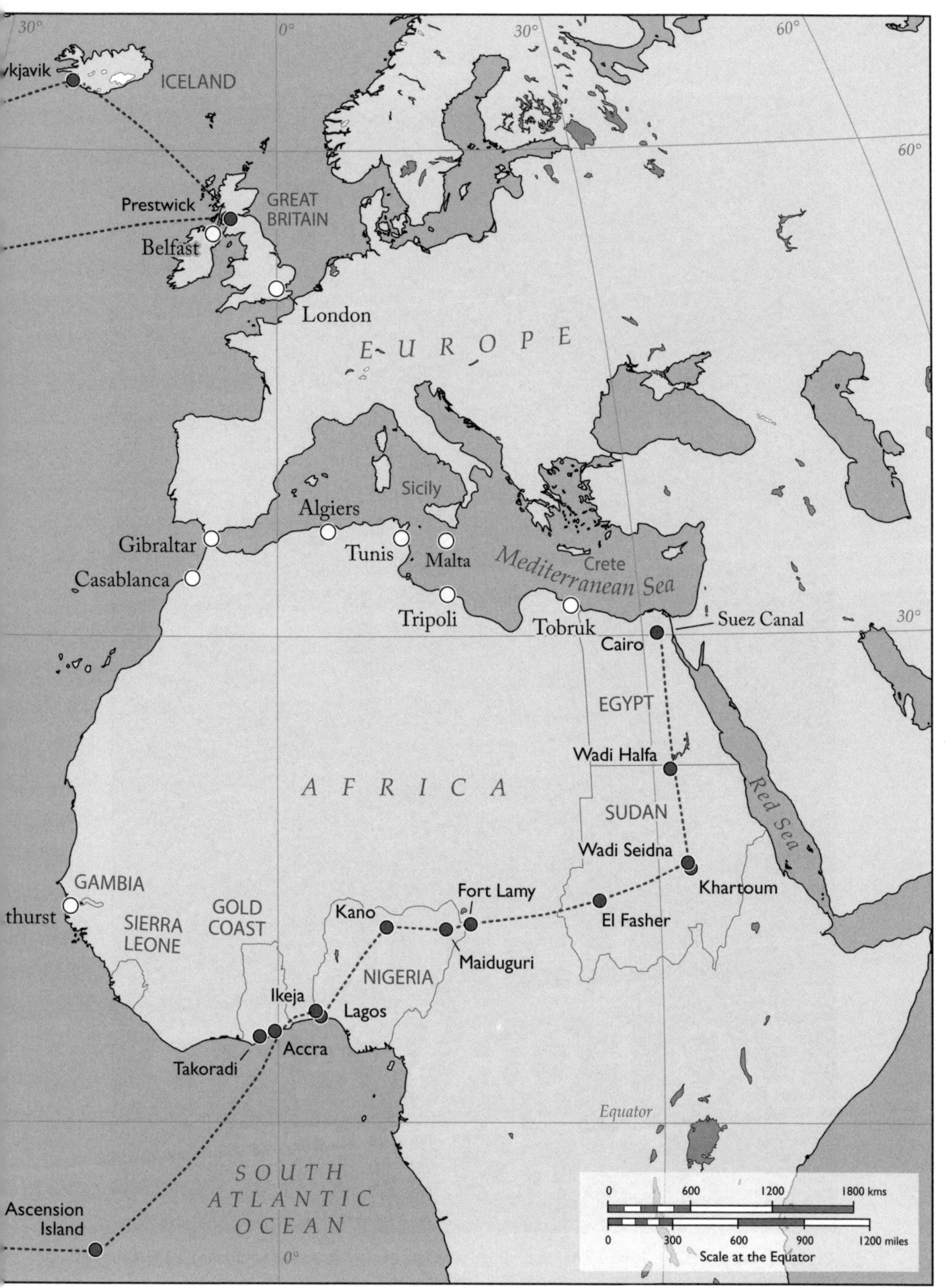

30°
0°
30°
60°
60°
30°
kjavik
ICELAND
Prestwick
GREAT
BRITAIN
Belfast
London
E U R O P E
Sicily
Algiers
Gibraltar
Tunis
Malta
Crete
Mediterranean Sea
Casablanca
Tripoli
Tobruk
Suez Canal
Cairo
EGYPT
Wadi Halfa
A F R I C A
SUDAN
Red Sea
Wadi Seidna
Khartoum
GAMBIA
Fort Lamy
El Fasher
thurst
SIERRA
LEONE
GOLD
COAST
Kano
Maiduguri
NIGERIA
Ikeja
Lagos
Accra
Takoradi
Equator
SOUTH
ATLANTIC
OCEAN
Ascension
Island
0°
0
600
1200
1800 kms
0
300
600
900
1200 miles
Scale at the Equator

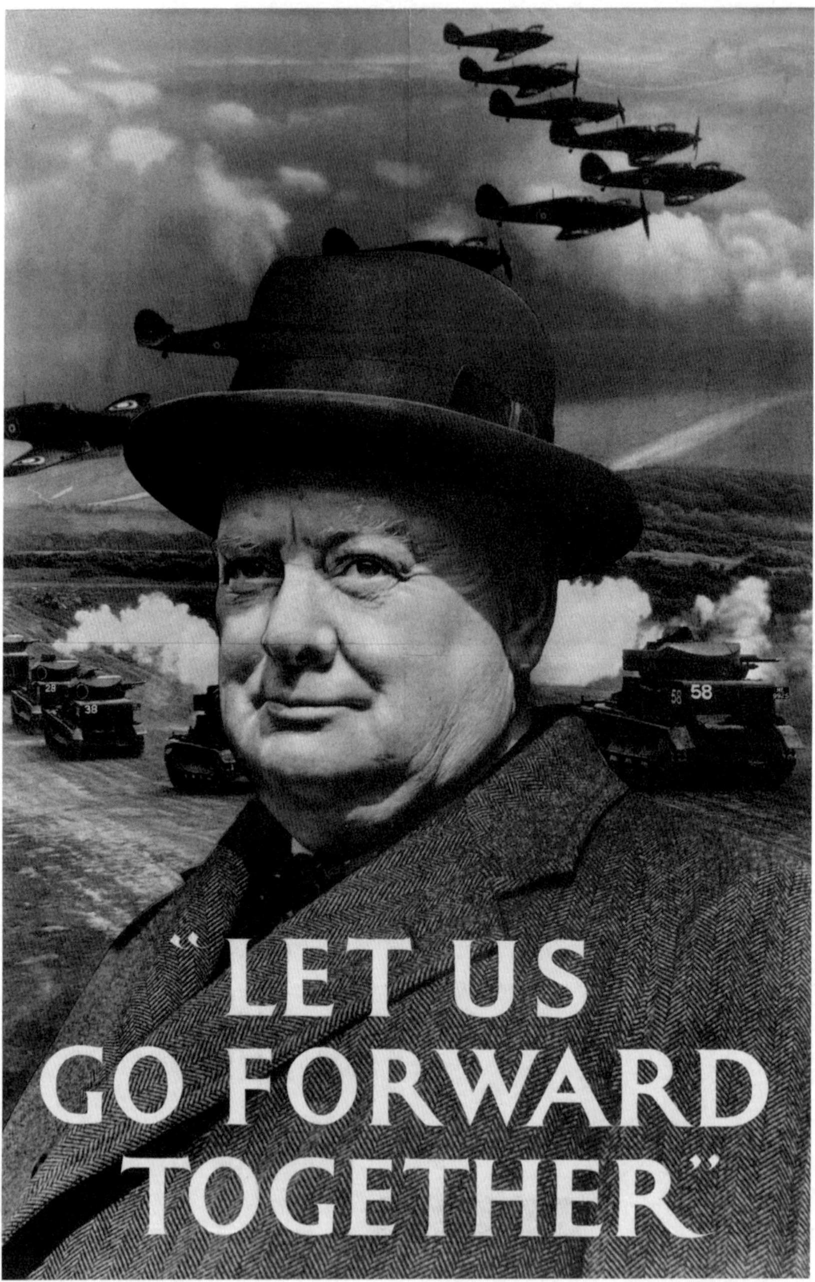
"LET US
GO FORWARD
TOGETHER"

Churchill dominates this Ministry of Information propaganda poster, just as he dominated British politics once he became Prime Minister in May 1940. He and his advisers were prescient in realizing early the importance of establishing the Takoradi Route once Italy entered the war on the Axis side, threatening British positions in the Middle East.

PREFACE

The Diary that forms the centrepiece of this book turned up unexpectedly in a desk drawer in the summer of 2020. Its author, Vivian Ridler, had lived in the house where it was found – 14 Stanley Road, a large, yellow-brick Victorian detached property in East Oxford – from 1948, when he and his wife Anne moved here on his appointment as Works Manager at the University Press. Over the subsequent decades, as Vivian became successively Assistant Printer then Printer at the Press, retiring in 1978 (he died in 2009), he and Anne brought up four children in the house: Jane (b.1941), Alison (b.1943; who now uses her second name of Kate) – both often mentioned in the Diary – Ben (b.1947) and Colin (b.1952). Although, as his children, we all knew that he had served in the RAF in Orkney, Nigeria and Germany during the war, and we enjoyed his occasional amusing anecdotes about that time (our father had a great sense of humour, teasing and laughter being a regular feature of mealtimes), we none of us knew of the existence of this little Diary recording part of his wartime service in Nigeria. He simply didn't mention it.

The Diary is certainly small enough to be easily overlooked – a mere 5 inches tall and 4 inches wide. Drafted almost daily in neat but tiny pencil writing, it is not always easy to decipher. In a way, that has been one of the main reasons for transferring it to print, for otherwise no one – except perhaps some future very diligent researcher into our father's biography – would bother to try to read it. He never wrote a memoir of his life, unlike his wife Anne, so by producing this brief account of at least part of it, we may catch a glimpse of one of the most dramatic and formative periods in his career. In its own modest way, too, the Diary sheds fresh light on a little-known aspect of the war – the crucial supply of British and American aircraft to the war front in North Africa via Ghana and Nigeria during 1941-43, when the Allies were fighting Rommel. Indeed, it is no exaggeration to say that without this supply route – which became known as the Takoradi Route for its base of that name on the Gold Coast (modern Ghana) – the Allies might well have lost the Desert War and conceivably the entire World War II itself. The Introduction below fleshes out this story, as well as giving a short narrative of Vivian's life up to that point.

To complement the Diary, relevant surviving letters of the period covered by this book (1942-46) are interwoven with the chronological account. In the Prologue Anne writes to the literary critic John Hayward – a regular and important correspondent for her during the war who valued her poetry – in July and December 1942, recounting how Vivian (who for 14 months had been at an RAF camp in Orkney) has suddenly been inoculated against malaria and despatched abroad to an unknown destination somewhere in the tropics, possibly even the dreaded Far East. Two wonderful poems of the time by Anne are included to show how she could transmute into art some of her anguish at parting, perhaps for ever, after only four years of marriage (they convey too just why she was regarded as one of the foremost young poets of her generation).

Then, for the Diary itself – which covers the calendar year of 1943 while he is in Nigeria – we have the tantalizingly few extant letters that Vivian wrote to Anne (4 out of 60), one from him to Anne's parents Violet and Kit Bradby, two more from Anne to John Hayward, but alas none of the 60 she wrote to Vivian, which perhaps lie so far undiscovered in an uncatalogued library archive.

For the story of what happened to Vivian when he left Nigeria and returned to Britain just before D-Day in 1944 we then turn in the Epilogue to Violet Bradby's vivid weekly diary of events for the final years of the war (her full diary begins at Christmas 1938). Written from the Home Front – she, Kit and Anne are living at Ringshall End, just outside Little Gaddesden in Hertfordshire – and with a novelist's eye for arresting detail, we follow the progress of the war as the Second Front opens on the continent, German flying bombs land around them, and family members – a naval officer and Royal Army Service Corps major among them – both visit and send reports of their activities. Vivian at last gains a commission as an intelligence officer and is posted at war's end to Germany. And one letter of Anne's to John Hayward expresses her joy at Vivian's safe return.

As the Introduction explains, Vivian's closest friend from his earliest years growing up in Bristol was David Bland. During the war David serves as a navigator in RAF bombers, making perilous flights over the continent until he is shot down in August 1943 and imprisoned in Stalag Luft III. His son Roger Bland has kindly made a short selection from the letters David sent to his sisters between 1941 and 1945, focusing here on references to his exchanges with Vivian as well as describing two of his bombing raids over Germany and Italy. These letters form Appendix 1.

In order to provide greater depth to the story of the Takoradi Route and the aircraft that flew along it, Appendix 2 then gives details of each of the 20 planes that Vivian mentions in the Diary, from fighters such as Spitfires, Hurricanes and Tomahawks to bombers such as twin-engine Blenheims and four-engine long-range Liberators and Flying Fortresses. The four-engine Halifax bomber in which David Bland served as a navigator is also described. The appendix concludes with a list of how many of a dozen or more aircraft types were assembled at Takoradi from crates shipped there by the Allies over the base's lifetime (September 1940 to October 1943). The total is an impressive 5,262.

The story of the Takoradi Route also forms a prominent part of the substantial Chronology in the endmatter. It is striking how quickly Churchill and his advisers decided to establish the Route, during the very month of June 1940 that Mussolini brought Italy into the war on Hitler's side; for the British knew that their vital supply of oil in the Middle East was now threatened by Italian forces that would advance from their base in Libya, an Italian colony. Allied aircraft sent to North Africa from Britain could no longer easily or securely come via the Mediterranean, subject as the region was to attacks from U-boats and Italian ships and aircraft. Furthermore the resulting inability now to bring supplies safely by sea through the Suez Canal meant all Allied shipping to and from the East had for the time being to be brought round the Cape of Good Hope, necessitating a 4,000-mile journey that was risky, slow, costly in terms of precious fuel, and required an additional million tons of scarce shipping. The new Desert War simply had to be won, and for that a cross-Africa aircraft supply route was desperately needed.

In typing out Vivian's Diary, I have by and large rendered it in the manner and style in which my father drafted it – written in the moment, with all the doubts and uncertainties of a posting where at any juncture, in the 'chaos of war', commands from on high might change. Nevertheless, I know that were my father alive, he himself would have felt (particularly with dissemination of the Diary) that occasional terms used by all servicemen of the colonized in that era were now inappropriate. I have accordingly adjusted the language slightly in a few places. And days have been omitted for which there are no written entries.

There are numerous references in the Diary to people or events or books or films that may seem obscure. Here I have had the immense help of my brother Ben, who has undertaken the task of adding fascinating notes about the extraordinary range of books and films our father read or saw. More generally, throughout the relatively long gestation of this book Ben has provided the essential encouragement and critical input without which it might never have seen the light of day. I for my part have added brief explanations of RAF terms and often cryptic references, to people, to events, as well as to types of aircraft. In the last case, where strictly correct designations require hyphens (as in DC-3 for that ubiquitous transport plane), I have followed the more digestible style (ie DC3) used both by my father in the Diary and by *The Oxford Companion to the Second World War* (Oxford, 1995), a magnificently comprehensive and informative reference work on which I have drawn substantially to check many points. All these additions are shown in parentheses in smaller type.

The two poems by Anne referred to above, together with the few short lines from my mother's poetry that have been included in the Introduction, are taken from Anne Ridler, *Collected Poems* (Carcanet Press, 1994); they appear here by kind permission of the publisher, Michael Schmidt.

My sister Kate Wilson, who like Ben is far more knowledgeable about our mother's poetry than I am, has helped me engage with Anne's rich literary legacy, including the letters to John Hayward. And it is thanks to Kate and her late husband Richard – who became the owners of the family house in Stanley Road at our father's death – that both Vivian's and Violet's diaries came to light (the first part of Violet's diary of the war years, ie from 1938 to June 1943, is held in the Bradby of Hamble papers at the Hampshire Record Office in Winchester).

Jane Scott, eldest of the Ridler children and the stimulus for some of Anne's finest poems during the war, such as 'For a Child Expected', holds many of the family photographs from this period and earlier – including a vital small album of 'box brownie' photographs that Vivian took in Nigeria, which are our only visual record of his time there and several of which we reproduce in this book. My grateful thanks to both Jane and Kate for their help in very many ways.

Ben and I have shared moments of hilarity in attempting accurately to transcribe and interpret the handwritten texts in both diaries. Vivian had a most elegant italic script, easy to read when he used a fountain pen as in the letters, but less so in the Diary written in pencil. Violet used a fountain pen, but her loops and swoops for capital letters especially could be challenging. In one instance we puzzled for days over two words, abbreviated as, it seemed at first, Prof Wolf, or Inf Welf. Was the latter Infantryman Welf and, if so, why were Violet and Anne taking the children to hear or see him? It took a sudden brainwave to crack the code – of course, Inf Welf was short for Infant Welfare! Not that either of us had heard of it, nor dear reader does it feature even as an abbreviation in this particular and heavily shortened version of Violet's diary of the war's latter stages.

Colin Ridler

Established and up-and-coming figures in the world of book production enjoy an outing in the Tintern Valley during the summer of 1936. Left to right: Vincent Stuart, John Johnson (Printer to the University, Oxford), Thea Brown (artist), Vivian Ridler (aged 22, and shortly to join the Press at Oxford as Johnson's assistant), Bruce Rogers (great American typographer) and David Bland (Vivian's partner at the Perpetua Press, shortly to join Faber in their production department).

INTRODUCTION

Printer, Typographer, Airman

Vivian Hughes Ridler (1913-2009) was a young man of 29 when he began writing a daily diary of his experiences as an aircraftman in Nigeria in 1943. His father, Bertram Hughes Ridler (1865-1934), had been Superintendent of Avonmouth Docks before he fell ill and had to retire early. (On his appointment in 1917 he had been given the following encomium in a public notice: 'His pleasing personality, genial disposition, impartiality, and willingness always to hear "both sides" have made him exceedingly popular amongst shipowners, shipmasters, seamen, and the public generally.' Those attributes were inherited by his son.)

As the Diary records, Vivian wrote regularly to his mother, Elizabeth (née Best; 1883-1955), but she was something of a recluse at their house in Trelawney Road, Bristol, often obsessively scrubbing the front steps. He never felt able as a Bristol Grammar School boy to bring friends home. Happily, as we shall see, he established a close friendship with a near neighbour and contemporary, David Bland (1911-1970).

Vivian had an elder sister, Mildred Hughes Ridler (1911-1965), who may have experienced greatest satisfaction in life from the years she spent during World War II both at the codebreaking centre at Bletchley Park, and as a secretary at the BBC to the future world-famous publisher George Weidenfeld. As an extremely dynamic 20-year-old Austrian immigré who spoke many languages, Weidenfeld was hired by the corporation to help monitor enemy broadcasts and write summaries and scripts. Decades later, when I encountered him after a talk he gave at the Double Crown Club (for the DCC, see below), he remembered Mildred most warmly. She and Vivian corresponded regularly, as the Diary shows. His aunt Ada Ridler (1870-*c.*1947) also features. She must have been one of the more prominent women of her generation, achieving a degree in Philosophy and Maths at the University of Wales, a 1st-class diploma in teacher-training, and speaking in 1915 on a panel in connection with the National Bureau of Political Information for Women. Otherwise, and apart from some Best cousins living in Birmingham, Vivian seems to have had little in the way of wider family with whom he was close.

By contrast Anne Bradby, whom he married in July 1938 (and who would soon make her name as the poet Anne Ridler: 1912-2001), belonged to a large extended family. Not only did she have three older surviving brothers (Matt, b.1899, Christopher, b.1905, and Edward, b.1907 – all of whom appear briefly in the Diary; another brother, Dan, b.1896, had died on the Western Front in 1917), but there were numerous cousins, uncles and aunts, not to mention Anne's parents, H.C. or 'Kit' Bradby (1868-1947; a former housemaster at Rugby School) and Violet Bradby, née Milford (1871-1956; a writer of fiction for children). Violet's brother, Humphrey Milford (1877-1952), was the highly influential and successful London Publisher at Oxford University Press. Vivian was welcomed wholeheartedly into this new, broader family (Kit told his daughter that she had a young man 'with lots of go'), and quite clearly the feeling was reciprocated. Hence, when we read in the Diary of letters written by Vivian to Uncle H. or to M & F, he means Anne's Uncle Humphrey or her Mother & Father (his father, after all, had died in 1934).

Apart from his beloved wife, however, it was to his dear friend David Bland that Vivian felt closest, as the Diary entry for VR's 30th birthday on 2 October 1943 makes clear (David has been shot down over Germany on a bombing mission, and Vivian doesn't know whether he is alive or dead). The two shared a passion for printing and typography (the design of type or 'print' on a page). This had been nurtured many years before in their Bristol days, when in their spare time they had run a tiny private press they had named The Perpetua Press, after the new typeface Perpetua designed by the famous letterer and carver Eric Gill, whom they met. It was an exciting period to be involved in the world of books. Since the

1920s there had been a renaissance in type design, led amongst others by the bibliophile Stanley Morison, who was hired by the Monotype Corporation to advise on new typefaces the firm might introduce for its typesetting machines. Hence the creation of Gill's Perpetua, but also his now-ubiquitous Gill Sans (ie without serifs), which Vivian refers to in his entry for 4 February 1943 as he letters a truck. (As a side-note I must record how fine a letterer my father was; he could draw accurately and with ease the precise way a title page should look; and his beautiful handwriting is admired by all who see it.) All the great book designers and printers of the day – Morison, Francis Meynell, Herbert and Oliver Simon, Holbrook Jackson, Bernard Newdigate and many others – attended regular dinners of the elite typographers' club, The Double Crown Club, where they held animated discussions about printing history and the new typefaces. It was thus an honour for Vivian – who first attended a dinner in 1935 – to be elected a member, along with David Bland, in 1943 (see Diary entry for 9 November).

Although Vivian and David had established The Perpetua Press in 1931, and together produced several fine books which they designed and printed themselves (*Fifteen Old Nursery Rhymes* was chosen as one of the Fifty Best Books of the Year by the First Editions Club in 1935), it was not an enterprise that could provide a living for either of them. So Vivian took on an apprenticeship at the packaging printer E S & A Robinson in Bristol, while David studied for a degree at the university there. In 1937 David joined the production department at Faber & Faber, and that same year Vivian was lured from Robinson's to Oxford University Press by John Johnson, Printer to the University (a post that my father himself would hold with distinction for 20 years from 1958).

Johnson was a respected figure, not only head of probably the finest printing works in the world, but a scholar of typographic history, President of the Double Crown Club in 1933, and collector of printed ephemera (the Bodleian Library in Oxford now holds the major collection that bears his name). He was, however, a tyrant in the workplace. Worse still, as it turned out for Vivian, he had a jealous rivalry with the London Publisher of OUP – in the person of none other than Humphrey Milford. So, when

Johnson discovered in the autumn of 1937 that his new recruit had got engaged to Milford's niece, he promptly gave Vivian three months' notice (without revealing to the young man the real reason for his being fired). This was a devastating blow to my father – who was about to be married, yet now without an income to help support them both (moreover he had given up a promising career at Robinson's thanks to Johnson).

Although Vivian did quickly find employment with a bibliographer called Theodore Besterman in London, for whom he set up a private press in 1938, the Bunhill Press – named after Bunhill Cemetery located nearby (where Blake and Bunyan are buried) – this too proved to be short-lived. In January 1941 the press took a direct hit in a German bombing raid during the Blitz, destroying all the stock and machinery. Thus it is not surprising, after these years of uncertain employment, to read in the Diary numerous references to exchanges with a well-known and admired printer, James Shand of Shenval Press, who might offer Vivian a job after the war (as indeed Shand does at one point: 10 September).[1]

THE MAKING OF AN AIRMAN: FROM BRITAIN TO NIGERIA (AND BACK)

At the outbreak of war in September 1939, both Vivian and David joined the Auxiliary Fire Service, watching for enemy aircraft at night while continuing with their previous daytime work; they shared a flat at 15 Taviton Street in central London with Anne. She meantime carried on at the publisher Faber & Faber, where she was secretary and assistant to T S Eliot, the dominant figure in the world of modernist poetry. Other figures who joined the Fire Service included writers such as Stephen Spender, a protégé of Eliot's and a contributor to the new literary magazine *Horizon* edited by Cyril Connolly, which Vivian read avidly while in Nigeria and where some of Anne's poems were first published.

In June 1940, however, just at the time of the Fall of France to the

1 I cannot resist including for posterity my father's marginal note in his copy of James Moran's 1974 history of the Double Crown Club that, at Vivian's first attendance at a DCC meeting in 1935, Jimmy Shand – yet another member – mocking the flood of new typefaces, 'was delightfully rude to Morison and the Monotype Corporation. He called for the introduction of contraception at Monotype House, which caused SM great offence, as intended.'

German Blitzkrieg, Anne became pregnant with their first child (Jane). Feeling extremely sick and unwilling to stay at Taviton Street without Vivian once he was called up, she moved in July to her parents' retirement home in Hertfordshire, Ringshall End near Berkhamsted. Later that summer air raids on London began; in mid-September a land mine was dropped near the Taviton Street flat, forcing Vivian and David to join Anne at Ringshall, from where the young men commuted to London. In her poem 'For this Time' that October, Anne gives a vivid sense of the ghastly new reality that confronted them: 'Now country people look towards town,/ And awestruck see the crimson stain/ Spread on the cloud, and London's burning/ Say in grief as once laughing'.

David Bland was soon called up, and began his training as an RAF pilot at Pensacola in Florida. During subsequent flying practice in Texas he only just survived after his plane hit an overhead cable. For a week they feared he had lost an eye. Thankfully skilful plastic surgery reconstructed his cheek – but it meant he would become a navigator, not pilot. Appendix 1 gives brief extracts from some of his letters to his sisters as he helped carry the fight to Nazi Europe in his role as a navigator in Halifax bombers, before being shot down in August 1943 and incarcerated at the infamous prison camp at Stalag Luft III.

Vivian was sworn in by the RAF that December, and the following month, on 23 January 1941, he departed for Padgate in Cheshire to begin his training as a wireless operator, subsequently moving to Cranwell for further training. He missed Jane's birth on 4 February, and carried a keepsake of her hair with him all the way to Nigeria, placing it carefully wrapped within the pages of the 1943 Diary where it still resides. Jane's godparents at her christening in April included Anne's cousin, the composer Robin Milford; both he and his wife Kirstie were the recipients of numerous letters from Vivian during his time in Nigeria, as the Diary records. (They suffered the agonizing loss of their only child, Barnaby, aged five in a road accident in May 1941.)

Vivian now received his first posting, in May 1941, to the RAF camp at Kirkwall in Orkney, where he was put on the watch for enemy aircraft that might attack the Royal Navy's main base at Scapa Flow (where as a youthful naval officer in 1918, Anne's brother Matt had witnessed the unexpected scuttling of the German fleet after it had surrendered at the end of World War I). Here he was billeted with 18 other men – 'Neck by neck in a Nissen hut', as his wife put it in a poem to mark his 28th birthday – until the following April when Anne, with baby Jane, joined him, and they moved together into lodgings in the house of a vet. As Anne records in her *Memoirs* (2004), Vivian had made a number of friends (all called Shearer or Smith it seemed – perhaps indeed including Victor Smith, to whom he wrote often from Nigeria as the Diary shows), and they were invited to their houses. Working on a day-night shift, Vivian was often free during the day, and one person they visited was the prolific novelist and poet Eric Linklater (1899-1974). Linklater, who had served in World War I, commanded a Royal Engineers unit protecting the Scapa Flow defences from 1938 until mid-1940, and his *The Northern Garrisons* (1941), an official 'instant history', described the life of British servicemen in Orkney. It is intriguing to note that Douglas Fairbanks, Jr, like Anne arrived at Scapa Flow in April 1942.[2] The 32-year-old film star was posted to the aircraft carrier USS *Wasp*, part of an American task force supporting the Royal Navy. 'The first grey, misty sight of all those ships of two mighty navies lying there in that huge, landlocked sea shelter . . . was breath-taking', he wrote in his memoir, *A Hell of a War* (1993). 'In a setting of much drama in both world wars rode about every type of warship and naval auxiliary. . . . widely dispersed buildings ashore served as command and communications headquarters. . . . The base looked to be what, in fact, nothing in war could be – invincible.'

Vivian's life in Orkney came to an abrupt end in the autumn of 1942. He had been seeking a commission in photographic intelligence, but was to be bitterly disappointed as Anne despairingly recounts in two letters given here in the Prologue that follows this Introduction. The inoculation he received against yellow fever and new tropical kit made the dreaded Far East seem a likely destination. Yet even as his crowded troopship left

2 How Vivian, as a devoted film buff, would have loved to encounter the star of *The Prisoner of Zenda* (1937) and countless other movies! Fairbanks sailed with the *Wasp* in May 1942, bound for the Straits of Gibraltar, from where it launched more than 60 Spitfires destined for the beleaguered island of Malta. Like Anne and Vivian, he survived to see the new millennium.

Blackpool that October, the men had no idea where they were headed. Two destroyers escorted them a short way, but then their ship was left on its own. They virtually crossed the Atlantic to avoid U-boats, my father told me many years later, before swinging back across the ocean to Freetown in the British colony of Sierra Leone. They had been incredibly lucky. Both the troopship ahead of them and the one behind were sunk. Later Vivian learned that October 1942 was one of the worst, indeed possibly the very worst, for shipping losses of the whole war. The Germans had added an extra rotor to their U-boat Enigma cipher machine that February, and until December 1942 the Bletchley Park codebreakers were unable to use Ultra decrypts to track wolf-packs.

Vivian was assigned to a Belgian air squadron 349 in Hastings, Sierra Leone. (The RAF allocated the 300 numerals to squadrons operated by foreign nationals in exile, their countries having been overrun by the Nazis.) In fact, my father told me, there were few Belgians in it, except for NCOs and officers. From Sierra Leone the squadron joined another troopship as it made its way around the southern coast of West Africa, reaching the RAF staging post of Takoradi on the Gold Coast (modern Ghana) on 4 January 1943, as the Diary records. As the next section explains, Takoradi gave its name to a crucial route for ferrying aircraft (arriving from Britain and after 1942 from the United States as well) via staging posts in Nigeria and further north up to the battle front in North Africa, where British desert forces were fighting first the Italians, and then from February 1941 the Afrikakorps, with combined Italian and German divisions, under Rommel. This was why Vivian had been posted here – to help fully establish staging posts in Nigeria.

Not that such a role is immediately apparent from the Diary. For the first four months of 1943, there seems to be constant confusion as to precisely what the Belgian squadron's purpose is.[3] In the humid, tropical heat they help construct an airfield at Ikeja, near Lagos, it is true, but rumours persist that they may be posted to the Far East, or to the Belgian

3 By this time – several months after the crucial British victory at El Alamein and successful Allied landings in Morocco and Algeria – Rommel and the Axis forces were in full retreat in North Africa. Questions will therefore have arisen as to whether the Takoradi aircraft supply route and its air squadrons needed to be maintained now that the Allies could begin again to fly planes direct to the Mediterranean theatre.

colony of the Congo. They contract malaria, Vivian among them, but are kept working in the broiling sun by a brutal Medical Officer, until several of them collapse and they are allowed to go to a hospital in Ibadan. Using his skill as a typographer and artist, rather than as an airman, Vivian finds himself lettering trucks and signs. News of the birth of his second child, Alison, a redhead, on 10 April brings joy but also sadness because of his distance from home. (Anne vividly compares the two girls in her poem 'Aquarius, Aries', which begins 'My Candlemas first-born, cherry in a field of frost;/ My second, copper and gold in an Easter garden'.)

Finally, in May, the squadron is broken up, and Vivian is posted to the much more congenial RAF station at Kano in northern Nigeria, where he works as a radio operator in the Control Tower, guiding the hundreds of aircraft of all types as they come in or take off. He finds time with chums to explore the ancient walled city of Kano (see not only the memorable account in the section below, but the Diary entries for 9 October and 8 December). And he establishes an active cultural life, going to the cinema several times a week, reading countless novels, and maintaining a voluminous correspondence, especially with Anne. Jack Benny and Larry Adler fly in on 30 July to entertain them, as does the Gang Show on 23 December. Meantime Vivian keeps an ear out for news on the radio from the North African and Eastern Fronts, and listens to Churchill several times, though not uncritically (see 23 September).

The Diary ends on 1 January 1944 and, if Vivian kept a new one for that year, it no longer survives. However, he told me (in 1995) that he had returned to Britain in May 1944 via Gibraltar. They sat for a long ten days at the Rock, cooped up in their troopship – meant to hold 600 men but packed with 4,000 (or even 6,000 as Anne records in a letter of 12 August 1944 reproduced in the Epilogue) – as they waited for an escort vessel. Depth charges were dropped throughout each night around their ship to scare off possible attacks by midget submarines. (This was not an implausible threat: three Italian midget submarines had penetrated Alexandria harbour on 19 December 1941, severely damaging the only two battleships Britain had at the time in the Mediterranean.) Eventually the escort vessel arrived and they made their way along the west coast of

Britain. Moving up the Clyde during the last week of May, Vivian saw several battleships passing en route for what proved to be the D-Day assault (6 June), as well as flotillas of vessels filling every cove.

To Vivian and Anne's delight he was now assigned to the RAF camp at Westcott, within bicycling distance of Anne and her parents at Ringshall End (see Epilogue). After the German surrender in May 1945 he was busy round the clock at Westcott, using his expertise learned in Nigeria to guide aircraft repatriating British former prisoners of war, for which he was 'mentioned in Dispatches'.[4] Later that summer he applied for, and got, a commission in Intelligence, attending a short course at Caen Wood House in north London before being posted to Herne in the Ruhr. Here he spent the winter and following spring, inspecting German factories for armaments that Britain might wish to acquire, and guiding officials around the area. (Was it here or in Nigeria that he gained the RAF nickname of 'Jimmy' as in Cockney rhyming slang 'Jimmy Riddle'?) Finally, in June 1946, he was demobilized and returned to Britain.

Vivian never did join Jimmy Shand at the Shenval Press. Instead he took up the enjoyable if somewhat precarious life of a freelance designer, working for Lund Humphries and as art editor for the short-lived magazine *Contact*. This had been set up by George Weidenfeld, who thus by a curious twist of fate employed both Vivian and Mildred at different times in the 1940s (see above). (It was a small world: *Contact* shared offices with Poetry London, run by Tambimuttu, publisher of *A Dream Observed* (1941), Anne's second collection of poetry.) Vivian also derived much satisfaction from his part-time appointment as the first Lecturer in Typography at the Royal College of Art.

What happened next – his surprising return to the University Press in Oxford in 1948, where a decade later he gained the prestigious appointment of Printer – belongs elsewhere. (A full account may be found in his *Diary of a Master Printer*, The Perpetua Press, 2022.) At this juncture we need to return to tropical Africa before and during the war, for a fuller explanation as to why exactly Vivian found himself there in 1942-43.

4 In two months, some 34,600 PoWs were brought back to Westcott aboard Lancasters, Dakotas, Stirlings, Commandos, Liberators, Halifaxes, Flying Fortresses, Ansons, Mosquitoes and a Hudson – making in all 1391 separate flights of 10 different aircraft types that had to be guided in to land.

THE ATLANTIC BRIDGE AND TAKORADI ROUTE

(Many of the details about the Bridge and Route that follow are derived from the excellent HMSO publication of 1945, *Atlantic Bridge*, the 'Official Account of RAF Transport Command's Ocean Ferry', written by the historian John Pudney.)

After the fall of France to the German Blitzkrieg in May 1940, Britain and her Empire stood alone against the Nazi onslaught. The Soviet Union had a pact with Germany, which kept it out of the conflict until the German invasion of June 1941. The United States was officially neutral – though increasingly supportive of Britain – until the Japanese attack on the naval base of the US Pacific fleet at Pearl Harbor on 7 December 1941, at which point Hitler unwisely declared war on the Americans too. The beleaguered British, as an island nation, badly needed supplies of all kinds from across the Atlantic – food, weapons, ships, oil, aircraft – which, with the terms of Lend-Lease, instituted officially with the Americans in March 1941, led by 1945 to the transfer of goods, food and oil to the value of over $31 billion ($525 billion in today's money). Yet the Atlantic route was desperately vulnerable to attacks on shipping by German U-boats. Aircraft despatched by sea from the US might take three months to arrive, or not arrive at all, sent to the bottom of the ocean.

Thus arose the novel idea of setting up a transatlantic air crossing for planes (in an era well before regular transoceanic air travel), a so-called Atlantic Bridge. Late on the evening of 10 November 1940, seven Lockheed Hudson light bomber /maritime patrol aircraft flew successfully overnight from Newfoundland to Prestwick in Scotland, thus initiating a North Atlantic air bridge that – with other airfields en route in Labrador and Iceland – supplied Britain with 722 aircraft in 1941 rising to 1,450 in 1943.[5] After the Hudsons, long-range four-engine Boeing Flying Fortress and Consolidated Liberator bombers were added to the route, followed by many other types.

However, once the Italians entered the war on the German side in June 1940, their colonies in Libya and Somaliland became the focus of

5 It is an amusing fact that these first seven planes, manufactured in neutral USA, had to be drawn across the frontier into Canada by horses, so that customs proprieties could be observed.

conflict with the British, leading to extensive desert warfare in North and East Africa from 1941 onwards for which the RAF required large numbers of aircraft. While initially these came via the sea route from Britain, through the Mediterranean (and therefore vulnerable to Italian and later German air and naval attack), it saved two months' journey time and in any case was safer and more logical to fly American planes direct from the US factories to West Africa – in hops via airfields newly established in the Caribbean, Brazil and Ascension Island[6] – and from there up to the desert war front in North Africa. Aircraft from Britain, on the other hand, made the more perilous journey via the North Atlantic and round the West African coast, disassembled in crates on board transport ships.

As it happened, this West-to-North Africa route had been pioneered by the British as long before as 1925, when Squadron Leader Arthur Coningham (who was to become the brilliant commander of the Desert Air Force in 1942) made a survey flight from the Nile to Kano in northern Nigeria, which a decade later led to the creation by Imperial Airways of a regular civil air service from Cairo to West Africa. Britain had colonies in the Gambia, Sierra Leone, the Gold Coast (modern Ghana) and Nigeria. Within a month of Italy's entry into the war, an RAF advance party arrived at the trading post of Takoradi, 'built at the top of red cliffs on the outskirts of the Gold Coast bush', as John Pudney puts it in his account. His vivid description of what ensued is worth quoting at length – the creation of the base for what became known as the Takoradi Route (or to give it the more cumbersome official RAF name, the West African Reinforcement Route):

> The existing facilities had to be rapidly extended: new workshops, hangars and runways were made. Living accommodation had to keep pace with a staff which by 1942 had been increased to more than three thousand men ... The station at Takoradi ... has become an

6 A fascinating 1975 study of the origins of the Takoradi Route by Deborah Wing Ray (*Journal of American History*, vol. 62, no. 2, pp 340–358) explains how skilful not to say devious President Roosevelt was in circumventing the strict terms of American neutrality until Pearl Harbor in December 1941 brought the US formally into the war on the Allied side. In particular he secretly mandated the civilian airline Pan-American to greatly expand and strengthen its airfields in the Caribbean and Latin America, ready to take the heavy bombers that would cross the Atlantic. Indeed, after Pearl Harbor the Takoradi Route proved to be the only way for several months that aircraft of any kind could be supplied – via Africa and India – to General MacArthur's beleaguered forces in China and the Pacific that were fighting the Japanese aggressors.

air-oasis upon that tropical coast, surrounded by the palm trees and rank vegetation of the bush, by mosquito-breeding swamps and pools, and by the hazy, shark-infested sea. The climate is humid, unvarying throughout the year, with a temperature between seventy-five and ninety degrees. There is the constant threat of malaria and other tropical diseases.

Within three months of their arrival, the advance party sent off their first reinforcement aircraft. Within fourteen months, they had passed more than 1,400 'up the line' (as they call it) to the Middle East. All along the route, bases and landing grounds were extended or brought into existence. . . . The Nigerian Public Works Department, for example, has built seventeen entirely new airfields since June 1940, and carried out extensions to nine existing ones. . . .

Deliveries from Britain to the Middle East were accelerated by two months by the opening of the route from Takoradi. The deliveries fall into two categories. Most of these early reinforcements were fighters carried in crates by sea. Takoradi, and later the Apapa airfield at Lagos, in Nigeria, were used as unloading and assembly points for sea-borne cargoes. The ground crews, working fantastically long hours in the humid heat, were able to assemble a Hurricane ready to take off on test within twelve hours of its wooden crate passing over the side of the ship. Pilots had to sit in the cramped space of a fighter cockpit in blinding sun, in the harmattan dust storms, or in tropical rain, and fly thousands of miles in formation following a navigator leader in a Blenheim or Bisley light bomber. While the Mediterranean was closed, except for the gallant staging post of Malta where they handled longer-range bombers, the earlier deliveries all followed the sea-air route from Britain, by way of West Africa, to the Middle East. And wholly successful, owing to pre-war foresight, was that method of delivery.

The second category of ferry aircraft naturally developed with the creation of the South Atlantic Bridge. Besides fighters and all the light bombers which could be spared from Britain, the Desert Forces needed the Marylands, Baltimores, Bostons and Mitchells manufactured in America. For those the southern route across the Atlantic was opened [in December 1942]. They arrived in one piece, not needing the services of the assembly plants at Takoradi and Apapa. Their arrival base became Accra, a peace-time airfield built by the Gold Coast Public Works Department and extended since the war . . . to be an important airport, the Americans supplying some of their own equipment.

The reader of the Diary will appreciate how helpful this description by Pudney is to a proper understanding of both Vivian's sometimes cryptic entries, and the context of his role in the airforce in Nigeria, at first around Lagos and later in Kano. The observant reader will also note that, at Kano, he encounters even more aircraft types than those listed by Pudney, including the big four-engine American bombers the Flying Fortress and Liberator. All told, between September 1940 and October 1943 the RAF ferried more than 5,300 aircraft from West Africa to Egypt. And in 1943, 1,336 aircraft flew via the South Atlantic Bridge from the USA to West Africa, up from only 127 in 1942.

I shall include one final extensive extract from Pudney's account. It introduces the reader to some of the other places that feature in the Diary (Ikeja, Maiduguri etc.). And it is so rich in colourful description that it conveys some of the sense of adventure, even in the midst of adversity, ill-health, homesickness and often ennui, that must have been felt on occasion by a young man as he recorded his impressions over a year in this tropical land during a world war.

From Accra, the route most likely to be followed by the light bombers is first along the surf-beaten coast, dotted here and there with the square, turreted castles of the old slave traders. Following round the Bight of Benin the aircraft strike inland over mangrove swamps and put down at Ikeja, the first staging post in Nigeria, a short distance inland from the port of Lagos. Thousands of natives hacked the runways of Ikeja out of the jungle.[7] When the station was first opened the airfield-control unit inhabited a Hurricane packing case close to the runway; the staff's cinema consisted of a sheet slung between two palm trees under a roof of stars: but they were proud of their private orange grove, which supplied the messes with fruit.

The next leg of the flight is over dense jungle, becoming more sparse toward the north of Nigeria. Close to its confluence with the Kaduna River, the Niger reflects the sun with an oily bronze lustre. A landing may be made at Kano, one of the most romantic cities in all Africa, built of reddish clay and compassed by a wall eleven miles in perimeter, ruled by an Emir from a palace covering thirty-three acres. In clouds of red dust the aircraft pour in and out of the airfield, which is sited upon the sparse plain on the outskirts of the city.

7 Apapa was the original airfield for Lagos, lying close to the sea. In 1941 it was being extended by a dredger, but when this hit an enemy mine and sank a safer airfield at Ikeja, about 10 miles inland from Lagos, was established. Here Vivian was stationed from January to May 1943.

It is a mere staging post in the traffic of the air: but for centuries it has been a staging post for the land traffic which moves across the Sahara and south into the Congo, and written history carries the records of its kings back to AD 900. It is during this part of the flight that the delivery crews are most likely to encounter the harmattan, a persistent wind which raises a haze of Sahara dust sometimes to 10,000 feet, often blotting out visibility. An encounter with the harmattan always endangers convoy flying: only constant cross-checking by radio can keep the units together.[8]

They pass over dense jungle again to reach the staging post at Maiduguri, over territory which is so dense as to make a forced landing inconceivable. Possibly an aircraft which has landed at Kano, however, may fly on direct to Fort Lamy in Equatorial Africa, where the French flag flies[9] . . . Beyond, the ground grows more sparse, more yellow, and the going is steady, monotonous, gruelling.

El Fasher is the next stop – a cool rest-house built on the sand near the airfield with plain white rooms, scarlet blankets, and silent, attentive Sudanese. Into the dining room will drift men from India, from the Mediterranean fronts, from America, to spin a yarn or two before taking off again at dawn. It is an easy lap to the Nile, to the confluence of the White and the Blue Niles by Omdurman and Khartoum. Then comes the magnificent flight down the Nile; the crews cut off the corners where the river winds, but they may catch sight of the cataracts, Luxor, the Valley of the Kings. Finally the Pyramids loom up ahead, and the vast smudge of Cairo spreads beside them. The aircraft drop down over minarets to their destination.

For a vivid first-hand account of flying the whole Takoradi Route as a ferry pilot, the reader is referred to Humphrey Wynn's *Wings Without Weapons* (2008). Wynn spent a year on the Route from December 1941 ferrying mostly Hurricanes and later Kittyhawks in convoys of eight fighters at a time – experiencing four crashes all told and malaria – before progressing to an Aircraft Delivery Unit near Cairo that took planes of many types along the North African coast right up to the war frontline. In 1941 Wynn encountered the Middle East Air Force Commander-in-Chief,

8 Britain's wartime Foreign Secretary, Anthony Eden, later wrote in his *Memoirs: The Reckoning* (1965, p. 166): 'Aircraft flying to Egypt across Africa on the Takoradi Route at times sucked into their engines so much sand that they had to be stripped right down.'
9 From August 1940 this was de Gaulle's Free French flag, not that of the Vichy French who collaborated with the Nazis. Thanks to this development ferry aircraft on the Takoradi Route were able to refuel at Fort Lamy; without it the Route might not have functioned.

Air Marshall Sir Arthur Tedder, who told him that the Takoradi Route ferry pilots were 'our lifeline'. Indeed Montgomery's victory at El Alamein in November 1942 could scarcely have been achieved without the 530 aircraft Tedder was now able to throw into the fight, giving vital air superiority over the Germans.

The Takoradi Route, developed and constantly adjusted through painstaking planning and the hard labour of thousands of ground staff and hundreds of brave pilots during the three years from 1940, had fully proved its worth. Without it the North African campaign and perhaps the entire war would have been lost.

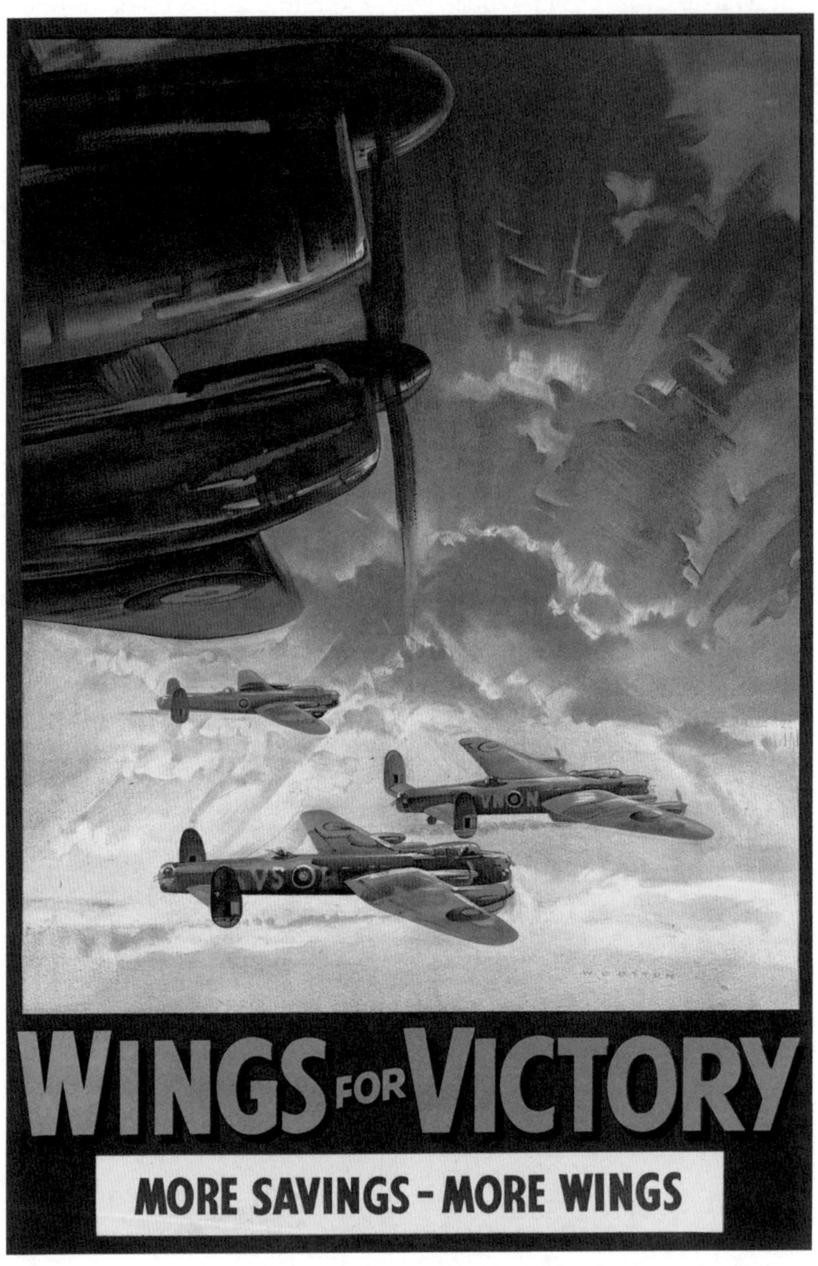
WINGS FOR VICTORY
MORE SAVINGS - MORE WINGS

The importance of air power in the conflict is emphasized in this British propaganda poster. Both Vivian and his closest friend David Bland became RAF recruits.

PROLOGUE

News of a Posting Overseas

As we saw in the Introduction Vivian had joined the RAF in January 1941, and been posted to Orkney as a wireless operator the following May. Here he was stationed at an RAF camp protecting the vital Royal Navy base at Scapa Flow. Anne – who had since the Fall of France in 1940 moved from their London flat to live with her parents at Ringshall End near Berkhamsted – herself went up with baby Jane to Orkney in April 1942 where she could now share lodgings in a house with Vivian when he was not on duty.

The two letters from Anne which follow reveal what happened that autumn to shatter their hopes for a more fulfilling role and posting for Vivian. They are written to John Hayward (1904-1965), a highly influential literary critic. He had made his name as the editor of Donne and Swift in the early 1930s and – though afflicted by crippling and progressive muscular dystrophy that confined him from young adulthood to a wheelchair – he nevertheless through his literary acumen and wit came to be indispensable as a critic for very many writers of the period. Not the least of these was T S Eliot who, as an American by birth, relied on Hayward amongst other things to filter out any Americanisms in his poetry and prose. (After the war, they shared a flat until Eliot married in 1957.) Thus it is possible to imagine how grateful Anne felt as an aspiring young poet, when in early 1939 Hayward approached her indicating that he admired many aspects of her work – thus initiating a long period of regular correspondence that lasted essentially until she and Vivian moved to Oxford in 1948. Anne would show drafts of her work to Hayward, and found his supportive but critical insights invaluable as she came to find her own voice as a poet: not that she necessarily agreed with or adopted all his suggestions for alterations. Such frank advice was all the more valued by her since Eliot (the towering literary figure of the age for whom she worked directly at Faber from 1938 to 1940, and subsequently as an adviser) always responded to her about her poetry and plays in such an enigmatic way that she was never quite sure whether he approved or not, as her letters and later *Memoirs* (2004) reveal.

It is in this light that we should interpret the otherwise quite surprising warmth and effusiveness of her opening and closing greetings to Hayward in her letters to him. Moreover, isolated as she was in the countryside for so many years during the war – particularly during the agonizing separation from Vivian – to have John Hayward's intellectual support must have been a source of great comfort.

We are lucky to have these two letters and two other relevant ones from Anne to Hayward of 1943 which are included within the Diary below, because none of hers to Vivian during that year survive – whereas for the preceding and succeeding war years some 37 have come down to us. Sadly, only eight of Vivian's war letters survive, five of which were written in 1943 and are reproduced below.

16 July 1942
Ringshall End, near Berkhamsted, Herts

Dearest John,
This is a mere note to let you know that I am in the South again. On the first day of summer in the Orkneys, and the fourth anniversary of our wedding day, came the news that Vivian was to go overseas. We were having a picnic on Scapa Beach when we heard, so it will always be one of those marvellously cruel sunny days in my memory – how cruel, depends upon the sequel, of course. So we packed up the pots & pans in a hurry, & sent the scattered bits of our life there by post & passenger train, & travelled to Inverness, where we found that it was only a 'preliminary warning', & V was to have 10 days' leave & then

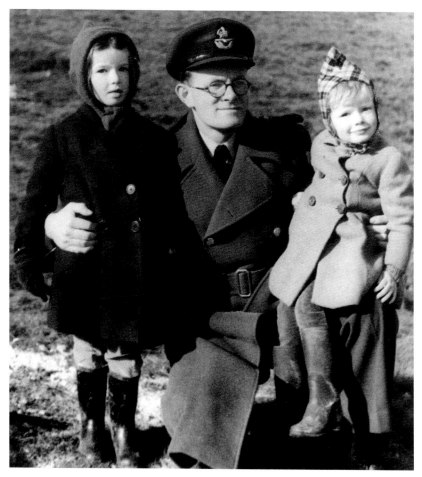

Youth and maturity: *TOP* **1** Vivian Ridler as a very young man, early 1930s.
ABOVE **2** The RAF intelligence officer with his daughters Jane and Alison (Kate), 1945-46.

Close family: *ABOVE* **3** Vivian's parents Bertram and Elizabeth about the time of their marriage in 1910. Bertram became Superintendent of Avonmouth Docks in 1917, but fell ill and had to retire early. *RIGHT* **4** Vivian's aunt Ada Ridler in 1894, aged 24. She was among the first women to gain a degree.

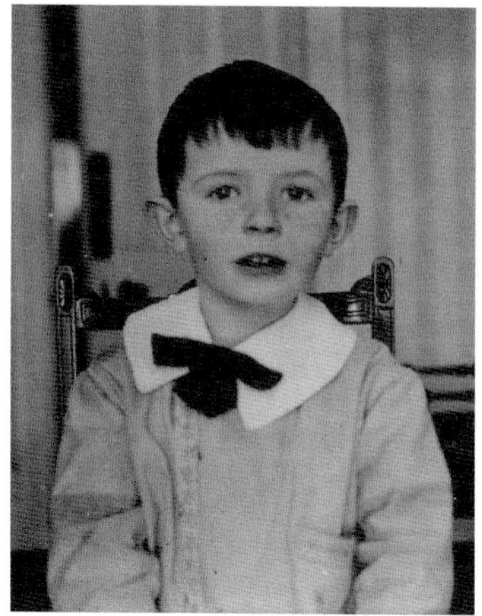

Ridler siblings: **5,7** Vivian as a boy with his sister Mildred, who was two years older. *ABOVE RIGHT* **6** During the war Mildred worked at Bletchley Park, the secret code-breaking centre.

Close friends: *LEFT* **8** David Bland and the artist Barnett Freedman relax in Anne and Vivian's flat at 15 Taviton Street, central London. *BELOW* **9** David Bland at Porlock in 1940, shortly before he joined the RAF.

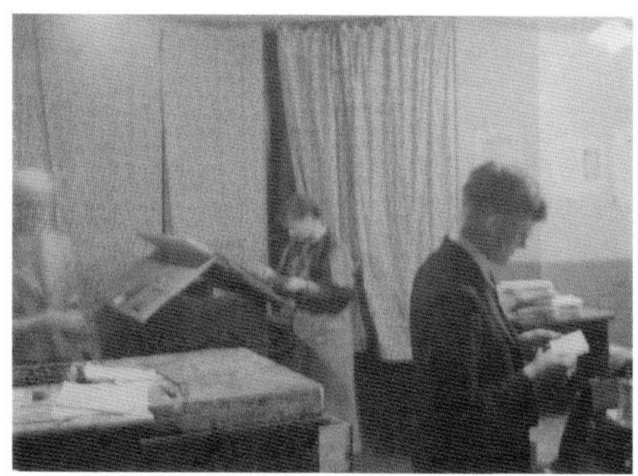

ABOVE **10, 11** The Perpetua Press in Bristol, 1935-36: David and Vivian (artist friend Thea Brown in the background of the first image) check proofs in their modest printshop at David's parental home, a vicarage.
RIGHT **12** The Bunhill Press in London, 1938: here Vivian printed books for the bibliophile Theodore Besterman until the Luftwaffe destroyed the premises in January 1941.

13 The Bradbys: a family group in 1928, with 16-year-old Anne in the centre, her mother Violet to her right, and brothers Matt and Edward to her left.

14 Two years later: Kit and Violet (seated at left and right) enjoy their newly built retirement home at Ringshall End near Berkhamsted, with their sons Christopher and Edward (latter standing), and Matt's wife Jan.

15 The intense gaze of mother and children: Vivian's fine portrait of Anne with Jane and Alison (Kate) in 1944. As the war draws to a close Anne – already by now with two well-received volumes of poetry to her name – has begun to write verse dramas for live performance and BBC broadcast.

16 Home Front family: on leave in the summer of 1942 from his RAF posting in Orkney, Vivian poses (back right) for this group photograph at Ringshall End. Nellie Pinner, housekeeper, stands beside him, with Kit Bradby to her right. Seated are, left to right, Jan Bradby, Anne with Jane on her lap, and Violet Bradby, while at their feet young Dan and Diana (Jan and Matt's children) are watched over by the family dog, Pooh.

await instructions. It is particularly bitter, because on the day the order came through, he became eligible to train as a photographer, which is what he has tried for from the beginning. We are doing our best to get the order cancelled on this account, but we have very few strings to pull. (I don't suppose the name of anyone who might help occurs to you?) Everyone at Kirkwall was puzzled at his going, because no one of his trade has been sent overseas from there, within the 14 months of his stay at any rate; when he first arrived, he & 6 others were only 'attached' to the station, & for some reason, when the others were regularly posted, Vivian remained as an attachment, in spite of requests from the Kirkwall people to have him posted. It makes one feel as if he were the luckless hero of a Kafka story; especially as his application for a commission was turned down because of his being in the wrong Grade.

If I have been tedious, forgive me: you can see that I have been turning these matters over & over in my head, however much I try to concentrate upon the incomparably greater sufferings of the Russians!

Well, thank you very much for your letter. We had better to continue to think of the Orkneys as we did, especially now that I have left them. Anyhow, I did not see the Atlantic side & the cliffs & tides of Hoy until we were coming away or heard the wind howl as you get out into the Pentland Firth.

All blessings,
Your loving
Anne

PS: We visited Russell Sq yesterday to discuss V's alphabets

22 December 1942
Ringshall End, near Berkhamsted, Herts

My dearest John,
Here are Vivian's two little alphabets, with Christmas good wishes from us both, particular blessings from me – & there should be something from Jane,

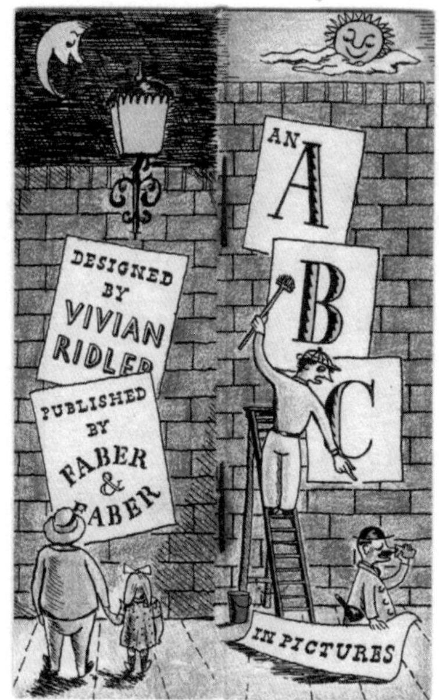

Vivian had been commissioned by Faber for their children's list to write, illustrate and produce two slim colour booklets he called *An ABC for Jane* – of which 50,000 were printed – and subsequently *An ABC in Pictures*, both priced at 6d. So popular were these booklets with his messmates in Nigeria in 1943 that several entries in the Diary record his requests home for more copies. See also pp234-35.

since after all the ABCs really belong to her, but I can't think what the right phrase would be. The Curwen Press did the lithography, & we think they made a very good job of it; the long-shaped one has lost most in reproduction, because it was meant to be a folder, but had to be made into a book to avoid the 66% Purchase Tax.

Our affairs have gone miserably. After various cat-and-mouse scares, Vivian was really expecting to escape from being a telephone robot & start his photographic course, when his Inverness HQ suddenly ordered him overseas. He rang up the Air Ministry from Kirkwall, & they immediately cancelled the order, but this was much too unorthodox for Inverness, who told V he had broken the King's Regulations, stuck an injection into him & packed him off to Blackpool. I didn't know where he was, but was assured by the Air Min that everything had been satisfactorily settled; however, after a series of telegrams from V telling me to come at once if I wanted to see him before he went, I finally went up to Blackpool, & arrived just 24 hours before he and his draft departed, on the night of Oct 24th in a gale & sleet. What an odd thing it is that one consents to these things; I am still puzzled to know what part of the will is affected, & how it controls the rest. It was a strange 24 hours too – almost happiness, since we were together after so many cross-purpose telegrams & censored letters, & because we thought we might still have a few days together; & Blackpool was such a joke, tho' a grim one, with the spray flying over the empty Lunar Parks & the Fairy Grottoes, & Epstein's Jacob & the Angel in a booth on the promenade advertised as so many Tons of Sensation. And then there were the other wives & husbands, so pathetic & inarticulate, & so patient that it made one ashamed to be bitter – not that Vivian ever was.

At that time I did not feel as if I should see him again in this world, but now – it seems a little better, since he has arrived safely in West Africa, & two months have gone by. He is somewhere in the jungle, quiet enough, but also unpleasant enough, with the sweat pouring off you by night & day, nothing to read except what you could carry with you, not a soul to talk to – not talk, I mean – & giant spiders, cockroaches, mosquitoes, jigger flies everywhere, & even the flowers full of enmity.

You will forgive my telling it all to you in such detail, since it is a comfort to me, won't you? I wish you could see our Jane, who is really very nice now. I am going to have another baby – it should be early in April. No time for more, if I'm to get this to you for Christmas Day. God be with you.

With love as always –

Anne

A POEM BY ANNE

Anne's consummate skill as a poet was to be able to transmute her (and Vivian's) feelings into art. In this wonderful, lyrical poem she shows her gift for self-expression within traditional forms, echoing folksongs ('My bonny lies…') and riddling verse across stanzas of neatly growing length that use rhymed and half-rhymed tetrameters, with a closing pentameter directly referencing Robert Burns's love poem, 'A Red, Red Rose' ('Till a' the seas gang dry, my dear, And the rocks melt wi' the sun').

Bring Back

Salt sea, sweet sea,
Bring my lover back to me.

Then will winters lose their sting,
The dumb sorrow depart from spring;
I shall rise easy in the morning;
The endless afternoons will bring
No sick weariness to me;
I shall be beautiful and free.

I shall not hate the baby's crying –
I shall hear the turtle sing.
Taste shall equal scent; rejoicing
Really be now, not past or coming;
Having outdo desire, and longing
Lead to delight; all poetry
Emerge as it was meant to be.
And to be good will be easy.

If he returns across the sea
Shall all these mercies really be?

Shall we see raindrops upward rain,
Figs grow on thorn, and an end of pain,
Because your lover comes again?
Affluent hearts have power through
Their alembic to make love new –
But likelier life goes on as before.
Love can do all, but needs more
Than fortune and a rapturous hour.
Tedious and rare tasks are done
Ere rivers run dry and rocks melt with the sun.

'In the climate of tropical West Africa no man can work as hard or as long as at home.'

WINSTON S CHURCHILL 11 MAY 1941, IN CHURCHILL *THE SECOND WORLD WAR* (CASSELL, 1950), VOL. III, P.681

THE DIARY 1943

1212727 LAC Ridler VH (Leading Aircraftman, a non-commissioned rank in the RAF – see 13 & 19 February, below)
RAF West African Forces
349 Squadron (VR crossed this out after moving to Kano, when he was no longer part of the Belgian Squadron 349)
RAF Kano

January 1943

Friday 1 January

At sea off West African coast. Strong wind blowing. After breakfast learned the description of Cleopatra from *Antony & Cleopatra* (1607). Had intended to do this for months, so felt pleased with myself.

Had a rotten New Year's Eve. Couldn't sleep in usual place on deck owing to rain. Slept on narrow promenade deck with beer bottles being broken around me.

Reading short stories by Gissing (1898 & later). Just read some Chekhov stories, including the superb 'At Home' (1897) & 'The Princess' (1886).

Acting as Librarian. Hours 10.30 to 11.30.

Chatted with Cpl Carter yesterday. Shall try to cultivate his acquaintance I think. One of the few people I like in this squadron so far.

Took part in Quiz. Dinner tonight: liver sausage, fried cod, duck, green peas, yams, apple sauce, apricot tart.

Saturday 2 January

Wrote to Anne 10.

Learnt more Shakespeare poems.

Our concert party gave a concert to the African soldiers. It was much appreciated, particularly the choruses, many of which they could sing.

Read more Gissing. On the whole not very inspiring, tho' the characters are painstakingly drawn. But after Chekhov . . .

Slept on deck. Slight shower in night.

Sunday 3 January

Took part in Spelling Bee. Tho' we won, I put up a bad show.

Tomorrow we dine below the salt, alas. Canteen equipment already issued.

Finished learning Epilogue to *Midsummer Night's Dream* (1595/6). Also Gissing *Stories*.

Monday 4 January

Docked at T this evening (VR is referring to Takoradi, a city and RAF base on what was then the Gold Coast – modern Ghana – and gave its name to The Takoradi Route: see Introduction). From the sea the coast is quite flat, without any of the beauty of Sierra Leone. It seems much cooler here in the evenings. Many rumours going around as to how long we shall stay. I hope it won't be long, because eating between decks is almost intolerable. I seem to have lost my appetite, tho' I stuffed at each meal in the dining room.

We had a little exercise, hauling the boats in before docking. The RAF station looks very fine from the sea – its NAAFI especially: reputed to have been built by the Americans (Navy Army & Airforce Institute that provided canteens, shops etc for the armed forces).

The railway is wider in gauge than the SLR.

Heavy dew in the morning. Little wind and no clouds. Slept above.

Tuesday 5 January

Hung around all day while supplies were loaded up. Everyone now feeling fed up, what with losing our dining room and being confined to a small portion of the deck.

This evening at 17.30 we went ashore, marching up the hill in the background in column of route. The roads and houses are altogether cleaner and more spacious than Freetown's. We stopped too long at the RAF Hospital NAAFI and had to return in the dark. We came back by a different way and got lost. It suddenly seemed strange to find myself stumbling along a railway line, with shouts of 'Mind the wire' and 'Mind the hole'. We did get back, sweating like horses.

Wednesday 6 January

My shirt was so soaked with dew this morning when I got up that I had to change it.

Wimpy brought up a pail of tea – very sweet, almost like syrup! Then we watched the locals arriving for work. The police look elegant in their dark blue uniforms, with crimson belts and caps.

As I was on guard this afternoon, I saw a native pedlar on the quayside. He had spread out an antelope skin in the mud under a crane. On it was a little attaché case and some beads. Half an hour later I looked down & he was fast asleep on the skin.

Reading a ponderous novel *The Son of Marietta* (1936) that I had brought from Freetown. Written by a Dutchman, Fabricius. Stodgy & slow-moving, with exasperating technical devices, continual asking of rhetorical questions, etc. But it passes the time while I am on guard. Don't finish duty till 9 tomorrow.

Thursday 7 January

The ship we are waiting for came this evening. It seems we shall get away tomorrow.

In the evening talked with Cpl Smith, Wimpy & Chris about studying some subject as English while we are at Lagos. I like the idea, tho' I doubt it would be kept up for long.

Lofty Williams showed me the first part of his detective story. It is quite hopeless unfortunately.

Friday 8 January

Pulled alongside the liner this a.m., a fascinating operation to watch. One of our men threw some officers a tin of cigarettes. They were most grateful – just like natives.

Expected to leave this evening, but for some reason it was postponed.

Saturday 9 January

Left early this a.m. Took part in Officers v 349 Quiz this p.m. Some answers: William Tell wrote 'Merrie Eng' (Wing Co.). One officer didn't know who wrote *Robinson Crusoe*. Another Wing Co. the capital of Poland.

Slept on deck. Officers falling over us for about an hour.

Thought about working for Shand (James Shand of Shenval Press – see Introduction above, and entries for 10 September & 20 October below). Think I must write him soon.

Sunday 10 January

Arrived at Lagos just before dark. Moved slowly up wide river, set with many palms in the distance. After dark spent 2 ½ hours playing at word games.

Monday 11 January

Reveille at 5.30 – quite unnecessary as it happens, because we don't leave till after dinner. Spent the morning watching the natives diving for money – one girl was particularly good. The boats they use are made from one tree trunk and carved out.

Seems much hotter today. Had my first pineapple for dinner. Not quite ripe but very good. (A favourite reminiscence of VR's, many years later, of his time in Nigeria was how tired they all became of the semi-ripe local pineapples, and how delighted they were when an American ship docked, disgorging great boxes of sweet, tinned pineapple chunks!)

Left by small lighter after dinner. Landed on jetty of Lagos Yacht Club. Elegant country houses and good roads. Many multi-coloured lizards. By bus to camp. Arr. about 16.00 (at Ikeja, where they were helping to establish a staging-post on the Takoradi Route – see Introduction). Taken straight to huts. Vegetation very thick around camp. Warned about snakes.

Tuesday 12 January

The huts here are good. Mahogany planks – 36 to a hut in 3 sections of 12. Canvas camp beds, locker, mosquito nets but no proofing. Showers and lavatories connected by covered passage. Managed to get in with friends, tho' Cocker is separated from us. Quite good NAAFI – expensive for some things such as cigs and toothpaste.

Received 3 cables from Anne, Mother, and Mildred (Mildred Ridler, VR's sister, see Introduction above).

Addressed this a.m. by our Belgian C.O. (Malengreau – see 8 May); then the Admin officer spoke & introduced some officers.

Took out *Queen Elizabeth* from Library.

Reading *Story of an African Farm* (1883, Olive Schreiner) – most moving so far.

Wednesday 13 January

Received Advent p.c. Letters 5 & 6 a, b, *Eliz. Plays*, from Anne this morning.

F.F.I. (a check for Free From Infection) at 11 a.m.

Working at preparing parade ground this p.m. Buildings at present in being are 3 packing cases. Cpl Proctor drove us back to billet in a 60ft wagon & came to grief at a corner, nearly cutting a palm tree in two.

Lecture by Col. Holman James this evening.

Started letter 11 to Anne.

Letter No. 11 from Vivian to Anne

13/14 January 1943

1212727 ACI Ridler. 349 Squadron, RAF,

West African Forces

My darling,

At last!!! Today will live in my memory, for I received the Advent Sunday p.c., letters V & VI, & the six Elizabethan plays – all at once, this morning. You can imagine how carefully I saved them until I got back to the billet. I opened the parcel first, as comparatively the least exciting. Then I read the letters, very slowly, going back to the beginning immediately to start all over again. Now I have read them I feel an imperative wish to talk with you – for hours & hours. My pen is so sluggish and I am so lazy. I shall never be able to put down one quarter of what I feel – you must imagine that, I fear.

How shall I begin? First of course, I am relieved and overjoyed to know that you are well & safe, honey. Trying to catch up with my mail, I began to think that if anything were to go wrong with the infant (Alison, due in April) *to affect you, I might not hear of it, the cables just going aimlessly up and down the West Coast. Now I feel fairly certain of being here until after the baby is born at least & so closer to you. This part of the world corresponds more with the tropics of one's imagination: date palms by the thousand, and long lines of surf licking at the beaches. We were led to expect a better climate than our previous one* (at Freetown in Sierra Leone). *So far I find it worse: in the morning there is an amazingly heavy fall of dew which leaves everything damp, practically wet. The mist caused by the sun acting on this hangs around almost until mid-day, and never disappears entirely. I don't think it can do one much harm. My clothes are always damp the next morning anyway. But it must be just the climate for rheumatism, nevertheless.*

The dew while we were in the ship was also heavy. One's bed left a dry patch on the deck when it was rolled up. Incidentally, you will remember my description of the luxurious food we had. Well, it didn't last the voyage, because the dining room was usurped by a hoard of officers. Our food below decks was such a contrast that for the first time I felt really bitter about such divergence of treatment between men & officers. Rank may differ, but stomachs don't; and when you consider that we as taxpayers indirectly help to pay their salaries, as they help to pay our pittance, such an extravagant standard of feeding is intolerable. One of the ship's officers had the astounding impertinence to protest at the scandalous right of airmen eating in such style!

Fortunately our accommodation here is splendid. I am not supposed to describe the billets in any detail, but I think I can tell you that they are made of mahogany planks that wd look superb in an English dining room if polished up. As it is, I keep imagining myself in a Swiss châlet – until I look out upon the endless date palms, or try to get my shirt off my back! We also get the native service here which we heard about coming over, but didn't get at our last station. Boys clean our shoes, make our beds, tidy lockers, sweep up, wait on us at table, and in general create the illusion that there is something to be said for service overseas! Our chief boy styles himself Manuel – why, I don't know, and appears in the morning wearing a Khaki shirt and an elegant pair of green flannel shorts with a pale green stripe; rather like Daks cut down. He talks English quite well, and has tact enough to keep us well supplied with enormous pine-apples, oranges & bananas. . . . I have been lucky to get in with people I like, so I think life will be fairly happy. In my more detached moments I stare out at the jungle, watching the local people not working and wondering whether their rhythm of life is not the right one – the only one – for this climate. We call them lazy, but if they can support life why should they behave like mad dogs and Englishmen? I know we are supposed to have all the right answers, but surely colonizing from the Phoenicians onward is fundamentally selfish? Isn't it the subtle human mind that calls up all these imperative reasons? Perhaps the speculation is too Hamlet-like to stand everyday wear. I should like to read Wilberforce on the subject.

Now we are settled I shall have plenty of hard work, I hope. At the last station I had every other day off. It might be a luxury in some circumstances, but not out here. But for the time being we have to walk over a mile to work; and when you consider going back to dinner, and the close atmosphere, you can understand how tiring that part of it is. Yet I believe conditions will soon alter. I like the look of our officers, and our senior NCOs (our Warrant Officer is an exceptionally good type, always working with us on hard jobs, not standing around giving orders; it is a simple & efficient way of getting loyalty – but how rare!) are on the whole a good crowd. Food should be better, but that never bothers me, and never will, I hope.

I will give myself the pleasure of going back to your letters. So far no letters addressed to my APO number have arrived. Some may have been lost between the dates I gave you, and some will probably arrive fairly soon. But, naturally I have to take certain of your references as read; and you may have to do the same.

What will you think of me, writing so much without having mentioned the poem? But I am the child with the Christmas tree, not knowing where to turn or how to count my blessings. The poem moved me deeply at the first reading, and it is indeed as perfect as any you have written. Of course the shorter ending is the better. It is right to sustain the lyrical outcry to the end, and the metaphysical touch of 'we may divide the sum' has the effect of snuffing it out, cutting it off. I think you should alter the 'dose to dampen lust' if only for the reason that it is speculation among 'plonks' rather than proved fact. I can't tell you how lovely it is to have another poem from you after so long. I was amused at yr mention of 'Hence, you long-legg'd spinners, hence', because I learnt that only the other day, in the ship. I also got two other fellows to learn it as well. It was delightful to hear these two, who had dropped poetry after leaving school, solemnly spouting Shakespeare! Another I now know is the wonderful Epilogue to the Midsummer Night's Dream – or have I told you that already?

Thursday 14 Jan.
As a new order has just come out withholding our address, which we had previous permission to give, I have had to re-write the first part of this letter. It is really most exasperating. It seemed such a relief to tell you where we were, but I must just bow to the inevitable.

I pored over your lovely description of our darling Jane & her new games. I have yet to learn the date when she first began to stagger about. It must be in one of your earlier letters. Really, that is the hardest part of this business, missing Janey's early development. I find it difficult to picture the cautious Jane I left behind in September dancing round the room and singing to the Byrd Mass. And soon she will be two! O, bless her from me many times for that birthday. I can feel her in my blood as I write the words, the darling.

Until yr earlier letters come I don't quite follow what has been happening with Matt & Jan, tho' I realize Matt must have been posted to Liverpool. (Matt Bradby was AR's elder brother, serving with the Royal Navy in Ceylon/Sri Lanka, then East Africa before returning to Britain aboard the battleship *Duke of York* and being posted to Birkenhead to join the staff monitoring U-boat activity in the Atlantic. Jan, his wife, had returned ahead of him in June 1942, together with their young children Dan and Diana.) *It must be trying for you all to have to deal with Diana & Jane at the same time. I wish I could send you all some gift or other. I may find something here if export restrictions allow. Meanwhile I shall probably send £10 home soon, and more a little later.*

Well my darling, unless I want a censor's suicide on my conscience, I must stop. Thank you so much, dearest, for sending me the book and other delights yet to come; and for the wonderful letters.

'So shall thy unfailing love, Guide, & support, and cheer me to the end!' (the closing words of Home at Grasmere, part of the unfinished Part One of Wordsworth's projected trilogy *The Recluse*)

Your Vivian X

NB The poem is greatly admired in the billet.

PS Reading JM Neale's life of Elizabeth. She equalled Hitler in duplicity it seems! Also Story of An African Farm. *You must certainly read this if you haven't done so. A Penguin.*

The poem of Anne's referred to by Vivian in the letters above is reproduced below in its final form, as published in *The Nine Bright Shiners* later in 1943. It is interesting to note that Anne has changed 'dose to dampen lust' to 'drug to dampen love', following Vivian's criticism of the original version – indicating just how much she valued his literary advice (evident from other letters too). John Hayward, the professional literary critic who corresponded regularly with Anne, particularly admired this poem, learning it by heart.

Remember Him

Remember him when the wind speaks over a still bed
In restless report: remember
Him faring afar in danger –
Neutral stars and enemy sea – sped
By the will unwilling, steaming against the heart, against the blood,
Faring for ever, and unimaginably far.

And this is foolishness, for
No parting is for ever,
And all divergence meets in a round world.
Yet it is now more vivid
Than hope of ultimate good
From this evil; while our dearest, filed
Numbered inoculated comforted
By a drug to dampen love, are forwarded
To endure the life-giving sun, or to be killed.

Tropic of Cancer: yet even this we willed, though not foreseeing.
It is now to remember
The glory even there
Where boredom, heartache and discomfort are.
Not in the News, where hills are plains and battles plain in meaning,
The risk all past – but a senseless, timeless war.

O all you lovers, listeners, when
The strange sea flings him back again
Into your arms, these histories hear
Only as a wind that shakes the door
And makes more grateful the good fire.
I pray that comes: but now remember
Him in loneliness and danger,
And let the wind fill your ears,

For if imagination shares
His pain, he bears only
A divided burden, and a grief less lonely.

Thursday 14 January

Working on parade ground again. Still much useless speculation as to where we are going, N or S. It doesn't look as though we shall be ready for at least six months – there is so much to do in preparing stores etc.

Censorship regulations were altered today. I had to rewrite my letter to Anne in part.

Pay Parade. £3.

Friday 15 January

Room Orderly today. Chased the house boys around. They are an artful lot.

Wrote to Mother 4.

Saw an ENSA show in evening: 'The Music Box'. Excellent conjuror & pianist. Fair comedian. (Entertainment National Service Association established in World War II as part of NAAFI to provide shows for British armed forces.)

Saturday 16 January

Marched 3 miles to Stores this a.m. Unpacking wireless equipment. There seems to be enough to equip 3 complete squadrons. Impressed by the organization at the other end – not by ours, alas.

Received a letter of enclosures from Anne. Sent books for repair.

Sunday 17 January

Worked at Stores in a.m. Finished *Queen Elizabeth* in the afternoon. Very good indeed.

Sent 1 shirt, 1 slacks, 1 hank.

Monday 18 January

Arranging stores in Signals section all morning.

Suddenly put on guard beginning at 16.00. Not too bad, tho' working 2.40 on and 4 off. Day off tomorrow.

While on guard talked with Nigerian watchman. He said faces were marked with traditional mark so that children could be bought back by parents if they had been taken for war or slavery.

Tuesday 19 January

Went to Lagos this a.m. Bought *History of Tropical Africa* at Cath. Bookshop. *History of Nigeria* & *Maps of Africa* at CMS Book. Had lunch of ham, onions, cucumber, tomato & lettuce in K. George V Memorial Gardens. Watched lizards catching & eating bluebottles. Horrible buzzing and crunching sounds!

Streets are wider & cleaner than Freetown's, & buildings better near waterfront. But local shops no better.

Argued fiercely in second-hand bookshop over *Complete Shakespeare*. Bought Penguin *Loom of Youth* (1917, Alec Waugh – elder brother of Evelyn) & *Back to Methuselah* (Shaw, 1922). Came back to Ikeja by train. Sat in guards van surrounded by locals & guinea fowl.

Wrote to Anne 12.

Wednesday 20 January

Fixed up 1084 in Officers' Mess. Started lettering trucks and lorries in the afternoon. Previous people had made a hopeless job of it.

My pillow, ordered from Manuel, came – 2/6.

Took out Shakespeare and Plutarch's *Lives* (? tr Perrin 1914) from Library.

Hear I may go on RT watch soon (presumably Radio Transmitter watch).

Planes shd arrive tomorrow.

Thursday 21 January

Continued lettering trucks. Squadron half-day, with run to Lagos. Stayed at billet to finish *The White Devil* (Webster, 1612).

Read Plutarch on Antony.

Friday 22 January

Still working on trucks, surrounded by locals, all of whom claimed to be painters. Their work suggests otherwise.

Two of our aircraft arrived today – and crashed.

Paid £6.10.

Saw *She Knew All the Answers* (1941) with Joan Bennett – awful.

Began reading *Othello* (1603) again.

Saturday 23 January

Still lettering trucks. Local said: 'He call you good massa because you laugh and talk with everyone.' They are on a good scrounge anyway.

All given large wooden lockers.

Heard of the fall of Tripoli on the 5 o'c news (part of Allied advance in North Africa against Rommel, after Montgomery's victory at El Alamein and Allied landings in Morocco and Algeria, both in November 1942).

Everyone complaining of the bullshit. Wonder if it will last? No Liberty run tomorrow because of untidy billet.

Laundry returned.

Sunday 24 January

Finished *Othello* and learnt Othello's deathbed speech.

Bull inspection at 15.00 ('Bull' – 'cleaning' in RAF parlance).

Started *Antony & Cleopatra*.

Wrote Anne 13.

Monday 25 January

Continued working in M.T. (Motor Transport). My work (ie lettering) shows improvement I think.

On guard at 4 o'c this afternoon.

In the evening the watchman brought his sister & a friend, offering them in a businesslike way at 10/- each.

Read a little of Shaw's preface to *Methuselah*.

Tuesday 26 January

Went to Lagos. Bought a large camel leather bag for 25/- & a jewelled handbag for 26/-.

Visited the US War Inf. Bureau & came away with many good specimens (ie of typography).

Dined at Tugnells House Canteen – tongue & salad; fruit salad.

Returned at 5 o'c.

Wednesday 27 January

Went on Liberty run to Lagos in evening. Saw Leslie Howard in *Pimpernel Smith* (1941 British anti-Nazi thriller, produced & directed by its star) – good & well photographed. Delightful ride back. Air very cool, quite like home.

Thursday 28 January

Finished *Antony & Cleo.*

Lettered a large board for the M.T. section.

The commission business has come up again. Doubt now whether to put in or not. Probably not, now that I have thought it over.

Began *Coriolanus* (between 1605 & 1608).

Wrote to Robin (Robin Milford 1903-59, AR's first cousin, a composer & son of Humphrey Milford, London Publisher at Oxford University Press; see also Introduction).

Friday 29 January

Tremendous fight in wash house with buckets of water – mainly between Nobby Warman (the Lacey Man) & Jack Smith.

Saturday 30 January

Inspected my documents. Nothing of any interest in them. Could not see document dealing with Cranwell marks (where VR had been on a training course, see Introduction).

Wrote to Anne 14.

Sunday 31 January

Began *Back to Methuselah.*

Many rumours flying around.

Took part in Brains' Trust against my will. Poor show.

February 1943

Monday 1 February

Rumour that we may go to Burma. Heaven forbid. Now working on sign-boards for the Orderly Room. Painted several good ones, but hampered by brush. Now have to do large fascia sign about 14 feet long.

Heard our aircrew were in New York after having been torpedoed.

Tuesday 2 February

Painted more signs for Squadron HQ. Spent afternoon looking for planks. Will have to try M.T.

Finished *Coriolanus* & *Back to Methuselah.*

Wednesday 3 February

Started on a 12 ft sign for Squadron HQ. The wood I have is called abora, & it is rather like satin walnut in texture, but whiter in colour. The local carpenter has planed it well. I can now settle down to enjoy myself.

Started *Troilus & Cressida* (probably 1602).

Thursday 4 February

Jane is 2 today.

Continued with the sign. Drew in the letters with chalk: 10" high & roughly Gill in shape (ie Gill Sans; see Introduction). Now held up for paint, as the white paint in the Stores is n/s. I nearly ruined one letter in trying to use it.

Went in Liberty to Lagos. A rotten evening. Intended to see *Dangerous Moonlight* (1941, in which aerial scenes were actually filmed in combat)) & had to see *Wizard of Oz* (1939) instead. Awful.

Friday 5 February

Paid £1 today. Otherwise did nothing except begin *The Loom of Youth*.

More bull from Clarke. He is a weak man, I fear, with no understanding of when to rebuke or praise. But I still think he is well-intentioned.

M.T. moved out today. Stores go tomorrow. Mad! Mad! Mad!

Saturday 6 February

M.T. now out in open on side of runway, in thick sand. Still unable to continue with board owing to lack of paint.

Wrote to Anne 15.

Wrote to M & F ('Mother & Father', meaning AR's parents, Violet & Kit Bradby, since VR's own father had died in 1934).

Letter No. 15 from Vivian to Anne
6 February 1943
1212727 ACI Ridler 349 Squadron, RAF
West African Forces

Darling,
Well, Jane's birthday has come and gone without any present from me, alas. Nothing I looked at seemed suitable, so you must comfort her with kisses and an extra birthday hug. I am sure she must have changed out of recognition during the past three months, and will have quite grown-up ways by the time I get back. Perhaps you will have taken some more photographs by now.

Next week I am sending off a present for you, and a leather (camel skin) travelling bag for M&F. You are not to tell them what it is, because it must be a surprise; but I am telling you because I want to suggest that they have it cloth-lined if possible since the joints don't look over-strong. I would have kept both presents for a suitable occasion, only mildew is so bad here that I feared to spoil them. As it is, I have to take all my kit out of the locker frequently, to air it; otherwise, even if it shows no mildew it acquires the most awful, musty stench! Spraying with insecticide helps to keep the smell down, tho' not entirely. Another reason why I am glad to have left the camera behind.

My letter-painting job continues. At the moment I am working on a big sign, twelve feet long. For it I managed to get a fine plank of wood, called (at any rate by the native carpenter) 'abora': it is rather like our satin walnut in grain, but paler in colour, & even green in places. It is also very soft, in common use for sheds & suchlike. I have to work with the most primitive tools, which shouldn't really matter, considering the relative importance of the work; but I am trying to make a careful job of it, and it isn't easy. My technique has much improved since I started, nevertheless.

These last few days I have been reading Troilus & Cressida *again, interspersed with Plutarch. Memories of our evening at the Westminster theatre rushed back while I was reading. It is a satisfactory play. I remember being thrilled by it when I first read it in 1932.*

'So, Ilion, fall thou next! Now, Troy, sink down!
Here lies thy heart, thy sinew & thy bone.'

And all the play with these stupendous Greek names! O, it is marvellous.

Plutarch's figures bob up & down in a sea of blood, while he, in spite of his philosophy, neither approves nor disapproves unless at some blatant treachery! I don't remember being shocked either when I did Ancient History, tho' I did question the appellation 'great' at times!

I still wait, & long for your letters. It is no good asking you again whether you are safe & well, so many months will separate me from the answer; but I pray with all my heart that you are, my darling.

Tropical kisses from your

Vivian XX

Sunday 7 February

On guard tonight. 4 hrs at a stretch. Very grim indeed.

Finished *Loom of Youth*. Read *Midsummer Night's Dream*.

Monday 8 February

There has been a row between Chambers & Clarke about my working for other sections. Clarke has taken the sign away in a huff for his own Cpl to finish. Ah well.

Nearly killed myself sawing wood for Signals Hut.

Hear we are moving to N. Africa in max. of 6 weeks. Wonder whether this is true.

Read *Duchess of Malfi* (Webster, 1612-13).

Attended first half of rhythm club meeting.

Heard C.O.'s Parade a flop.

Tuesday 9 February

Started in Receiver Trailer today. The whole thing is not too well organized, but with Wing Commander Chambers & Sgt Evans it is best to say nothing. I have a poor opinion of the latter, & he panics over trifles. His

R/T (Radio Telephony) style is bad & unnecessarily complicated. Altogether there are 5 of us in the cabin to do one simple job (ie to guide aircraft in & out of Ikeja over the radio, VR having trained in Britain as a wireless operator).

Took out Vol. I of *Men & Memories* (1932/1935, artist William Rothenstein's anecdotal recollections of figures such as Beerbohm, Verlaine, Degas, Whistler & Singer Sargent; his portrait of AR's aunt Barbara Hammond – see 25 February – hangs in Lady Margaret Hall, Oxford, where she was a fellow). I bought Vol. II in 1935, always intending to get Vol. I secondhand too. (See also letter to AR of 13 February.)

Started *Richard II* (c1595).

Read *Duchess of Malfi* in bed this a.m.

Wednesday 10 February

Plenty of panic this a.m. over aircraft control. Quite unnecessary but Chambers panics like mad. Gave it up as a bad job. Stayed in the trailer for lunch to avoid the long walk to lunch which made me very tired last night.

I was thinking today how aerodrome runways are a queer counterpart to the great landscape gardens of 18c times. The contrast of the flat, grass runway, with its tiny native figures watering the soil, makes a fine picture set against the palm trees & bush. They run for their lives when an aircraft approaches.

The station crash truck dresses its crew in scarlet shirts which makes them look quite comical, poor fellows.

Thursday 11 February

Went to the bathing pool in Lagos for the first time. Water very warm & fairly clean-looking. Bought a pair of bathing trunks in the George V Canteen for 3/11. Also had a good meal of roast chicken, salad & trifle there for 1/4.

Have not been eating any lunch for last few days as I have no appetite.

Began *Men & Memories*.

Friday 12 February

Took the Belgian flag to the tailors to have the RAF mandrils cut out & sewn on. Hoping the tailor understood as well as he said.

My sign has been completed – very badly indeed – by Cpl Cartwright. It looked well at a distance, but when I had a close look I was dismayed at the mess.

In *Men & Memories* I was sorry to see him misquote Henry James's remark about 'cadaverous charm' as 'beauty' (mentioned more fully in letter to AR of 13 February).

Finished *Richard II* and learnt one of the speeches. Also swotting some radio stuff.

Saturday 13 February

Received letters 7 & 8 from Anne. Also the 1st Alphabet (presumably the first of the two amusing alphabet booklets VR wrote & illustrated for Faber) & a letter from Mother.

Wrote to Anne 16.

Swotting for LAC now (VR was studying to gain the rank of Leading Aircraftman) & quite enjoying life in the Receiver Trailer.

Letter No. 16 from Vivian to Anne

13 February 1943

1212727 ACI Ridler 349 Squadron, RAF

West African Forces

My dearest Anne,

Earlier this week some mail came in for the squadron, but containing none for me, to my great dismay. Coupled with that came the news that mail posted in the UK between Nov 8 & Nov 20 had been lost. You can understand how depressed I was feeling. But the silver lining turned up unexpectedly this morning, when I received the first alphabet, a letter from Mother (his own mother) *(so ecstatic about you that I could have wept for joy), and your letters nos 7 & 8 of Dec 10 & 18.*

In Music Ho! *Constant Lambert said rather cleverly that Duke Ellington could be taken as the inventor of a new musical form – the 3-minute or 10-inch form. Taking a tip from him, I think I shall confine my letters to the Air Mail or 10-minute form: it suits my lethargic nature, and has the great advantage of being more quick and more certain than the usual landborne variety. If you have been getting all my letters as quickly as my Nov 27 one, we certainly cannot grumble.*

All this is a prosaic & matter of fact opening to a letter which should really be chaotic with delight! I shall spend the next few air cards in answering yours!

You were amazingly astute over the Arabian Nights, and we can take that position as now finally settled.

Now darling, I must say how wonderfully sweet of you it is to write so fully to Mother (again, VR's own mother). *I knew you wd write, but I didn't realize, as I should have done, that you wd be so VERY thorough. It makes such a difference to her, and in consequence I get lovely things to read about you from her. David* (Bland) *has called in once or twice* (ie on VR's mother, living in Bristol). *Characteristically she says he 'looked thinner'. Another typical episode describes taking her latest cat to the vet to be castrated, poor Tom. I can't help laughing at her account of such things, it is all so seriously done.*

I see you are sending me a grand set of books. As I told you, only the Eliz. Plays have so far arrived, but more mail is now expected. But I SHOULD like the History of Greece, *especially after reading Plutarch. I am in the middle of the first vol. of Rothenstein's* Men & Memories. *The second vol. I read nearly ten years ago when I bought a 2nd-hand copy in Salisbury. It is just charming, and most interesting in places, tho' he does misquote yr favourite Henry James remark into 'cadaverous BEAUTY' – much to my annoyance. He makes up for it, however, with a magnificent letter from James which begins like this:*

'Dear William Rothenstein,

I am afraid I am condemned, in answer to your note, to inflict on your artistic sense more than one shock; therefore let the outrage of this ponderous machinery deaden you a little at the start to what may follow.'

There is also a good drawing by him of Max Beerbohm, and an interesting note about his brother (Herbert Tree's) insistence that Max couldn't draw & shd learn. 'In vain I explained that Max's manner of drawing was adapted to his needs; that it was, in fact, for its purpose, excellent drawing.'

Your description of the Madges' tea party has served to whet my appetite for their acquaintance. (Charles Madge, the surrealist poet and co-founder of Mass Observation, was married to the poet Kathleen Raine from 1938 to 1942; she became Alison Ridler's godmother – see 7 June, below.) *And of course I am proud to know that Ben Nicholson likes your work. Your reference to some new paper is also interesting – as for ALL the passages dealing with our dear, darling Jane – well, there is no need for me to tell you their effect on me. How splendid that she can now enjoy picture books! And how unbelievable to a father who has only seen his daughter trample on some innocent Faber ducks! Do send me if you can a copy of Mrs Parson's 2nd alphabet (or whatever); and more copies, if possible, of my own, because several of the men would like them.*

Funny that you don't remember Berridge. He was in the next form to me, at a time when we had most of the black sheep. I looked him up once before I left England, but didn't have more than an hour or two with him. He was just the same.

Just finished Richard II. *Also learnt one of the speeches. I shall learn more soon. Quite well, & happier now that I am doing my own job again, with less bullshit. Sent off parcel last Monday. Writing again in a day or two.*

Love & inexpressible joy, my Tobie,

Vivian

Sunday 14 February

Wrote to Mother (Air).

Monday 15 February

Wrote to Anne 17 (Sea).

My day off today.

Finished *Men & Memories*.

Wrote a 'thank' letter to Diana (presumably Diana Bradby, then aged 7, AR's niece, staying with AR and AR's parents at Ringshall End in Hertfordshire, having been evacuated from Ceylon/Sri Lanka the previous year together with her mother Jan and brother Dan. See also Vivian's letter to Anne of 14 January, above).

Tuesday 16 February

Received *N.E.W.* (*New English Weekly*) (Dec. 17).

Saw another T. crack up (must refer to the US-built Texan, a training aircraft – hence the frequent crashes? The RAF and Commonwealth version was known as the Harvard).

Began Wilkie Collins's *Haunted Hotel* (1879). (Collins, 1824-89, was a friend of Charles Dickens, 1812-70, who mentored him & published his early work; his *The Moonstone*, 1868 – see 16 June – is widely referred to as the first modern English detective novel.) Took out E.E. Cummings's *Enormous Rooms* (autobiographical novel about the author's temporary imprisonment in France in WWI) from Library.

Rumours of moving have died down now, & it seems that we may stay here.

Wednesday 17 February

Hut Orderly. A native boy rushed in shouting: 'Massa, plenty big worm!' I went outside to see a crowd of Nigerians around the men on a mound of earth. One had a big snake by the tail, tugging hard while the other waited to pin its head down when it was pulled out of its hole. It was about 5 feet long with black, brown & white markings. There were 10 large eggs with it, stuck together. A man cut off its head.

Thursday 18 February

Working on a big Flight Board for the C.O. Not making too good a job of it, I fear.

Saw another T. prang.

Received photos, letters 9 & 10, & 2nd Alphabet from Anne. Quite bewildered by all the answers I shall have to give. Jane's latest photos again give me the feeling of a strange little girl, so different she looks now.

Received letter from David & Victor S. (David Bland was VR's closest friend, then serving as a navigator in RAF bombers; see Introduction, entry for 2 October and Appendix 1.)

Friday 19 February

Finished C.O.'s Board. He is more pleased with it than I am.

Pay Parade: £3.10.

Letters from Anne (Oct. 26), Ripper & David. Also a copy of *Poetry* with exciting drawings by Henry Moore. Annoyed to see Jennett has pinched his typography from me! (Sean Jennett was a typographer at Faber who later wrote *The Making of Books* (1951).)

Took 'LAC Board' (ie 'exam'), a farce really, as Chambers just asked what I had been on & then put me through. Anne will be pleased (ie that VR had now become a Leading Aircraftman).

Saw *Boys from Syracuse* (1940 US musical based on *The Comedy of Errors*). Came out before end.

Saturday 20 February

More mail: Anne's no. I. David's Orkney. Mildred I. *Horizon* (a British monthly review of literature and art, edited by Cyril Connolly and published 1939-50).

3 parcels: 2 from Anne: shaving cream; Boswell (*Life of Samuel Johnson,* 1791 – see 13 March) & Daudet (see 19 March). OUP *Elizab. Transl.* Tolstoy: *Army Life* (*Tales from Army Life* tr Louise & Aylmer Maude, World's Classics, January 1943).

Wrote Anne 18 (Sea).

Sunday 21 February

Half-day. Finished *The Enormous Room*. Started Boswell again.

Monday 22 February

Received from Anne her New Year's Eve note with many enclosures & letter no. 11. Also letter from Victor.

Wrote to Uncle Humphrey (Milford).

Still feeling sick. Took a no.9 to see if it wd help.

Tuesday 23 February

Wrote to Nellie (Nellie Pinner was the faithful cook-housekeeper to Violet & Kit Bradby at Ringshall End; she had worked briefly as a clerk for the publishers Hutchinson, in London, but had had to return to Hertfordshire to look after her father, a retired gamekeeper, after her mother's death).

Received *N.E.W.* 31.2.42.

Wednesday 24 February

Day off. Went to Lagos. Bought camel skin bag – 35/- & *ABC of English Usage* (PI Reed, 1938) – 2/6.

Good feed in King George Mem. Garden. Back by train. A woman lay on one seat with her breast out. Her child stood on the floor, its chin on the edge of the seat & sucked vigorously!

Wrote Anne 19.

Thursday 25 February

Wrote to Uncle Lawrence (Hammond (1872-1949), a social historian and highly influential political journalist who with his brilliant wife Barbara (1873-1961), younger sister of Kit Bradby, wrote *The Village Labourer, 1760-1832* (1911), followed by *The Town Labourer* (1917) and *The Skilled Labourer* (1919). Together, these three volumes by 'the Hammonds', as they were always known, shaped the modern view of the Industrial Revolution as well as pioneering what was later called 'history from below'. Vivian had read Lawrence's masterpiece, *Gladstone and the Irish Nation* (1938), back in England soon after it came out (sadly the remaining stock was destroyed in the Blitz, though it was reissued in 1964). Barbara was the first woman to achieve a First in Mods and Greats (ie Classics) at Oxford in 1896. The great historian Arnold Toynbee called the Hammonds 'a precious part of mankind's human treasure').

Clarke sent a foolish letter round the billet about saluting officers & standing to attention before N.C.O.'s. He IS a silly man.

More Belgian aircrew arrived.

Painted Signals sign. It looks well.

Friday 26 February

Next week we start a weapon training course. Rumour has it that an assault course a mile long will be included eventually. Cannot believe THAT in this climate.

Feeling less sick but still not right.

The Burma rumour came up again today. A nasty blow if true.

Saturday 27 February

Idled most of the day. Lettered some leather bags in the evening.

Still feeling slightly unwell.

Sunday 28 February

Went to Church in Lagos. Quite pleasant service, but choir dragged hymns very badly.

March 1943

Monday 1 March

According to Chambers, the curious story of the Governor of the Congo (a Belgian colony) refusing to admit this Squadron because it is mainly English is true. It is one explanation of the enigma, but I still do not believe it entirely. Surely the Belgian government in London does not take orders from a colonial governor?

Another T. (ie Texan) hit the dirt this a.m.

Started the Aircraft Control Board.

Tuesday 2 March

Cpl Wolfenden nearly fired the Armoury & all the other huts this morning. When he told me he was going to engage in 'Arson', I warned him of the Armoury. 'O, I shall only burn the brushwood in small piles' was his reply. He couldn't control the blaze which had to be put out by the fire tender.

Chambers most pleased with my Control Board.

Finished Philaster.

Still very sick.

Wednesday 3 March

Day off. Wrote to Anne 20.

Chambers added to his story re the Squadron. We were to have given protection over a new convoy across the Congo. This is just as convincing as the 'Propaganda Tour' story.

Feeling worse this evening.

Thursday 4 March

Took out Haldane's *Possible Worlds* (1927, essays on science by JBS Haldane, 1892-1964) from the Library. Now reading *Spanish Tragedy* (between 1582 & 1592, Thomas Kyd, 1558-94) with enthusiasm.

Heard news of destruction of large Jap convoy in Bismarck Straits.

Film show *Mask of Zorro* (1940). Too bored to stay long. Returned to Boswell instead.

Noted Leonardo's invention of movable bed for hand-press in *Life*: 17.7.39. See my copy.

Friday 5 March

Feeling UNUSUALLY indolent these last few days, I hope owing to not being well. My skin is now yellow, as well as my eyeballs.

Chambers is putting up the D.F. (probably Direction-finding) Station at last. The new Adjutant, when he saw this, said 'You will probably just finish it before we are disbanded.' This remark has of course set another crop of rumours going.

Williams came in drunk but was VERY funny.

Paid £4.

Saturday 6 March

Intense longing to be with Anne & Jane again today. Feeling generally frustrated & idle.

Have been overreading.

Thought about preparing a Royal College syllabus (ie typographic).

Could do with much more work.

Monday 8 March

Read a Simenon: *The Disintegration of J.P.G* (tr Geoffrey Sainsbury, 1937). Also Hazlitt's *English Comic Writers* (1819).

Stores have orders to begin repacking. The C.O. is said to have written to A.M. (Air Ministry) about getting us re-equipped & into action, complaining of the mens' health etc. Large percentage with this jaundice complaint.

Dieting & feeling better on the whole.

Tuesday 9 March

Wrote to Mother.

Wednesday 10 March

Wrote to Anne 21 (Sea).

17 Toiling in the tropical heat: Nigerian workers tar and gravel one of the newly constructed runways at Ikeja, a Takoradi Route airbase just north of Lagos, 1942-43. It was here that Vivian and the Belgian 349 Squadron arrived in January 1943.

Ikeja scenes, Vivian's snaps with a box camera: *FROM TOP* **18-21** An RAF hut; group photo, Vivian (back left) and messmates; local village hut; two of the house boys.

ABOVE **22, 23** Two views of RAF huts amongst palm trees; attempting to undertake physical work in the intense heat and high humidity of the tropics was a constant challenge. *RIGHT* **24** Observing the local wildlife proved a pleasant diversion for Vivian and his messmates when off-duty.

The wireless operator:
LEFT AND BELOW RIGHT **25, 26** Vivian at his control board.
CENTRE LEFT **27** Vivian in the camp hut, working at the desk he made himself.

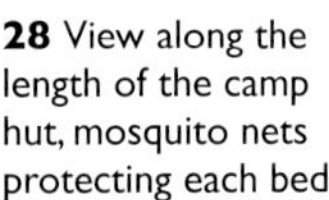

28 View along the length of the camp hut, mosquito nets protecting each bed.

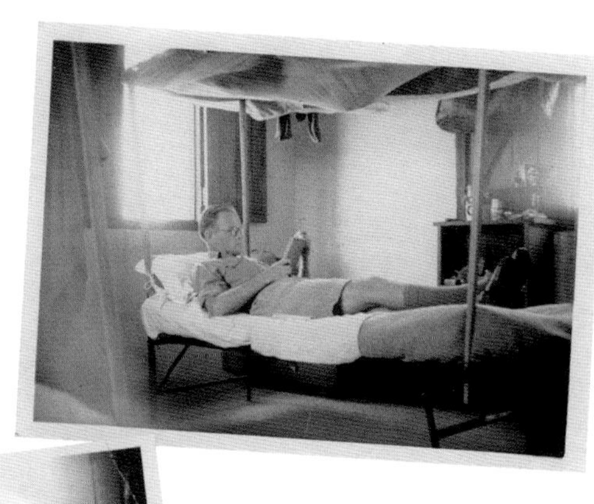

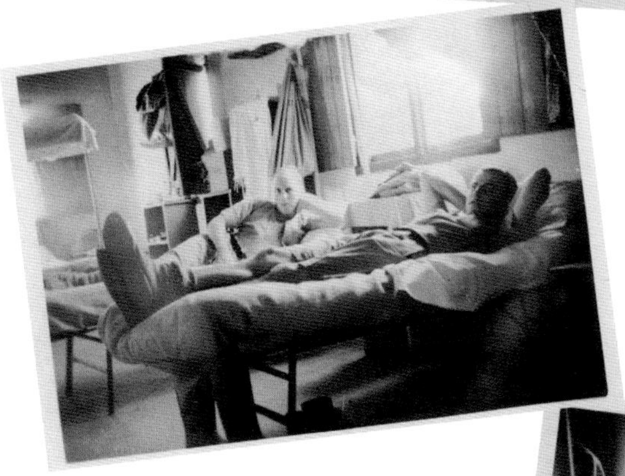

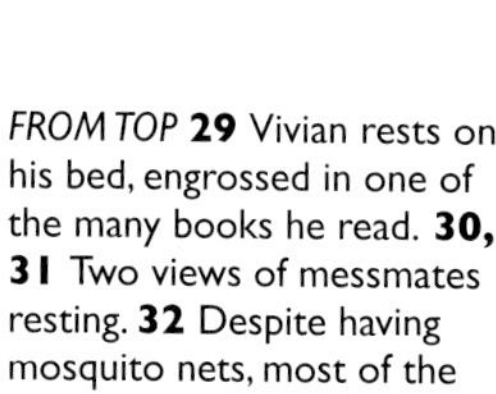

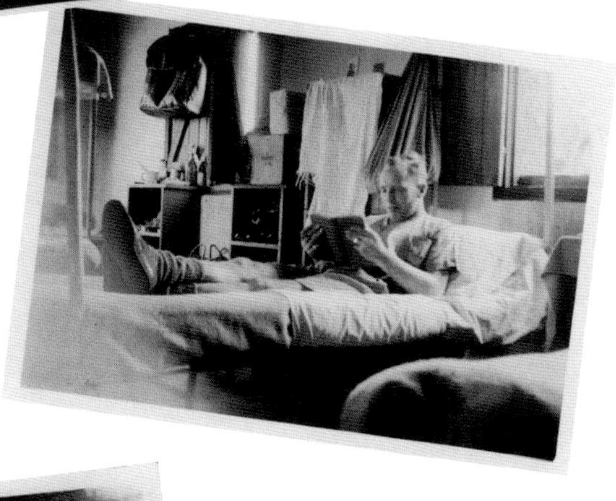

FROM TOP **29** Vivian rests on his bed, engrossed in one of the many books he read. **30, 31** Two views of messmates resting. **32** Despite having mosquito nets, most of the men contracted malaria.

33 The historic and impressive walled city of Kano: an aerial photograph taken in 1930-31. Vivian much preferred the less humid conditions here in northern Nigeria when he was transferred from Ikeja in May 1943, though there could be dramatic storms.
OPPOSITE **34** When off-duty, Vivian sometimes ventured into the city, witnessing scenes such as this or cycling round the perimeter walls.

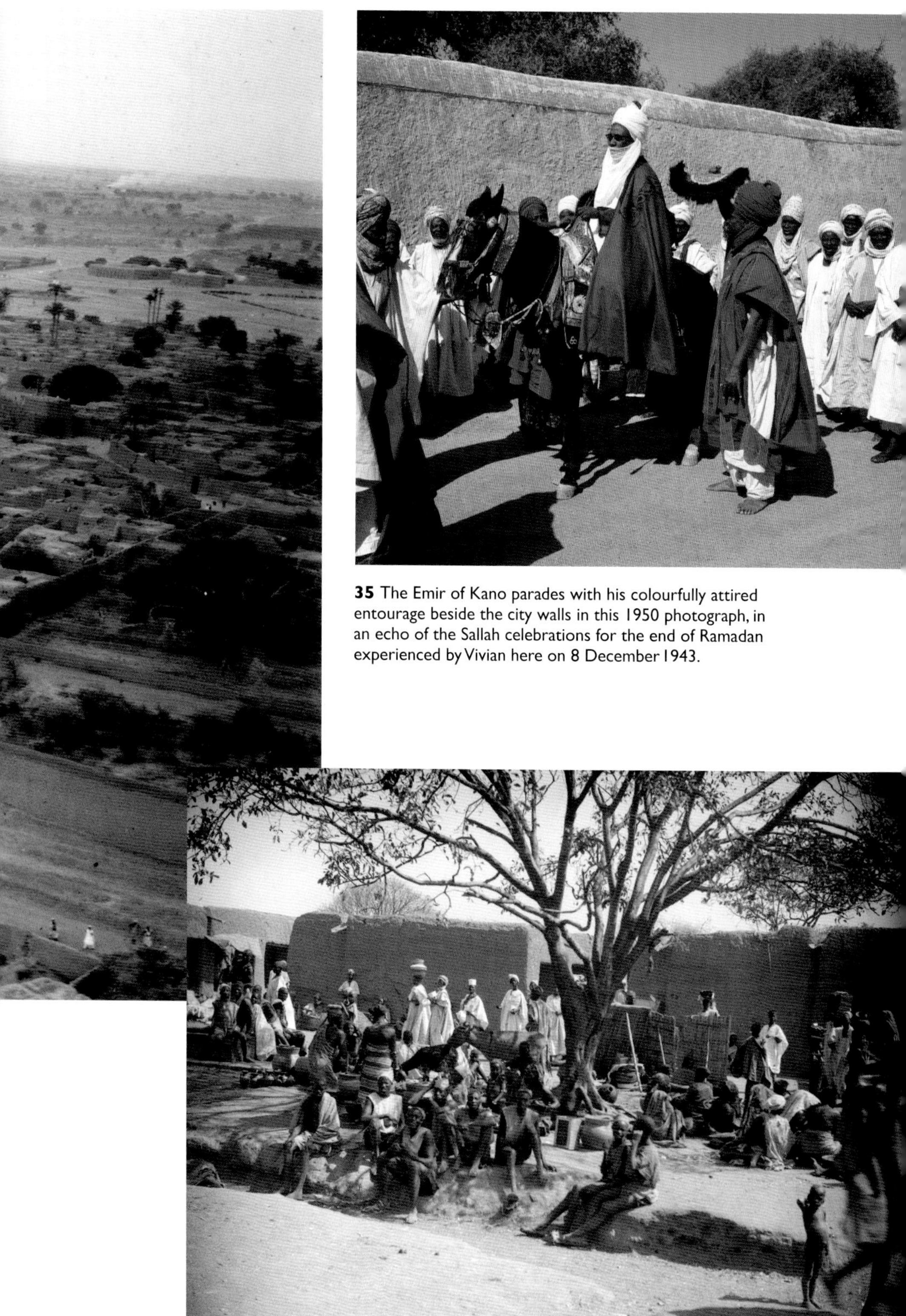

35 The Emir of Kano parades with his colourfully attired entourage beside the city walls in this 1950 photograph, in an echo of the Sallah celebrations for the end of Ramadan experienced by Vivian here on 8 December 1943.

Entertaining the forces: *TOP* **36** Jack Benny and Larry Adler, American fiddle and harmonica players respectively, flew into Kano on 30 July 1943, but Vivian – on duty – missed the fun. *ABOVE* **37** Vivian did catch the Gang Show when they performed on 24 December; note the presence in this photograph of a young Peter Sellers, fourth from right.

Have gone much yellower again today, but my appetite improved.

Delighting in Boswell.

Lofty Williams reported sick this morning & has to go to Ibadan tomorrow. This is because our Belgian M.O. (Medical Officer) is in dock (ie hospital), & the sick parade was taken by the Station M.O. who has different – & sensible – ideas.

Thursday 11 March

Reported sick this morning. The M.O. gave no immediate decision, but told us (8 of us!) we should be advised later. When I returned from work at 5.45 I had to fill in a form at once, as we are all going to Ibadan tomorrow at 7 a.m.

Started Fanny Burney's *Memoirs* (?*Memoirs of Doctor Burney*, 1832).

Friday 12 March

Left Iddo 8 a.m. 1st class coaches – seat too small for 2, too large for 1! Miles of bush with single tall trees rising from it. Abeokuta – hundreds of barn-like houses spread around a large hill formation rising out of the flat plain.

Reached Ibadan at 2.30. Ambulance took us to hospital. Situated on hill. Well laid out & QUIET. Had tea at 4. Issued with kit – heavy woollen pyjamas, shirt etc. Native Sergeant acts as Orderly & prepares food. While Sister looks in now & then, but native takes temperature & attends generally.

M.O. has not been round yet. Lights out 9 o'clock.

Decent chop of fish, beans & jelly. Also bottle of soda water.

Saturday 13 March

14 in our ward. Tea at 7 a.m. Breakfast 7.30. Tea at 10.30. Lunch at 12.30. Tea at 3. Proper tea at 4. Chop at 7. Tea at 9!!

Tremendous appetite. Feeling TOO well now.

Finished Boswell, alas. I shall dip into it again often. Curious that so devout a man as Johnson shd have bolstered his fear of death on Scripture when St John was against his argument so plainly vide Comm. for Sick.

Sunday 14 March

Finished *Letters of Madame d'Arblay* (married name of Fanny Burney, 1752-1840; *Diary & Letters of Madame d'Arblay* published posthumously, 1842-46). Re-read *Crome Yellow* (1921, 'Crome' being a lightly veiled Garsington frequented by the Bloomsbury Group; Aldous Huxley, 1894-1963). Well-written but it seems very slight.

Also read *Henry IV Part I* (by 1597).

Monday 15 March

Joy! This morning received letters 13 & 14 from Anne, enclosing letters from Barkis, Aunt Ada (Ridler – see Introduction) & Mildred. Also *N.E.W.*: 21.1.43 & *Musketeers* in French (1844 *Les Trois Mousquetaires*, Alexandre Dumas *père*, 1802-70). Letter from Mrs Smith.

Am allowed to get up now, which is a pleasant relief. Dressed in white shirt, THICK blue trousers & red tie – exactly as those at Bonar Law College (set up in 1929 by the Conservatives for the study of political science & history at Ashridge House, not far from Ringshall End).

W.O. Clarke & Alec Raeburn came in this a.m. Another T. (Texan) has been crashed, this time by P/O MacDonald, who has already pranged 2 others. He was injured but is now out of danger. Clarke brought no real news, but still says we are not staying in W. Africa. Thinks we shall go North, when our 18-month term would no longer be valid. But why worry now?

Eating tremendous meals of chicken & asparagus.

Reading Belloc (1870-1953): *But Soft*...etc (*But Soft: We Are Observed*, 1928, a satire on living targets and contemporary governments).

Tuesday 16 March

Tomorrow I go on ordinary diet. Have also asked to see the Dentist.

Started a letter to Anne 22.

Now reading *Le Petit Chose* (see 19 March) & trying to keep up a chapter a day.

Also reading *Henry VIII* (?1613), mainly because Dr Johnson agreed with Mrs Siddons that Queen Catharine was the most natural of S's characters.

The view from the ward has an almost English atmosphere. The rough grass gives an illusion of fields, while the low hills remind me of Montgomeryshire or even Malvern.

One of our orderlies calls himself Cornelius!

Wednesday 17 March

Finished letter to Anne.

Read *A Time to Keep* (1934, 2nd of 3 volumes of autobiography) by Halliday Sutherland (1882-1960, Scottish doctor who fought tuberculosis & opposed eugenics) & *Go She Must!* (1927) by David Garnett (1892-1981, novelist member of the Bloomsbury Group & co-founder of the Nonesuch Press) – this has an interesting reference to Little Gidding. Later in the evening began *Merry Wives of Windsor* (before 1597). There is little to do but read.

The Sergeant Orderly is a teacher in a Roman Catholic Mission School at Ibbo in civilian life. Looks a bit artful to me.

Thursday 18 March

Went to Dentist. Nothing wrong with my teeth, but I have to have them scaled.

Finished *Merry Wives*. Also read *The Shadow Line* (1915) by Conrad (1857-1924), a book which begins slowly but held my attention to the end. The descriptions of the sea are fine.

Friday 19 March

Getting on well with my French. Reading *Le Petit Chose* by Daudet (Alphonse Daudet, 1840-97). It is fairly simple & I find it easier to remember unusual words than I expected. The story is quite interesting in a mild way. (The title of Daudet's 1868 autobiographical memoir was his school nickname, rendered in translation as Little Good-For-Nothing or Little What's-His-Name.)

Started Beeding thriller – *The League of Discontent* ('ideal for light reading' – *Spectator* review of 26 April 1930. Francis Beeding was the pseudonym of collaborative writers John Palmer, 1885-1944, & Hilary Saunders, 1898-1951, who between 1928 & 1943 co-wrote more than 30 novels).

Saturday 20 March

An inspection from the C.O. this morning. Told I am to be discharged on Monday, but later the Dentist said he couldn't see me till then, so I may stay another day. I shan't be sorry.

Watched a cricket match in the early evening. That wicket Bowling screen made of cane. Low hills in background.

Sunday 21 March

Communion at 6.45. I was the only white man among African troops. Liked the Padre, who yawned heavily now & again to my surprise.

Monday 22 March

There was a storm last night. Smithies asked Cornelius whether the storm had abated. 'Yessir, there are more stars shining in the sky Sah.' 'Good', I said, and we went off to sleep. I was woken up by Cornelius. 'Please Sah, I know the meaning of "abated".' 'Yes, Cornelius?' 'It means "lessened", Sah.' 'Very good, Cornelius. Goodnight.' 'Yessah, goodnight.' He carries a Cassells dictionary about with him, & is easily the most charming African I have yet come across.

Finished *Le Petit Chose*. Started *Le Roi des Montagnes* (1857 novel by Edmond About).

When I returned from the cricket pitch, I was told that I should have to go tomorrow – without the dental treatment.

Tuesday 23 March

Left Ibadan on the 10 a.m. train with three sandwiches and a bottle of lime juice. Got off the train two stations from Ikeja, then got a lift back to camp.

Learned from Chris that an airmail service started from the U.K. on March 5. I hope Anne has heard of it.

No T's are now allowed to fly. That means we have 2 Harvards (the RAF name for the Texan trainer aircraft it had acquired – see 16 February).

The Eighth Army is doing well (ie pushing further into Tunisia from the southeast).

Don Hardcastle & Bill Irvine in dock with malaria.

Wednesday 24 March

Received letter 12 from Anne, sending *Horizon*, Nov & Dec; *ABC* by Nancy Innes. Encl. from Pringle, Kirstie & Thea (Alan Pringle, a Faber editor with whom AR had worked when at the firm; Kirstie Milford, Robin Milford's wife; Thea Jackson, née Brown, artist friend of VR's from his Bristol days). Last 3 photos of Jane.

Letter from Mother – Jan 9th

Letter from Victor – Jan 14th

Letter from Herbert Simon (of Curwen Press, fine art printers; and see Introduction) – Dec 11th

Gasc's *French Dictionary* (1939)

N.E.W. – Jan 14th

Wrote to H. Simon.

Saw M.O. & put on 3 days light duties. There is nothing to do anyway.

Played dominoes in evening.

Started French vocab properly.

Setback to Eighth Army (during the battle to break through the Mareth Line and drive forward into Tunisia).

Thursday 25 March

Wrote to Anne 23.

Received airmail: 20 from Anne & one from Mother i-l.

Saw a very poor Formby film: *Let George Do It* (1940, US title *To Hell with Hitler;* VR would later take his son Ben to see George Formby, 1904-61, strum & sing at the New Theatre, Oxford).

Lettered 4 boxes for Signals.

Friday 26 March

Terrific rain this morning. Great pools outside.

Wrote to Mother.

Played my first game of table tennis. Beaten by Wisken.

Apparently the Army here are going to have jungle training for a few weeks before moving off. This sounds rather ominous for 349, but we must prepare for the worst.

Practically finished lettering tool boxes.

Saturday 27 March

Day off. Wrote to Thea, tho' can't remember her married name – must guess it.

Spent most of day on French & adding to my vocabulary.

As there is no flying, all Signals busy doing woodwork. One is making an a/c, another a mirror stand, another a yacht etc.

Sunday 28 March

Made a bench-hook in 1" mahogany.

Finished lettering boxes.

Going hard at French.

Read *A Woman Killed with Kindness* (1607 tragedy by Thomas Heywood) – very dull.

Monday 29 March

Received Letters 15 & 16 from Anne.

Our aircrew are now going to work for F.C. (presumably Ferry Command). There are of course more rumours about our movements, with India being spoken of. But no one has any accurate information.

Don Hardcastle came out of dock. We went to NAAFI & played over some dull swing records, after listening to the Eighth Army's success in the Mareth Line.

Food has been better these last few days.

Took out Scott's *Journal* (1825-32, published 1890).

Tuesday 30 March

Received letter from Mother 14.2.

The M.O. Corporal told me today that we had as many as 50 in dock last week, & over 40 now. I have now got prickly heat, and to make things worse tinea (ie ringworm) has appeared again.

Still working on D.F. Control Board.

News from Tunisia very good.

Wednesday 31 March

Started letter to Anne 24.

Made a rack for bins this morning. Also started painting the Control Board.

Football match between Signals & Maintenance at 5 o'clock. We won 2-1.

Our blitz on the African house boys started. They didn't know what had hit them. But they badly needed shaking up – our own fault of course.

Letter from Anne to John Hayward

31 March 1943 Ringshall End

Dearest John,

... I should have written before if I hadn't felt so sick and tired of letter-writing lately. The chief reason for that was the sensation of pouring endless words into the wind for Vivian: letter after letter with all the trivial details of our life, & none of them reaching him. Now at last he has received some, & they have started an air-mail-form service to West Africa, so that our correspondence is less one-sided. I think from one or two hints that he is at Takoradi on the Gold Coast: it is shrouded in mist for half the day and is villainously hot and damp, but he lives in a hut made of fine mahogany planks, & has pineapples to eat....

Yes, I think this spring has seemed even more of a boon because it seemed to come unearned and undeserved. Or for me it may be partly Jane's pleasure in it: her first spring of scrabbling in the earth & carrying bunches of primroses, & fistfuls of grabbed-off flower heads. I have to lift her up so that she can touch the japonica buds & almond blossom with her forefinger. It is still more of a pleasure to hear her begin to use words: she pronounces them with the greatest care, pausing a little before the final consonant in a word like church – I get her to repeat such words as barley, honey, morning for the pure joy of hearing them so refreshed....

I expect you too were swamped by the manoeuvres, from which the countryside is just recovering. We had soldiers for a week in our garage & wood & garden: in return for our cooking their dinner & giving them hot water etc., they stole our remaining apples, and cut down & burnt Jane's swing in the wood. They left a very embittered countryside behind them.... (Exercise Spartan was the largest offensive military operation ever undertaken in Britain. Involving British and untried Canadian troops, it was designed to test the Allies' readiness for the invasion of Europe on D-Day the following year. Two forces – Eastland representing the Germans and Southland representing the Allies – faced each other across great swathes of middle and southern England, with Allied HQ in Oxford. The exercise revealed many shortcomings, as a result of which three Canadian generals were stripped of their commands. Sir Alan Brooke, Chief of the Imperial General Staff, recorded in his diary that the head of the Canadian Army, General Andrew McNaughton, had tied up his forces 'into the most awful muddle' and was 'quite incompetent to command'. See also Violet Bradby's account in her war diary, an entry from which follows this letter.)

My baby should be born in about ten days' time. It is very curious waiting for it: one knows it must happen & yet because the when & how are unknown, one feels it never will; it demands all one's activity & yet happens in spite of one; it was planned, foreseen & awaited, & yet takes matters into its own hands. You know that same sense of contradiction in the enduring of illness or suffering (John Hayward lived with progressive muscular dystrophy)*: it seems that one can choose whether to bear it or not, & yet it will be borne, whichever way one's will is set – death being more or less outside volition. . . .*

I know there is still much more to say: but for now I send you my love,
Anne

Extract from Violet Bradby's weekly war diary (written at Ringshall End)

12 March 1943

Extensive manoeuvres round us & streams of men coming for water, & to wash at the tap outside, officers to wash & shave inside. We put up an urn fire for one night & gave them dinner & a bath. Tanks allowed to go over fields & hedges, broke down our hedge in two places & damaged a good deal on poor Nicholes's farm. 1,000,000 men said to have been engaged.

April 1943

Thursday 1 April

Went to Lagos this a.m. The train unexpectedly stopped when some of our men thumbed it as they were waiting in the main road.

Bought: Groundwork of Fr. Comp. 2/-
Leather bag 3/6
War in Maps 1/6
2 watch straps 2/-
Cheroots 1/3
1 film 2/6
Tin milk 6d

Sent off letter to Anne.

Finished *Le Roi des Montagnes*.

Friday 2 April

Paid £8.

Captain Williams was particularly funny tonight. His hair has been cut convict-style, but not so short, giving him a ridiculous look. He was parading up and down the billet in his vest, holding a broom and trying to do bayonet drill. He fell over at every difficult move. He showed me his MS (4pp so far), which is quite touching in parts.

Felt dizzy after smoking one of my cheroots!

Saturday 3 April

Hut Orderly.

During the night a thief ransacked our billet & the next & the sergeant's. From ours he stole £62, including £18 from Gordon Hardcastle. My locker had been opened but my wallet containing £13 had not been touched strangely enough. As I write, investigations are being made, though I doubt whether anything will come of it. Chris lost £4.

Received James Joyce; NLT Telegram & bill from Bumpus (a well-known London bookshop on Oxford Street).

Sunday 4 April

Complained to Adjutant about telegram delay. He promised to do something about it. Incidentally he thinks A.M. don't know our address either.

Had fingerprints taken. Finished D.F. Control Board. Played cricket.

Monday 5 April

Record lot of mail in today. From Anne: 17, 18, AM 21, 22, 23, 24.

1 from Robin (Milford), David (Bland), Mildred (VR's sister), Mother.

2 from HCB (Kit Bradby, Anne's father).

1 from Shand (James Shand).

Horizon for Jan.

N.E.W 18 Jan & 25 Feb.

Books from OUP: Jane Austen, Gibbon & Dickens.

Sweated over to Stores for a pair of socks – uselessly, owing to usual muck-up.

Cricket practice in afternoon. French with Don in evening.

I feel bewildered with all the books. It will be a problem when we move.

Started making desk-top.

Tuesday 6 April

The grass runway is being widened. All down the side blue fires mark the destruction of bush & undergrowth. Scores of Africans are digging up the roots of palm trees, which are fibrous and closely knit: the red soil they dig up around the bole makes them look like enormous anthills. It is raining more heavily almost every day.

My tinea is giving me much trouble. I have also been bitten in the leg.

Wednesday 7 April

Played cricket tonight. Signals v. Maintenance. We batted first, making a total of 71. I was lbw – 0.

After the match I intended to write to Anne, and went so far as to mention a list of points, but my energy gave out at 20.30 and I retired to the NAAFI.

My new folding desk-top is a great success & has been much admired.

Our pilots have already pranged 3 Kittyhawks ferrying to Middle East (the Kittyhawk was the British name for the US-built Curtiss P40 Warhawk; see Appendix 2).

Thursday 8 April

Started backers-up course. We met in a glade, the coolest place I have struck. Taken by a pleasant Scotch corporal, though the lessons are not particularly good. Too much emphasis on learning names instead of actual handling of weapons. We use rifle, Sten and grenade. The two corporals, both Regiment fellows, shoot a bit of a line, but teach more clearly than I expected.

Owen Williams is now butterfly collecting. He spent part of the evening hoisted on two pairs of shoulders, bashing at moths on the ceiling with a butterfly net. Have promised to go with him to the Races on Saturday!

Cricket match: Maintenance all out 43.

Started long letter to Anne.

Friday 9 April

Completed letter to Anne 25.

Clarke has now been made S.W.O. (Senior Warrant Officer) and is binding the whole station. Tonight he snooped about the Dining Room to catch men with sleeves undone etc. He has already put three corporals on the hooks for slight offences.

Had to dismantle Sten blindfold. Not very successful as my gun jammed, but useful practice. Also threw a grenade for FIRST TIME! Assault course now being made.

Saturday 10 April

ALISON BORN AT 11 A.M. (added by VR later)

Received no. 19 from Anne. Also letter from Mother, 16.2.43.

Ended weapon course by shooting on the range. Distinguished myself, to my own great surprise, by winning three sweeps in succession, 8/- in all. My first score was 14/20 – no bull; 2nd 18/20 – 3 bulls; 3rd 17/20 – 2 bulls, thus beating the Station team. For the oral test I got 90%.

Also received: *Pierre et Jean* (1887 novel, his shortest, by Guy de Maupassant)
Little Book of Verse

12 *ABCs* (presumably comprising one or both of the two illustrated ABCs VR

produced for Faber)

Sunday 11 April

New baby due! Communion at 7.15 this a.m.

Wrote to Mother (Air).

Cricket practice.

Monday 12 April

Received Airmail from Anne 26. Also Airmail from Mother 28.3.43.

Started making box for my books. A crude effort, but it should do.

A Spitfire that couldn't get its undercart down circled the field; dropped its tank & made a good belly-landing without injury to the pilot.

Heard Sergeant O'Brant had been killed ferrying.

I can read *Three Musketeers* appreciably more quickly now. My vocab is almost on the 400 mark and I know the words pretty thoroughly.

Tuesday 13 April

Wrote to M&F.

Almost finished my book-box. Lined it with sheet cork which should help to keep damp out.

My moustache is coming on quickly.

Rumour (latest) is the UK on 21 June! But more Belgian personnel are arriving.

Attended sale of Sergeant O'Brant's things. Bought nothing though.

Wednesday 14 April

Lettered my box. Played cricket in the evening. It is a pity the evenings are not longer. It is delightfully cool, almost like a pleasant English summer; but darkness clamps down regularly at 7.15 or thereabouts. The rain has not been half so bad as I was expecting, though it may get much heavier.

Thursday 15 April

Wrote to Anne 26.

Went to Lagos.

Bought : Cloth 9/-

Cigars3/-

Sbroly(??) 9d

Watched cricket match between E&Ks (?) & Sergeants.

Received letter from Uncle Humphrey.

Friday 16 April

Paid £6.

Finished my book-box which now reposes under my bed. It will only just hold all my books as it is.

Learnt Auden's 'Lay Your Sleeping Head'. Took out *Tate Gallery Illustrations* & *Coastal Command* from Library.

Saturday 17 April

Roman is now back from England. Therefore we may soon hear of a possible move.

My usual day now is spent woodworking & lettering in the Maintenance Hut.

Sunday 18 April

Played cricket in the evening.

Monday 19 April

Received letter 4 from Anne, together with enclosures including a marvellous Patmore poem.

Spent the day collecting wood & making a bench.

The latest rumour with some appearance of truth is that we are to be posted back to the UK. I heard it via Cpl W. from Eg. Off (? Egypt Office); in the evening the news was also in Lagos – via Apapa (airfield at Lagos).

Took out *Notebooks of Samuel Butler*; returned *Hangman's Holiday* (1933 collection of murder mystery short stories by Dorothy L. Sayers) – it was too awful.

Tuesday 20 April

There has been a great fuss about the news leaking out, so it may be taken as genuine. A severe censorship is to be imposed on all letters & cables. Male (presumably abbreviation for Malengreau, Belgian commander of 349 Squadron; see also 8 May) was reasonably sensible, I think, in seeing that damage had already been done.

I have had mixed feelings: elation & disbelief that we SHALL get home so soon. July is being spoken of.

Football match against Transit Camp. We won again, 4-1.

Wednesday 21 April

Woke this a.m. with bad attack of screaming s. But I went to Lagos with Slim as arranged. Bought another piece of cloth, 16/3; 30/- worth of film; leather bag 15/-. Returned on ration wagon at 12, feeling much worse. Pulse & temperature both up. Saw M.O. who sent me to 18th Hospital with Observ. Mal. (observed as having malaria). Not much to choose between this place & Ibadan, though this was formerly Yabu College & thus has better buildings.

Thursday 22 April

Maundy Thursday

Found that Cpl Tarbert worked in Kirkwall early in the war (where VR had been stationed; see Introduction). He was working in the Royal Bank off Albert Street. Lodged opposite the school in one of the small cottages above photographers. But he bores me rather: WILL tell me the plots of novels he has read in the ward.

Couldn't sleep for sweating, so sat up for an hour while the night orderly tried to curdle my blood with tales of black-water fever: ''e was rotten inside, 'e was – finished'. Or again – 'When 'e came in 'e was just about ready for 'is box, you might say.' I refused to shudder.

Friday 23 April

Good Friday

Anne 27.

My blood test is negative. Man in bed next to mine told of character named Taffy Jones. Been out here 47 years, building for the Govt. When in his car he steers while a native alongside works the foot-pedals – an arrangement not without danger, especially when he turns corners. Keeps a black girl, even though he has a wife & 3 girls in England.

Also nice story of his little girl (ie the black girl). He spanked her one day, whereupon she threatened to leave 'and take me ration cards'.

RECEIVED NEWS FROM A.M. OF ALISON'S BIRTH.

Extracts from Violet Bradby's weekly war diary

16 April 1943

Anne went down to Nursing Home, The Grange NH, Berkhamsted on Friday (9 April) at 9pm & Dr Skelton telephoned next morning to say her baby had been born at 11am, both well, a little girl. Went down by bus on Sunday morning to see her, Alison weighed 6.9 lbs, a beautiful little thing with gingery down on her head. Cabled news through air mail friend of V's to him. Jane very good with us & sleeps all night.

Heavy raids with planes going over us all early night on Tuesday. Allies advancing in Tunisia & have reached Enfidavil on coast. Several Italian destroyers sunk & a battleship in Sardinian harbour. Hitler & Mussolini had conference.

30 April 1943

Fetched Anne & baby back on Saturday morning. . . . Miss Morty, a monthly nurse, came for a week to help Anne. Jane very keen on tiny baby.

7 May 1943

Miss Morty went & Miss Tookey came for a week. . . . Wonderful news from Tunisia of Allies taking Tunis & Bizerta on same day. . . . US & British seem to be working together marvellously, under Eisenhower & Alexander, Navy under Cunningham. Rommel has left & an Italian is in command.

Saturday 24 April

Received 30 from Anne.

W.O. Clarke brought in last night. Scotch journalist, Jacobs, talked on Oscar Slater. Spoke about Inspector Trench's diary, which gives motive for murder. Murderer was murdered woman's brother, a doctor by name of McBraid, whom she had disinherited in her will the previous night. Jacobs scooped an interview for B.U.P. (possibly Bristol United Press, owner of the *Bristol Evening Post*) with Slater by disguising himself as a waiter.

(Slater, a German-born Jewish dandy and gambler, was wrongly convicted of the murder of an elderly spinster in Glasgow in 1908. His death sentence was commuted to life imprisonment after a petition. Numerous journalists, lawyers and writers, including Sir Arthur Conan Doyle, took up his case, and he was eventually freed in 1928 after almost two decades of hard labour.)

Sunday 25 April

Easter Day

Wrote Anne (Air) 28.

Monday 26 April

Wrote to Edwards.

Have been feeling restless since the news about going home. We have to be in bed by 9, & every night so far I have not slept until midnight. But I have managed to begin Gibbon's *Decline & Fall* which seems to suit my mood unexpectedly.

Tuesday 27 April

Wrote to Mother.

In the evening saw *Love Crazy* (1941 screwball comedy starring Myrna Loy), out of doors in the hospital grounds. Still very funny after a 2nd view.

W.O. Clarke caused his whole ward to be confined for smoking before 12. He surprised me by talking freely about going home. Thinks we shall be kept as a Squadron in England.

Bought 2 leather bags @ 9/- each.

Wednesday 28 April

Discharged from Hospital this a.m. Recommended 3 days sick leave. Glad to be out, though it was comfortable enough.

Came back with Clarke via Lagos. He landed in trouble again through not having returned his kit.

Cpl Wolfenden & George Turner are now over at Stores packing wireless equipment.

Flight-Lieutenant Willmot died this a.m. after a mysterious scuffle during the Officers' Dance.

Thursday 29 April

Saw M.O. Given 3 days sick leave which I shall spend here.

Packed up parcel of cloth & books to send home.

Paid £4.

Friday 30 April

Went to Lagos by train. It was pouring.

Bought 1 leather bag 9/-

2 films 5/-

Cloth 16/3

Cloth 9/-

Beads 8/-

Polish etc. 2/-

=49/3

Saw the first batch of photos. Some are fair, but the box camera is too poor to make them really worthwhile.

Wrote Anne 29 (Air).

May 1943

Saturday 1 May

Spent most of the day reading a Robert Graves novel, *Antigua, Penny, Puce* (1937, a tale of sibling rivalry). I didn't realize that he wrote in this genre, light, witty & amusing.

Also took out *Zuleika Dobson* (1911, Max Beerbohm).

Feeling bad again.

Sunday 2 May

Interesting walk in the bush. Swamps with fish. Giant Travellers' Tree which gives water. Enormous tadpoles with red bodies like cherries. Took many photos. Owen & Don caught butterflies.

Monday 3 May

Received 31 & 32 from Anne. Also letter from M&F.

Finished *Zuleika* & a poster I had started on Saturday for Sports Day, showing two men holding up palm trees etc.

Felt very bad last night – temperature 99.6; but after Wolfie had given me some quinine tablets I was better this morning.

Think our departure is near now, judging by the activity.

Took photos of cook house buildings on HP2 (a type of black & white film).

Tuesday 4 May

Took photos of hut buildings.

Wednesday 5 May

Received letter 33 from Anne. Also no. 3. One from Uncle L. (Lawrence).

One from Mother. One from David.

Bought Quinine 9/-

Cloth 15/-

Soap 3/-

Pants 11/-

Shoes 2/-

Strap 8/-

Basket 6d

Plug 9d

Thursday 6 May

Hut Orderly.

Wrote to Anne 30 (Air).

Sgt Evans, like the unpleasant fool he is, has been trying to scare Signals by taking measurements for Bush hats! And talking about going East.

Wrote David.

Saw *Caught in the Draft* (1941) with Bob Hope (& Dorothy Lamour, co-star in the 'Road' films). V. good.

Friday 7 May

The rumour that we shall be broken up is now stronger than ever, and I am afraid it may be true. Although it wd be a disappointment after what we had been led to expect, there is something to be said for finishing our tour out here, in comparative peace, though it will also be v. irksome.

The air crew are all going to the Middle East. All the aircraft are being stripped, crated and sent eventually to Takoradi (the RAF base in modern-day Ghana: see Introduction).

Heard of fall of Tunis & Bizerta.

Took out *Mr Norris Changes Trains* (1935 novel by Christopher Isherwood, set in 1930s Berlin).

Saturday 8 May

Squadron photo this a.m. Sports were held on the runway at 3.30. Well organized & went without a hitch. Tea was served out of doors. At the end Malengreau made a sad little speech about the fate of the Squadron. 'I am trying to keep the Squadron together, for I should be very sorry to lose you, but time & distance are against me.' He then thanked us for our work (!) & mentioned the difficulties we had faced. Gave us Sunday off.

Sunday 9 May

Apparently the AHQ intervened after the A.M. (Air Ministry) signal posting us home. Malengreau was posted back, to reform the Squadron with a different ground crew. He has cabled refusing to do this without us. Male (?Malengreau) & Evans have both been posted to Wing (an RAF unit – VR does not specify which).

Monday 10 May

Chambers thinks that the W. Mechs (Wing Mechanics?) will go to Oshodi (not far from Lagos), where a large M.U. (Maintenance Unit) is being formed. This will not be until everything has been cleared from here, I imagine. The R.T.O.s (Radio Transmitter Orderlies) MAY go to Coastal (Command) at

Apapa (Lagos airfield), which wouldn't be bad as it is right on the sea. The runway ends only about 20 yds from the shore.

Chances of going back are now 50-50, so I have packed up the two pieces of Ishogbu cloth & a small leather bag for Mother.

Wrote to M&F.

Finished *Three Musketeers.*

Started *Decline & Fall* Vol. 2.

Sent Parcel.

Letter from Vivian to Violet and Kit Bradby, Monday 10 May 1943
1212727 LAC Ridler 349 Squadron RAF, WAF (West African Forces)

My dear Mother & Father,
Your airmail of 15 April reached me almost as punctually as usual, late last week; and I am very glad to have more news of Anne & the tiny Alison. It will be pleasant to have a red-haired child in the family, and I hope she will manage to keep her present colour when she grows up. I have already cabled Anne, and written an airmail, both saying that I received your cable in very good time, when you consider that it goes first to AHQ West Africa, then to Wing HQ, and then to my station. It was a little delayed of course through my being in hospital, but not by many hours. Air Ministry has to be notified of Alison's birth for the allowances etc., and this is done from this end. It appeared on the notice board rather humorously in this guise: LAC R etc etc: Born to the wife of, a daughter. Authority: AM Signal PX0000 etc.!

I mentioned to Anne that we had been taking some photographs. Many of them were taken while I was in hospital, but I appear in later ones, with most horrific mien, unfortunately, owing to my moustache. After seeing these pictures I lost no time in removing it, beautiful auburn tho' it was. Prints will soon be ready, and you may then judge for yourselves. We have also had a Squadron photograph taken which is quite good, although the figures are very small and in many cases only just recognizable. I will send on copies when they are ready.

The long-awaited news of the fall of Tunis & Bizerta came through over the week end. As usual, everyone is now being excessively optimistic, saying that the war is nearly over, and all that sort of thing. But I do think we now have a good chance of finishing Germany & Italy this year, or early next, partly because of the number of escort ships that can now be released for the Atlantic routes; and partly because Germany must now have an insuperable supply problem, with the Russians still in great strength in the east. A grim foretaste of what the Germans will have brought on themselves was given me by one of the Belgians with the Squadron. He was in a Spanish concentration camp early in the war. The Germans sent him a leaflet warning him that he would be shot if found in Occupied Territory. Since then he has had no word from his wife, & he fears that she has been sent into Germany for forced labour. He said to me: 'When I get to Germany, I take machine gun and I shoot anybody: women, children, anybody – I shoot them all.' It will be a very difficult thing to stop indiscriminate massacres like that, particularly if we carry out our intention of dropping light automatic weapons from the air, capable of taking continental ammunition.

Our house-boy, the cunning Manuel with green striped trousers like sawn-off Daks, has pulled one final fast one on us. He became so lazy that we threatened him with the sack. The next day a new house-boy appeared, and it was not until later in the day that we espied Manuel ostentatiously busy in the cookhouse. When asked by Chris Church why he had left, he replied darkly, 'Too much worry'. By whisking himself off to the cookhouse, he had deprived us of the opportunity to fire him.

I was relieved to know that Jane has been behaving well while Anne is away. I am now waiting to hear of her reactions to 'tiny baby': she MAY even be disappointed when she finds a non-celluloid one!

All love & good wishes from

Your affec. s-i-l

Vivian

Have now finished 3 Musketeers. *I enjoyed Vol 2 much more.*

Tuesday 11 May

From what I heard today, it seems that Signals will be kept together, though not on this station. It MAY be Oshodi, a few miles down the road, or Apapa in Lagos. I don't mind which. Apapa might be pleasanter as it is on the sea, but the billets at Oshodi are supposed to be very good. We shall do no work wherever we go, I can see that.

Understand Italian prisoners coming to Transit camp.

Started *Pierre et Jean.*

Wrote to Mrs Franklin.

Wednesday 12 May

Had first taste of a REAL storm this afternoon. A strong wind came up suddenly. The palm trees were bent over by its force. Not long after the rain came. It was much heavier than anything I have seen so far, and it lasted all the afternoon.

In the evening the atmosphere was unpleasantly humid. No one went back to work.

Heard that many Bisleys go to Turkey (the Bisley was the last variant of the British Blenheim twin-engine light bomber, and later renamed as the Blenheim Mark V; see Appendix 2).

End of Tunisian campaign announced on wireless at 10 p.m. Von Arnim (overall Axis commander in North Africa; Rommel had left on 9 March) taken with 150,000 prisoners (in fact some 240,000 captured, comparable to Axis losses at Stalingrad in February 1943).

Thursday 13 May

Day off. Wrote Anne 31.

Saw an awful film, *Kiss the Boys Goodbye* (1941 comedy) with Don Ameche & Mary Martin.

Received a prize of 6 linen handkerchiefs from the C.O. for winning Signals team in league competition. As there were 15 of us & the hanks must have cost 1/9 each, this was another generous act by our C.O., who spent £30 on Sports prizes alone.

Friday 14 May

Paid £4.4.

Many postings through today, Maiduguri, Kano, 298 & Dongla in Cameroon, Ponte Noir in French Equatorial Africa. Nothing through for Signals. Chambers still thinks we shall go home, but I know better. Nevertheless we may stay together, which would be pleasant.

Heard Churchill's speech to Home Guard from America. Nothing new. The HG will take the weight of Britain's defences when the armies go abroad; that was the main point.

Took out *Land of Wales* (1937, by Eiluned & Peter Lewis) from Library.

Saturday 15 May

The idleness forced on us the last few days is getting intolerable. We have to go to the Signals hut, why, nobody knows; and there we sit about & read or help with the tea swindle. I read & look forward to the news at 5, & then read again. We are all hoping to have our postings through soon.

Sunday 16 May

Atkinson has bought the *British Journal of Photography Almanac* for this year. I have been working out some of the formulae which may be helpful later.

Monday 17 May

Formula for Hyperfocal Depth H=1000 f/s, where f is the focal length, s the stop size. (DIARY THEN LISTS 4 MORE FORMULAE)

Received letters 25 & 27 (Sea), 34 & 35 (Air) from Anne. *Horizon.* Chess Book. *N.E.W.* (4). *French Dictionary. English Towns.* Bethell's *Literary Outlook* (published that year). Air from Mildred.

Tuesday 18 May

Wrote Mildred & Simon Nowell-Smith (a bibliophile based in Oxford and connected to AR through a cousin).

My own French books having come to a stop, I am trying to read *Quo Vadis* in French. It is so poorly written, however, that the effort is almost too much. I am trying the Aragon poem in *Horizon*, but it is difficult going as yet, & shows me that to be able to read subtle poetry, much more than a large vocabulary is needed.

The rain seems to have started in earnest. Heavy this a.m. Just sat around the Maintenance Hut until lunch.

Wednesday 19 May

Wrote Anne 32.

A new Sergeant discip (?disciplinary) from Hastings caused high feeling by making us go back from the cook-house to fetch our topees (pith helmets). He is a little bald-headed, unpleasant-looking man, and may be quite a nuisance until he gets tired.

Received note & odd letters from Anne, including my Royalty sheets from Faber (presumably payment for the two little ABCs he had designed and drawn for them to publish).

Heavy rain again.

Thursday 20 May

Went to Lagos.

Bought: Circuses 5/-
Optics 2/-
Album 4/6
Stones 6d
Photos 2/6

The prints of hut interiors have been spoiled by bad developing, & the printing was worse. But the boys have ordered 94 in all.

No news of postings for us yet. The others go on Monday.

Friday 21 May

Saw a dull film in the Transit Camp NAAFI – *On the Night of January 16* (1941, based on 1934 play by Ayn Rand). The NAAFI is a sumptuous-looking place, with high roof & mahogany panels throughout.

Read, in *Scottish Short Stories*, 'A Story of Orkney' by Eric Linklater (whom VR had met with Anne in Orkney; see Introduction), dealing with the Peerie Men (mysterious, slightly sinister folk)!

Saturday 22 May

Wrote to Peter Ripper.

Today all our wireless equipment was handed over to the station. Our postings are supposed to be in, though nothing has leaked out about them.

Read *Literary Outlook.*

Began studying optics for photography.

Complained strongly about the food.

Sunday 23 May

Wrote to Robin.

Signals learnt their postings this a.m. I am for Kano, which is reputed to be a good station. Church, Williams, Turner, Hibbert, Waugh, Axten, Atkinson & Cpl Wolfenden posted to Takoradi. The biggest laugh is Chambers & Bushell for Maiduguri, because C tried to shake Wolfenden by pretending he was posted there. Water is short & the C.O. is supposed to be mad, so it sounds pretty awful (see last section of the Introduction).

In the evening our C.O. gave us a dinner: soup, fish, meat, sweet, cheese, rolls & coffee. It was well organized & enjoyable. Cpl. Nevisson presented him with a watch for which we had all subscribed. The sing-song after was not so successful – probably because there was no beer – but the Belgian officers sang a song in French very well. We broke up at 10.15. I had been packing in the afternoon.

Monday 24 May

Went to Lagos.
Cabled my address home.
Bought *Lives of Poets* – Johnson Vol I
Dostoevsky *Gambler*

(Must have sent parcel with ptd (?painted/printed) cotton in it about this date.)

Tuesday 25 May

Spent morning getting cleared.

Went to Wing HQ in afternoon for pay: £4.4.

Warned for leaving tomorrow at 9 a.m. for 10.15 train.

My leather bag holds a great deal of stuff. Managed with one kit bag, box & bag; but am doubtful of handles on the bag – don't think they will stand much strain.

Wednesday 26 May

Entrained this morning at 12 o'clock. There was a characteristic mess-up about my berth, but I got one in the end, with Harris, Cpl Proctor & Cpl Robbins. The berths are not so good as our 3rds, & the fares are extremely heavy – £12 to Jos alone, without meals. The food is good, though portions are small. One sheet, blanket & pillow provided at night.

I did not sleep well, owing to the jabbering of Nigerians whenever we stopped at a station. Owing to a landslide below Jebba, we stopped this side of the Niger so as to avoid traversing it in the dark.

Country monotonous, without palms; however maize crops plentiful, & fine trees, but little irregularity in features of land.

Thursday 27 May

Reached Jebba South before midday. The Niger is crossed here by an iron bridge, to the north of which Juju rock overlooks the curve of the river. The river narrows here, but to the south-east there are stretches of sand on both shores. A large, clean-looking village stands on the shore just below the bridge. The railway station is dotted with those lovely trees with bright red blossom, & intricate trunk formation.

The country has changed in aspect now; large pointed ant-hills, red against the blue sky, are dotted among the trees along the line; no more maize crops. Clean stations & native huts, surrounded by woven screens. Minna station reminded me of Aachen!

Friday 28 May

Arrived Kano at 2.15. Caused row between two boys by giving one 1/- to share.

Put into Transit camp. Apparently no one expected us at the station. The billets are stone here, & this camp is really only intended for aircrew, so the food & attention are good. We had a good dinner with egg custard & coffee after.

A little away from the camp is a polo ground where some Hausa men & British officers were playing. Their ponies are lean but look strong. Horses can be hired for 2/6 per hour & bicycles for 6d.

Opposite the camp many Hausa traders sit near a large tree on the roadside, trying to sell the usual goods at prices much higher than those in Lagos.

I am in one room with Dobson, Dunsmore, Mitchison & Mathew. It is VERY hot at night. Washbasin in room. Vultures outside.

Saturday 29 May

Went to the camp this morning. Our billet for the time being is a newly built Restaurant adjoining the Control Tower & Admin block, both of which are quite sumptuously built. We look out over the runways where a great variety of machines is dispersed: DCs, Ensigns, Baltimores, Mitchells, Beaufighters, Kittyhawks & Liberators (see Appendix 2 and also: Ensign, 1 June, below; B25 Mitchell, 6 December; Kittyhawk, 7 April, above; B17 Flying Fortress, 6 November, below).

I reported to Signals, & was surprised to find Sgt Brid there, from Orkney. He came out in August.

Sunday 30 May

Started in the Telephone Exchange. Mitchell, the op., is a pleasant person, though a little too intellectual in a superficial way, & inclined to be superior about the common man. I am to go in from 8.30 to 1 until I know the board. Then we shall be on a 4-watch system which will give us almost too much time off.

Monday 31 May

Wrote Anne 33.

Met Evans this morning – a Welshman with an honest face & pale blue eyes. He told me how to buy a horse for £4.10 etc. etc!

The food is not good & the NAAFI the worst stocked of any I have yet seen. But the camp is easily run & has a pleasant atmosphere.

The Signals W.O. is said to be a bit of a bind, & I didn't take to him when I first saw him.

Took out *The Arabian Nights Murder* (1936 whodunnit by John Dickson Carr) from Library. Saw *Neutral Port* (1940 British war film) at the Rex. Very poor.

June 1943

Tuesday 1 June

Wrote to Mother. Sent her £10 via RAF.

The Maiduguri people are still in the Transit camp. They are supposed to be going tomorrow in one of the Ensigns. I had never seen one close to before, & they are gigantic machines & make a Liberator look small (British Armstrong Whitworth AW27 Ensign 4-engine civilian airliner, flown in support of the military during the war; only 14 were ever built, 8 of which were used on the Africa to India route; 114 ft long and with a huge wingspan of 123 ft; see Appendix 2). Mitchells take off at terrific speed – well over 130 I should say. One of the Americans told me there were 900 waiting to be ferried from the US.

It is the custom here for the boys to bring the tea round, so I sleep from 1 to 4 almost every afternoon now.

Wednesday 2 June

For the first time, changing camps has made me feel a different person, with different habits. I now want to go out every evening, & the idea of studying seems remote. Perhaps I shall settle down again, but at present I feel restless.

Went to the Canteen for supper, which consisted of 3 poached eggs, fried potatoes & tomatoes, & a delicious sweet.

Then saw *You Will Remember* (1941) at the Rex. A well-acted British film with Robert Morley & Emlyn Williams, & Nicholas Phipps, Anne's childhood friend playing an amusing part as the musical-comedy type British Earl. (Phipps, 'even as a small boy', Anne writes in her *Memoirs*, 'could keep the company in fits of laughter'.)

Saw AMOs (Administrative Medical Officers) 1250/42 deal with Airfield Controller. Remuster?

Thursday 3 June

Wrote to Anne 34 (Sea).

Into Kano, again in the evening. Saw *Hellzapoppin* (1941, musical based on a 3-year Broadway hit) at the Rex. Mildly funny, & with some interesting process shots; but on the whole a waste of time.

Reading some short stories by Coppard: 'Ninepenny Flute' etc, many of them delightful. They are truly TALES rather than stories: not many people can do such slight things so well. Wonder whether Anne has ever read them?

Friday 4 June

Went to cinema in American camp. Their huts are laid out in a similar way to ours, with better finish. Saw an AWFUL film *Syncopation* (1942, loss-making romance used as vehicle for a history of jazz, swing etc), which the American next to me said he had seen twice. The Americans are mostly v. friendly, but they DO behave like overgrown schoolboys. Their clothing & equipment are good. They also have plenty of transport.

Saturday 5 June, Sunday 6 June

Wrote Mr & Mrs Johnson (presumably John Johnson – Printer to the University, Oxford, who fired VR in 1937 – & his wife; see Introduction).

This morning went into Kano with Carlos. Hired bikes & cycled into the walled city. It seems immense inside, & we didn't have time to go all around, because Carl got a puncture. The huts are well made, along irregular streets, & have patterns either in low relief or just scratched in the wall. Goats, donkeys, lizards & children hang around the water pools. The outer wall v. thick & guarded by Hausa police. The Admin block & Emir's palace are modern European buildings.

Saw *One Foot in Heaven* (1941, starring Frederic March as a 1920s Methodist minister who at first thinks film sinful, but comes to see its moral potential) at American cinema. Interesting but slow. Subtle boost for films.

Monday 7 June

Alison christened +

Now working regularly in the Control Tower. Of my 3 fellow R.T.O.s (Radio Transmitter Orderlies), Walker, Williams & Newton, I like Walker. Williams boasts & has too much to say; Newton is a nice chap but very dim.

We share the Tower with the Yanks, who have typical Yank equipment. Everything of the best & on a big scale. They are friendly & v. willing to share anything they have. We envy particularly the iced water that is brought to them in pewter jugs.

Worked part of the morning in the Control Office learning the codes. At night the R.T.O.s have to take messages & decode them.

Reading *Henry VIII* (1929) by F. Hackett. Revising French also.

Extract from Violet Bradby's weekly war diary

11 June 1943

Alison was christened on June 6th. David Bland spent Friday night here, & he and Enrica Garnier could both be at the christening (as godparents). Kathleen Madge (the poet Kathleen Raine, also a godparent) arrived too late but came up to tea with her small boy. Bishop Barkway (former Little Gaddesden rector) was the other godfather. Mrs Wager decorated the font, Mr Wager (current rector) took service & Mrs Melville & Clarissa (her daughter) came too, & we had 'The King of Love' unaccompanied & they all came up to tea. Nellie (the home help who lived with them at Ringshall End) made a sponge cake with chocolate icing & Alison in silver balls on top. Lovely afternoon. Alison very good at the christening. She wore one of Bertha's little embroidered frocks (Bertha Bradby, who with her husband Edward – Anne's brother – spent the war in Ceylon/Sri Lanka where Edward was a headmaster).

Tuesday 8 June

Received letters 36 & 38 from Anne. 1 air from Mother. 1 from Nellie.

Wednesday 9 June

Wrote to Anne 35 (Air).

On night watch for first time. At 8 o'clock a Fulani (widespread West African ethnic grouping) by the name of Mameola came up with my supper.

Then he put down my bed & retired into the corridor to sleep. I was roused at 1.15 by an American who said some flare path lights were out; & again later to take a code. At 6.15 I was brought some tea. This is going on watch in luxury.

Thursday 10 June

Day off today. Spent most of it reading *Henry VIII*, but in the evening went to Kano for chop, & on to the cinema to see *Arizona* (1940), a dullish Western with Jean Arthur.

Friday 11 June

Wrote to Chris Church.

Saturday 12 June

Wrote to David.

Sunday 13 June

Received letter 40 from Anne.

Monday 14 June

Wrote to Victor Smith.

Read 4 short novels (*Four Stories*, 1935) by Rebecca West. Apart from her purple passages which are forced, 3 of them I thought good, especially *The Abiding Vision.*

We fear one of our Blenheims (British twin-engine light bomber; see 12 May and Appendix 2) has been lost. It set out for Lagos this morning & nothing has been heard of it since.

Tuesday 15 June

Wrote to Anne 36 (Sea).

The Blenheim crash-landed near Oshogbu, but we don't know how badly it was damaged yet.

Wednesday 16 June

Sent cable to Mother.

Carlos induced me to see an awful film called *Congo Maisie* (1940, second in a 10-film series about showgirl Maisie who in this one quells a native rebellion by doing magic tricks), which for sheer vacuity wd take some beating.

Began reading *The Moonstone* (1868, Wilkie Collins – see 16 February), as Anne says she is now doing so. Begins well.

Thursday 17 June

The Moonstone is good, though it is curious that the part Collins thought best, & which had most success, should be Miss Clack's narrative. It is amusing, but it is spoilt by the self-regarding self being Collins himself, & not Miss Clack, ie she is made to caricature herself in a way which defeats his purpose. Betteridge is the most successful character I think.

Friday 18 June

Received 41 from Anne. Received letter from David. David was over the Ruhr three times last week (he was navigator in a Halifax bomber, as part of a Pathfinder squadron that dropped flares guiding the planes behind them; see also Appendix 1). The AA (anti-aircraft fire) is still just as bad he says.

Read in *Popular Photography*, an American magazine, a way of securing great depth of field by using a pinhole over the lens with flash bulbs. Examples were astonishing. Might take this mag. after the war.

Saturday 19 June

Cycled around Kano in the morning. In the evening saw two poor films at Rex: *Paris Calling* (1941, with a Resistance-based plot) & *Phantom Raiders* (1940, a standard Hollywood spy film of the time).

Am starting Defence Course on Monday.

Sunday 20 June

Read *Furthermore* (1938 story collection) by Runyon.

Monday 21 June

Started on the Defence Course. Released after first hour as I told the Sergeant I had done the course recently.

Traffic has not been very brisk lately. One of the 2 Control Officers, the Canadian, has gone down with malaria. I'm glad it wasn't the New Zealander whom I like better. The other binds me, though the other fellows get on with him.

Cabled Mother & Anne.

Tuesday 22 June

Wrote to Anne 37 (Air).

Took out *Press Parade* (1936, about the 'newspaper racket') by Hamilton Fyfe (famed for his *Daily Mail* report on the 1914 retreat from Mons). Revising my French vocab, & studying a French grammar borrowed from Carlos.

Wednesday 23 June

Mother's birthday.

Saw *Top Hat* (1935) again, after about 8 years. It didn't wear well, although the songs by Irving Berlin still sounded good. Astaire IS an ugly-looking man. (In later years VR loved to watch him dancing onscreen!)

Thursday 24 June

Met a youth called Williams who has lived for many years in France. He has leant me some copies of *La France Libre* and a modern novel by one Robert Goffin called *Les Cavaliers de la Déroute* (1941). It deals with Belgium during this war, & so far is not very good.

Friday 25 June

Sent cable to Anne.

Received big batch of mail, nos 29, 35, 37 from Anne & many enclosures, including 2 photos of Jane. *Horizon* for March.

Airmail from Enrica Garnier (a one-time fiancée of the Faber poet Norman Nicholson, & Alison's godmother). Airmail from Victor Smith.

Books (received): *Selected Poems* (NN (presumably Norman Nicholson) etc)

Wife to Milton (1943 Robert Graves historical novel)

War Map

Saturday 26 June

Wrote to Enrica.

Saw a big hurricane last night. Unfortunately it fused the mains, which meant sitting in the dark watching the lightning. The dark sky before sundown was wonderful and gave a curious colour to the landscape.

Sunday 27 June

Read *Father & Son* {1907) by Edmund Gosse. It held my attention closely. His father's type still remains in the Rev THB.

Monday 28 June

Received airmail 42 from Anne.

Tuesday 29 June

Sent off 38 to Anne. Included photo of Kano, drawing for her poem & layout for *Nine Bright Shiners* (Faber book of AR's poems, published that year).

Went inside a Commando the other night. 4-bladed props. like a ship inside, with one big deck & hatches beneath (Curtiss C46 twin-engine transport plane, with a larger cabin capacity than the Douglas C27/ Dakota; see Appendix 2). The crew had a little honey bear, a creature with a long pointed nose, which they were taking with them to India. One of their number crashed about 300 miles away, but the crew got out alive.

Wednesday 30 June

Owing to a childish difference of opinion, Carlos now speaks to none of us. It was a question of moving up the beds to allow another two men in. Carlos refused, & since he was later told to move to the US camp without other men who are being taken off the verandahs, he thought this was a plot on our part. He has returned my books with a polite note.

Saw *The Man Who Lost Himself* (1941). Brian Aherne in a part made for William Powell. Not bad.

Heard recording of Churchill's speech. Nothing new except good U-boat sinkings in May.

July 1943

Thursday 1 July

Wedding Anniversary (in fact Anne and Vivian had married on 2 July 1938).

Received letters from Church, Turner & Slim Williams. Poor Church is on flight work, which he detests, & there seems to be too much for him anyway; but they speak well of the food & the recreation facilities. Slim's letter is in the oddest style, almost arch in parts – none of them tell me of course what I really want to know, but fill up with childish jokes. Turner certainly has beautiful handwriting. I have never seen a style similar to it.

Wrote to Mother.

Friday 2 July

Cycled around Kano again. It is a pity there is so little to do down there. Bought 4 *Time & Tide* & a new govt booklet *East of Suez, West of Malta*, dealing with Mediterranean naval battles. I notice it is printed by the Amalgamated Press, & as one would expect, it is not v. well done. These layouts aren't really GOOD, too effeminate for one thing. The Americans have developed offset (lithography) much better than we have for this sort of work. And even their cheaper-quality gravure is better, vid. *Detroit Parade*, & compare with *Picture Post*. *Everybodys* has turned itself into a kind of *Penny Journal* or *People's Educator*, but uses the most awful format like a succession of *Times* leaders, with the minimum of cross-heads & a shrieking second colour nearly always out of register.

If I rewrite my 'Artistic Printing' (see entry for 20 October), I must not forget to show a Woodbine packet, as it is one of the last remaining examples of the American imported patterns. An idea might be a continuation of Faber's 19th-Century Types into a series for the modern typographer. Must see Shand about this.

Saturday 3 July, Sunday 4 July

By the day, have now been married to my dear Anne for 5 years.

Starting *Wife to Mr Milton* after finishing the French novel.

Wrote to Chris Church etc.

Monday 5 July

Wrote to Mrs Smith. Wrote to Victor.

Took out *The Pasquier Chronicles* (1938) by G. Duhamel ('the French Galsworthy'). By a coincidence the last book we have is also in French – *Le Désert de Bièvres* (1937, fifth in the cycle), & I shall read it in that. Interesting to see the latitude taken by the translator, extravagant at times.

Saw *Battle of Britain* (the 1943 official US account, directed by Frank Capra) & *In Which We Serve* (1942, directed by Noel Coward & David Lean; Coward also starred and wrote the music and screenplay, the latter based loosely on Louis Mountbatten's experience as Captain of the destroyer *HMS Kelly*; Mountbatten was sufficiently pleased with it to watch it numerous times) at US camp. Think the latter quite good in spite of what David said.

Tuesday 6 July

Received a letter from Mother. It contains the alarming news that she has had a proposal of marriage from the Scotch Dr who attended her. She doesn't express her feelings fully about it; but I think she is still turning it over in her mind. If I knew something about the Dr I should be able to form an opinion. As it is I think the PRINCIPLE is a good one, from the point of view of her own happiness – in fact nothing could be better – yet so much depends on what he is like.

I will write in a few days; meanwhile I must try to work out carefully the best advice possible to me.

Wednesday 7 July

Airmail from Anne 43 (22.6.43). Sad news in it about Mary Gomm. Jane is now 34" high, & said suddenly 'Daddy loves Janey', which he does indeed. I measured out 34" against the locker by my bed. How tall it seems! I know I shall have a shock when I see her again; she will seem so strange & grown up. What a delicious prospect to dream about all the same.

German offensive seems to have begun in earnest in the Orel sector (on the Eastern Front, where the 'biggest tank battle in history' around Kursk was being fought; the Soviet losses were greater, but Hitler had to call off his offensive – and the new Panther tanks had proved a liability, breaking down).

Lord Swinton arrived yesterday (Conservative politician, Secretary of State for Air 1935-38, Minister of Civil Aviation 1944-45).

Thursday 8 July

Wrote to Anne 39 (Air).

A Liberator crashed south of Kaduna yesterday. All 10 men bailed out safely. In the evening a DC had to force land near Maiduguri. It was v. tense & dramatic in the Tower. He said he had only fuel for 25 mins, Maiduguri couldn't contact him. We were trying to get a bearing on him when he said he was about to land on a road. That was the last we heard.

Friday 9 July

Paid £4.4.

Saw *Flame of New Orleans* (1941), an American film made by René Clair. The whole story, which was very slight, cried out for a complete French cast (Marlene Dietrich plays the female lead). The witty immorality sat oddly upon Roland Young & Bruce Cabot, though the former was good. I noticed again how much of the particular Clair atmosphere is provided by the music. Only Preston Sturges seems to have attempted to help comedy in this way: his early films copy Clair closely, particularly in the rushing of people along corridors & up stairs etc. This film was hampered by the Otterson sets.

Saturday 10 July

Sicily invaded this a.m. at 2 (by the Allies; this was the largest amphibious landing ever carried out on a single day, with 160,000 troops and paratroops).

Looked over a Liberator C87 (the transport version of the B24: see Appendix 2). The whole interior is padded; seats of leather; lavatory at the back. All Libs through here go to India I think.

Sunday 11 July

Received airmail 43(ii) from Anne.

Baltimore crashed this morning. Leg gave way. Damage not serious.

Saw *Married But Single*, with Rosalind Russell (star of 1940's *His Girl Friday*; no mention of this title in her filmography). Vile behaviour of 3 Polish officers at the cinema.

Monday 12 July

Wrote to Mother.

Tuesday 13 July

Wrote to Anne 40.

The Control Officer told me that some of our Ferry Pilots had taken over 300 Hurricanes to Persia in six weeks. The Russians are using them in enormous numbers. (In total the British supplied 2834 Hurricanes to the Soviet Union, not that Stalin ever expressed thanks; nor as a relatively old design was it particularly popular with Russian pilots, though it played an important role in the battle for Stalingrad.)

News from Sicily still good. And the Russians are holding firm, which is even more important.

Wednesday 14 July

Visited the Library in the walled city with Malone. It is in a cool, thick-walled stone building. Unfortunately the only attendant was a Hausa who had no English. He unlocked the various rooms, but the Library itself is rather disappointing, and musty-smelling too. But it contained Charles' *Shadows of Ecstasy* (Charles Williams, OUP editor and writer, close friend of AR) & the *OED* (*Oxford English Dictionary*).

Sent home a parcel of books.

Thursday 15 July

Wrote to Cpl Williams.

Andrew, our new boy, told me a story of the chameleon & the tortoise which he firmly believes. The c & t meet in a wood and make a large bowl of soup. Just as they are about to eat it, the chameleon asks the tortoise to climb up a palm tree to bring down some oil. While the t is doing this, the c gobbles up the soup, then has a crafty shit in the bowl & claps the lid on. He scuttles off into the bush, leaving the poor old tortoise to remove the lid & find the worst.

Friday 16 July

Wrote to M&F. Received 44 from Anne. 1 from Ripper, 1 from Mother, 1 from Robin, & I from Edward (Anne's brother Edward Bradby, at that time in Ceylon/Sri Lanka where he was headmaster of a school in Colombo; the Japanese had bombed Colombo harbour on Easter Day 1942, but thankfully never returned; see also Violet Bradby's diary entry, under 7 June above, and Chronology).

Saturday 17 July

Received parcel from Bumpus, containing *Crère-Coeur* (?), Reynolds & *War & Peace* pamphlet.

Sunday 18 July

Saw *The Foreman Went to France* (1942). Rather feeble, & a poor performance from Robert Morley as a French mayor.

Monday 19 July

Wrote to Edward.

Another terrific thunderstorm cut off all the power again. It seems that this happens regularly.

A Baltimore nearly crashed in landing. It bounced 3 times, about 70 feet; the pilot pulled the wheels up on the 4th & just managed to get airborne again. His third attempt was very good.

Tuesday 20 July

Now have a small chameleon – really tiny, about 3" long. He seems able to change his colour over a greater range than Horace, unless Horace is lazy. He can go from black to pale yellow. They don't seem able to get near the reds at all.

Wednesday 21 July

Received parcel from Bumpus containing Balzac & Flaubert.

Saw *Judge Hardy & Son* (1939, last MGM film of the 1930s, starring Mickey Rooney) at the Rex. Funny in parts, but lots of awful sentiment.

Thursday 22 July

Finished Vol. III of Gibbon. I particularly liked this passage:

'the wants & even the desires of the Romans were liberally satisfied; and they seem to have been embarrassed by the singular politeness of Bleda's widow, who added to her other favours the gift, or at least the loan, of a sufficient number of beautiful & obsequious damsels.'

Friday 23 July

Paid £4.4.

Started the Flaubert, finding the vocab more difficult than any previous book.

Went over to Yank camp to see *Talk of the Town* (1942), with Cary Grant, Jean Arthur, & Ronald Colman. Came out before the end, though it began very well. Directed by George Stevens.

Saturday 24 July

Bought Developing by Jacobson in Kano, for 7/6.

Wrote to Anne 41.

Sunday 25 July

Heard of Mussolini's resignation at 11 p.m. Badoglio has taken over the Govt. Unless this is a tactful prelude to capitulation, I don't think this will be particularly to our advantage. (Marshal Pietro Badoglio led the Italian government till June 1944, when the Allies captured Rome.)

Letter from Anne to John Hayward

25 July 1943 Ringshall End

My dearest John,

I feel unutterably stupid after the usual day of cooking & washing & walking in a hot wood with Jane, but if I don't write soon I shall be thirty-one, & what's more to the point, my book of poems will be in proof before I've told you about it – you of all people. (Anne valued his critical insight and support for her poetry – see Prologue, above.) . . . *Can it really be four years since Mr Faber gave a dinner-party at which we first met? It might be four or forty years or four months to my sensations, for the war has destroyed all sequence. That summer seems stiflingly hot all the time when I look back on it, & especially August, & especially that evening when we must have been just holding our breaths before the war broke, when Vivian & I came to your flat, & you gave me my copy of Noctes Binanianae* (while at Faber Anne had typed this small book of poems named after Hayward's flat in Bina Gardens, where he, T S Eliot, Geoffrey Faber and the Faber director Frank Morley used to meet). . . .

[As for] my own book, TSE wrote & asked me for it in May. . . . TSE said the collection seemed to him 'all right', thereby in his own inimitable way leaving me guessing as to what precisely he meant. . . . I have called the book The Nine Bright Shiners, *from an allusion in Jane's christening poem. . . .*

[Jane] stands on a stool by Alison's cot, holding her hand & treating her to a raucous chant, which sounds rather like an unfamiliar Tate & Brady hymn of which one can't catch the words, until the patient Alison can bear it no longer & drowns it with a roar. She is *a patient, peaceful baby, very fine and small as yet, with red hair & thin long hands.*

Vivian is now near Kano, the Moslem walled city in northern Nigeria. He likes it much better than Lagos where he was before; & says the city is kept clean by vultures, whose roosting trees he avoids on his way back to camp in the dark.

Past midnight & I must end.

My love, good wishes & gratitude as always, Anne

Monday 26 July

Wrote to David.

Saw *Tales of Manhattan* (1942) at the Yank camp. On the lines of *If I had a Million* (1932, also an 'anthology' film with several directors), & just as uneven. But good on the whole.

Tuesday 27 July

Received 45 from Anne.

Started reading *Fifteen Discourses* (1790) by Reynolds.

Wednesday 28 July

Wrote to Anne 42.

Thursday 29 July

Received letters 39 & 45 from Anne. Also *Horizon* for April & May. And Airgraph from Thea. (Space for airmail was limited, so in 1941 airgraphs were introduced whereby letters were photographed, and the much lighter negatives printed out on arrival.)

Benedick brought me the Apron toilet set, & another fountain pen.

Friday 30 July

Anne's Birthday.

Jack Benny (1894-1974, catchphrase-loving comic star of US radio, film & later TV), Larry Adler (1914-2001, harmonica virtuoso and frequent wartime guest on

Benny's radio show) & company arrived by DC this afternoon. I watched them from the Tower, though I didn't get more than a glimpse. O'Brien rushed along & took 2 spools of film. Benny said, when he got out of the plane, 'What's wrong? I've been on the ground two seconds, & nobody's said "dash me".' Their show is on tonight, & it is rumoured we are to see them tomorrow. I shall be on duty unluckily.

Saturday 31 July

Wrote to Mother.

Heard part of Benny's show over telephone. Bob Derr fixed this for me. Not bad.

August 1943

Monday 2 August

The rainy season has now started in earnest. I don't like this weather, even though it is much cooler. It holds up aircraft, and that means even less for us to do than before.

More of the Ikeja boys passed through here on their way to Maiduguri. Some have gone to Libreville. They say Clarke is now the most popular man in the station. A moral somewhere.

Tuesday 3 August

Wrote to Anne 43.

Must attempt to read something by Arthur Koestler (1905-1983) after reading his article on Hillary in *Horizon*. Hillary's *Last Enemy* also sounds an interesting book (1942, seven months before 23-year-old Richard Hillary's death in a night-training crash over Scotland; the autobiography describes his being shot down in the Battle of Britain, and recovering after several operations).

Practically all the land in & around the camp is now well covered with green vegetation. I suppose it will soon go again when the rain stops.

Wednesday 4 August

Received *Treks & Palavers* (1938, Capt. R.R. Oakley's description of life in the administration of Northern Nigeria in the 1920s and 1930s) from Bumpus.

Thursday 5 August

Wrote to Mildred.

Friday 6 August

Today we were suddenly pushed out of the Reception Room by Flight-Sergeant Smith. W.O. Henshaw put him under close arrest for saying that he was acting on instructions from the M.O., which was untrue. The C.O. released him without prejudice. Meanwhile we were told to go down to the main blocks. We knew beforehand that there was no room, so we had to sleep in the verandah. The M.O. is getting us moved, we hope.

Paid £4.4.

Saturday 7 August

Received letters 46 & 47 from Anne, and letter from David. Wrote to Anne 44 (Sea).

Saw an appalling British film, *Ships with Wings* (1941, set in the 1940-41 Battle of Greece), & a Yank one, *This Woman is Mine* (1941, Oscar-nominated for Best Music).

Sunday 8 August

Moved into new billet. It was intended for a cookhouse, but is clean & spacious room enough for eleven of us anyway. We shall be on our own near the NAAFI cookhouse.

Monday 9 August

(Shows VR sketch and plan of the new billet: a rectangular building with a pitched roof and porch, plus eleven beds, washbasin, showers, store and large area of ovens.)

Tuesday 10 August

Received airmails from Nellie & Mildred, plus letter from LAC Williams & parcel from Church.

Saw *Slightly Dangerous* (1943) at the US camp. Lana Turner & Robert Young. Quite entertaining. (One sequence, in which Lana Turner's character has to work blindfolded, is said to have been directed by an uncredited Buster Keaton.)

Finished Flaubert. Began Balzac *Le Père Goriot* (1835).

Wednesday 11 August

Received *Horizon* & letter from Anne enclosing 3 photos. Also airmail from Mother & Mildred.

Very excited over Alison's photos. She looks a CLEAN baby, v. neat & trim, as Anne says. In one photo she looks like an elderly statesman.

Jane seems to have grown beyond all recognition since the last batch of photos. No more the baby (alas), but a sweet little girl, mischievous-looking!

Thursday 12 August

Received letter from Mother with 3 more photos. A most cheerful letter too. At last she is going to Ringshall to see the babies!

Also received 2 *Spheres* & *Listener* (*The Sphere*, a British illustrated weekly newspaper, published 1900-64; *The Listener*, a BBC weekly magazine, published 1929-91).

Wrote to Slim Williams.

Friday 13 August

Received letter from Church. And 2 *N.E.W.*s

Doing a bit of Morse lately. Maybe because there is so little to occupy my mind, it now comes much easier than at Cranwell.

Went to French class in the evening. Elementary of course, but I was interested in seeing Carlos teach. He is better than I expected.

Saturday 14 August

Saw 2 awful films at Rex: *The Spoilers* (1942 Western starring Dietrich and John Wayne) & *Tight Shoes* (1941) – the latter based on a Runyon story, so it should have been good. But it wasn't.

Sunday 15 August

Wrote to Anne 45 (Air).

Monday 16 August

The new draft out here were bombed by Condors 3 days out from home (the Focke-Wulf Condor was used by the Luftwaffe as a long-distance reconnaissance plane & bomber over the Atlantic; see Appendix 2). In the convoy of 3 ships, 2 of them were sunk with direct hits from 20,000 feet, while the third one was damaged. It happened between 8 & 9 in the evening. Catalinas escorting them (ie flying boats: Appendix 2) patrolled at 10,000 feet. The men were picked up by a destroyer & taken to Casablanca, where they were equipped by the Americans. Some of our men should be going home at the end of this week.

Tuesday 17 August

Sicilian campaign ended (but 60,000 Axis troops escaped with 40,000 vehicles across the Straits of Messina to mainland Italy).

Wednesday 18 August

Wrote to Robin.

Thursday 19 August

Saw another awful film at the Rex: *A Little Bit of Heaven* (1940, US musical starring the teenage actress & singer Gloria Jean who would use the same title for her 2005 autobiography). Came out before the end.

Finished *Le Père Goriot*. The vocab was much easier than the Flaubert & on the whole I enjoyed it more. In the Flaubert I was distracted from full enjoyment by the difficulties.

Friday 20 August

Wrote to Mother.

Idea for lighting switchboard (VR gives 2 sketches) for 15-amp circuit.

Saturday 21 August

Mosquitoes are now about in swarms, & I have been badly bitten already, though not always by malaria-carriers.

Some of the boys have gone back home, flying to Accra by air. More will go this month. There is a chance of our getting away in another 3 or 4 months.

Sunday 22 August

Wrote to Anne 46.

Monday 23 August

Wrote to Church & Bushell.

As a collection of books has come up from Kaduna I offered to arrange & catalogue them. The bulk are in very bad condition, but there is some interesting stuff, including C.S. Lewis's *Out of the Silent Planet* (1938) & *Portraits* (1931) by Desmond McCarthy. I have borrowed from the selection:

Modern Humour (1940, an anthology of comic essays, poems, anecdotes and literary pastiches)

England Made Me (1935) – Greene – good, but nowhere near as good as his later ones

Introducing Shakespeare

Story of My Heart (1883, 'spiritual autobiography' of nature writer Richard Jefferies)

Henry James *Short Stories*

Fiesta (1930) by Hemingway

Tuesday 24 August

I don't know whether it is the gradual effect of the climate, but lately I have been feeling very irritable. I have the greatest difficulty in tolerating the conversation of Dobson & Mitchison, my two bête-noirs. They reduce everything to their own level of cynical opportunism, made more unpleasant by the knowledge that I am not entirely above it myself, and so can see myself in what I most loathe. And Carlos gets tiresome too, mainly because the conversation must always turn on C.M. – often interesting enough, but as often not. He has a naivety about himself that I have tried to dispel.

Wednesday 25 August

Now reading Balzac's *Eugénie Grandet* (1833), not in French alas. I now have only the Aragon (Louis Aragon 1897-1982, surrealist poet) to work on in French, which is still difficult for me in parts, even after 5 readings, but I found his essay at the end interesting & clear. It did strike me as peculiar though that he should herald the use of modern technical words as something new for poetry, after the English experiments.

Thursday 26 August

Smith, the little cook-man in our billet, who has a wife who cannot speak, read or write, and whom he does not go to see when he has leave, has now left our billet; and the new arrival is from the draft which was bombed. He told me that the bombs dropped were oil bombs, and their ship, of 22,000 tons, was sunk because a fire, started in the engine room, could not be controlled. Then the cargo ship which picked them up was bombed the next night, on its way to Casablanca, but the fires were put out without injury to anyone. At Casablanca they were kitted out by the Yanks & brought to Freetown in a ship which had had Italian prisoners on board at Algiers. They were taken off and the ship brought round to Casablanca. From Freetown they sailed in the *Tamaroak*, supposed to have been sunk.

Friday 27 August

Received a letter from Ripper.

Sunday 29 August

Wrote Anne 47.

Monday 30 August

Wrote to Kirstie.

Owing to a boob on somebody's part down at Ikeja, about four convoys were sent up in bad weather. They got into an awful mess, landing & crash-landing all over the place. Some landed in the bush, while one whole convoy came down in French territory.

September 1943

Wednesday 1 September

Wrote Mother.

Thursday 2 September

Reading Siepman's *French Course Part 3*, Desmond McCarthy's *Portraits*, & Hemingway's *Fiesta* – a poor book indeed.

Friday 3 September

Paid £4.4.

Saturday 4 September

Received 50 & 51 from Anne.

Italy invaded this morning.

Monday 6 September

Wrote to Anne 47.

Started *Maud-Evelyn & Other Stories* (1900) by Henry James. His world is so completely his own, that I think, unless you are very near in temperament, a preliminary effort to enter it has to be made before tackling the style. I enjoy some passages, but I cannot help being irritated by the excessive FINESSE of the whole. Such extreme self-awareness does not appeal to me.

Tuesday 7 September

Read *Blenheim* by Winston Churchill (excerpt from *Marlborough: His Life & Times*, 4 vols 1933-1938).

Wednesday & Thursday 8 & 9 September

Announced at 5.30 that Italy has surrendered unconditionally. I heard it first as HITLER surrendered. It seemed so incredible that I refused to believe it & took a bet with Pickett of a bottle of beer. I was glad to lose in the circumstances. (Hitler had not of course surrendered, so final sentence here is puzzling.)

Wrote to WJ Turner re his article in the *Listener* on Berlioz. (Walter J. Turner, 1884-1946, was a poet much admired by Yeats as well as being a novelist & playwright, but he is best known today for his music criticism & biographies; these included *Berlioz: the Man & his Work*, 1934. Berlioz would remain one of VR's favourite composers.) My suggestion is that something might be done in the way of a Society on an Anglo-French basis, perhaps through *La France Libre* (set up in London in June 1940 by de Gaulle to support the Resistance in Occupied France). I also suggested that he select & translate B's critical writings.

Toscanini has given a performance in full of *Romeo & Juliet.*

British, American & Canadian troops have landed near Naples & are now fighting the Germans.

Friday 10 September

Received 52 & 53 from Anne & a letter from Shand directly inviting me to join them (ie join Shenval Press run by Shand) after the war. This is exciting news, & I think I shall accept, though writing in general terms at present. He talks about expansion once the plant becomes available, & that should mean plenty of scope.

Saturday 11 September

Wrote Anne 48.

Sunday 12 September

Went to Communion Service.

Monday 13 September

Walked out in bush with Pickett. The guinea-corn is now being cut,

& on all sides we could see the Nigerians cutting the long seed stalks & tying them in bundles. There was a dead donkey lying in the roadside with two vultures padding about on its back, accompanied by millions of flies. The smell was ghastly.

Tuesday 14 September

Read a novel by René Clair, *Star Turn*, written in 1925 (about a Hollywood star for whom the distinction between the real and unreal becomes blurred). Although slight, it has the same fantastic & delightful touch as his films. He intended to be a writer, & I should think he would have made a good one eventually. This book was published by Chatto in 1938.

Wednesday 15 September

Wrote to Shand.

Saw another poor American film, *They Met in Bombay* (1941), with Clark Gable & Rosalind Russell. It was unintentionally funny, particularly in the VC award.

Started *Seven Red Sundays* (1936 Ramón J Sender, translation Penguin 1938, about Madrid revolutionaries).

Thursday 16 September

When Torre took over the watch on his own, he mistook the weather balloon, which carries a small light so that its track can be followed at night, for an aircraft circling, & tried to bring it in on R/T. As he could get no reply, he rang up Ops, called the C.O., & had the flare-path lit up. He has not lived down the story yet.

Saw *Philadelphia Story* (1940, Cary Grant & Katharine Hepburn). Very disappointed after what I had expected.

Friday 17 September

Wrote to M&F.

The Spitfires & Hurricanes are now almost finished on the route. We should be getting Venturas, Mitchells & Marauders now (see entries for 15 November, 6 December & 25 September respectively, and Appendix 2).

Sgt Coussins has built us a most elegant control desk in mahogany, with all R/T controls now ready to hand, including the stand-by set.

Saturday 18 September

Saw *You'll Never Get Rich* at American camp (1941 musical comedy which made a star of Rita Hayworth, and revived Fred Astaire's career after his break with Ginger Rogers). Quite an amusing show.

Sunday & Monday 19 & 20 September

Started a new watch system as Newton is in dock. Much better too, as we finish when aircraft have come in.

Went to service held by Sudan Mission preacher. He amused us by referring to Zaccheria, a man of little stature, as a little dwarf. All the same, I liked him, though his methods were a trifle embarrassing for true-blue Englishmen.

Read *Bridge of San Luis Rey* (short 1927 novel by Thornton Wilder, filmed in 1929, 1944 & 2004).

Tuesday 21 September

Wrote to Anne 49.

French commandos in Corsica. Russians nearing Smolensk.

Wednesday 22 September

Heat now getting much more intense during the day. There have been one or two storms, but nothing really bad.

Pickett is now taking bets that we shall be homeward-bound by

Christmas. Some of the camp may be, but we may not be among them, as our draft was two months later than theirs.

Saw *Parachute Battalion* (one of a rash of 1941 Hollywood films about the various branches of the US Armed Forces). Same old stuff.

Thursday 23 September

Churchill said in his report to Parliament that no ships had been lost to enemy action during the four months up to September! This hardly agrees with the experience of the last draft here. Three of their ships were lost in the N. Atlantic in June. Perhaps he meant the English-American route, but he didn't say so.

Friday 24 September

Saw *Something to Shout About* (1943) with Jack Oakie, at the US camp. An awful woman called Janet Blair sang & danced. (Her character is *meant* to sing and dance awfully!)

Saturday & Sunday 25 & 26 September

Marauders landed here. They have a very fast landing speed, and are considered by their pilots as pretty dangerous. Their only advantage seems to be that of range. Otherwise they give a performance little better than Baltimores. (The Martin B26 Marauder, a twin-engine medium bomber, was introduced in 1941 'straight off the drawing board', without prior testing, and was initially known as the 'widow-maker' for its high number of accidents. But by the end of the war it had a lower attrition rate than any other US army aircraft; see also Appendix 2.)

Received 54, 55 & 56 from Anne, July *Horizon*, letters from Philippa (Kingsbury, close friend of Anne's since schooldays, who inspired her fine 1939 poem 'Now Philippa is Gone'), Isobel Smith, *Listeners* & *Sphere*.

Monday 27 September

Wrote to Anne 50.

Reading *Joining Charles* (1929) by Elizabeth Bowen. Got hold of *Crime & Punishment* (1866) from Library. Finished an excellent Agatha Christie, *Dumb Witness* (1937).

Main power off in Kano.

Wednesday 29 September

Received letters from Church & Turner.

Saw *Shadow of a Doubt* (1943) at US camp. Splendid performance by Joseph Cotten as the uncle-murderer. Hitchcock seems to have gone back to his old method of using as many outdoor shots as possible for realism, though it may be just wartime economy. Produced by Universal. Some exciting shots of a chase taken from a tall building. Poor ending. But one of his best, & not so upholstered as *Suspicion* (1941).

Thursday 30 September

Wrote to Philippa. Played tennis for first time out here yesterday.

October 1943

Saturday 2 October (VR's 30th Birthday)

Received 57, 58a & b from Anne & letter from M&F.

So I heard on this day of all days (ie his birthday) about David. I don't realize it fully even now; & I must cling to the faint hope that he baled out, or at least died without pain. Nobody can possibly take his place for me. It is awful having no-one here to talk to about him. We had marvellously happy times together, & at present I don't like to think of going back into printing without his support. Yet how much harder it must be for poor Mr Bland. I must write to him, yet it will be very difficult. O, if only he is still alive.

Sunday 3 October

Wrote to Anne 51.

Monday 4 October

Saw *Model Wife* (1941 US comedy with a happy ending, unlike the real-life marriage of its stars Dick Powell & Joan Blondell) at Rex.

Wednesday 6 October

Visited market inside walled city with Carl. A self-appointed dragoman took us around & bargained for us. There were horrible sights in the way of leprosy & deformities. I can see how Jesus must have been mobbed when it got about he could heal the sick.

I bought some little caps; & at the UAC (United African Company) some Zinder leather work; it is more expensive, but much more carefully made than local work.

Saw *Across the Pacific* (1942) with Humphrey Bogart (also Mary Astor & Sydney Greenstreet, his co-stars in John Huston's 1941 *The Maltese Falcon*; Huston directed till leaving to join the US Army Signal Corps).

Thursday 7 October

Received telegram from Anne saying that David was safe. What made me so angry was that the telegram had arrived in Kano GPO last Friday morning. If I had had it at the proper time I should have been spared the anguish. I now SUPPOSE David to be in England, as nothing was said about his being a prisoner. (In fact he was captured and made a prisoner in Stalag Luft III; see Appendix 1. Here he remained until forced to trek westwards by the Nazis in 1944 as the Russians advanced. He survived, however, and returned to the production department at Faber & Faber, where he became a director.)

Friday 8 October

Received 59 from Anne.

Saturday to Tuesday 9 to 12 October

Went again to Kano market. Our same dragoman met us. He took us through many winding & stinking lanes, with however the most photogenic walls I have ever seen – I longed for my camera – to see a trader in ivory & ebony. The room we were shown into was clean & very cool, with one bench for us, mats for the others, & a large tin trunk in the corner containing the ivory. We did not buy any because it was dear & not really very good.

One amusing incident happened when Carl handed out cigarettes. He seemed to be passing over our dragoman who hastily said, with a shy smile, 'Excuse sah, I also smoke.'

Then he took us to the dye pits. The dye is made by digging up the mud & then burning it in a wood fire. It turns first white, then red, & finally the indigo blue. It is then mixed with water in the wells. These have been made up to date with concrete sides & proper lids. They are dotted all over small areas at the roadside, similar to the goat-mountains at Regent's Park, though on a smaller scale. The strength of dye depends on the length of time the stuff is left in the well. A large piece of stuff costs about 1/6 to dye deeply.

On the same visit a Nigerian pursued me with a pair of shoes I didn't want. He asked 14/-, but when he saw I really didn't want them he came down to 8/-, which was such a bargain I bought them. They look well, but are a bit uncomfortable just now. I also bought some more caps for Anne.

Wrote Anne 52.

Wednesday 13 October

Wrote to Mother.

Saw good Henry Fonda & Barbara Stanwyck film, *You Belong to Me*

(1941, in which Fonda, a millionaire playboy, marries Stanwyck, a doctor, and becomes jealous of her male patients).

Finished *Crime & Punishment.* Translation poor.

Began writing article, with great effort, on design in printing. Maybe it will be finished one day.

Thursday 14 October

Reading *Five Victorians* (1942) by Lytton Strachey (witty critiques of Queen Victoria, Cardinal Manning, Florence Nightingale, General Gordon and Dr. Arnold of Rugby).

Friday 15 October

Received 60 from Anne & one from Enrica.

Paid £4.4.

Bought bag for David: 14/-.

Wrote to Turner etc; & to Allen asking for my £1.

Monday 18 October

Wrote to Anne 53.

Now playing tennis like a maniac. At first found it hard going, but I sweat less now.

Wednesday 20 October

Wrote to Enrica.

Revising my article on 19th-century printing (later published by James Shand in *Alphabet & Image,* no. 6 (January 1948), edited by Robert Harling, as 'Artistic Printing: A Search for Principles').

Saturday 23 October

Have now taken over the Library from Webber, whose commission has come through. I can't do very much with it except in small improvements. It has been arranged queerly for a library.

Thursday 28 October

Carlos has got his clearance chit, and should be going tomorrow. Six armourers came up, which means that all now here can go. I feel most envious.

Saw *Pride & Prejudice* (1940 US adaptation, with Greer Garson & Laurence Olivier). Very good, much to my surprise.

Received *Geog. Mag*, *Sphere*, letters from Simon (presumably Nowell-Smith), & a Working Men's College man, Gee by name.

Friday 29 October

Wrote to Anne 54. Received 61 & 62 from her, & letter from Mother.

Sunday 31 October

Saw *Reluctant Dragon* (1941 mix of live-action and animation, a Disney showcase) for third time.

November 1943

Monday 1 November

Read *Put Out More Flags* (1942 Evelyn Waugh, set in 1939-40).

Tuesday 2 November

Reading *Cauldron Bubble* (1934, a fantasy novel of uprising & war) by Leslie Reid (1895-1977).

Wednesday 3 November

Received 63 & 74 from Anne.

Friday 5 November

Took part in Doubles Tournament. Failed at second round, but thoroughly enjoyed it, and didn't really do too badly. But I improve slowly, only my service having got much better.

Reading *The Escaping Club* (1926) by A.J. Evans (about the author's various escapes from PoW camps in WWI).

Saturday 6 November

Received letters 65 & 66 from Anne.

Russians captured Kiev.

Looked over a B17F, fitted for photo mapping. Can map with 3 cameras 10,000 sq. miles per hour at 20,000 feet, cruising at 190 mph. (Boeing B17 known as the Flying Fortress, the most famous American heavy bomber; see Appendix 2).

Sergeant told me he had seen B29 in US. About size of our Ensign. (The B29 was the formidable Boeing Superfortress, a high-altitude, long-range bomber introduced from autumn 1943; see Appendix 2). Also arsenal Liberators & Fortresses.

Received parcels & letters. Wrote Anne 55. Wrote Ripper & Isobel.

Monday 8 November

Wrote Nicky.

Stone & Flower (1943, Poems 1935-43 by Kathleen Raine with drawings by Barbara Hepworth) is giving me great pleasure. I don't agree that Barbara Hepworth's drawings are entirely inappropriate, though I think all should have been in colour.

The air war, flying in formation: *TOP* **38** A convoy of single-engine Hurricane fighters, carrying long-range fuel tanks, is guided by a Blenheim twin-engine bomber en route from Takoradi to Cairo. *ABOVE* **39** US Army Airforce Liberators on a bombing mission over North Africa.

At Takoradi: *ABOVE AND RIGHT* **40, 41** Hurricanes are removed from the packing cases used to ship them from Britain before being reassembled and flown in convoy to Cairo. *BELOW* **42** Airmen at Takoradi work on the engine of a US-made Tomahawk fighter.

Desert showdown: *TOP* **43** General Montgomery led a reinforced and reinvigorated Eighth Army to victory at El Alamein in November 1942. *ABOVE* **44** Field Marshal Rommel, Afrikakorps commander, had long outfoxed the British, but met his match in Montgomery.

ABOVE **45** Allied commanders at Algiers, 28 May 1943: left to right around Churchill, Eden (Foreign Secretary), Brooke (CIGS), Tedder (chief, Middle East Airforce), Cunningham (chief, Royal Navy Mediterranean Fleet), Alexander (C-in-C, Middle East forces), Marshall (US Chief of Staff), Eisenhower (US military C-in-C), Montgomery (standing).

RIGHT **46** Tehran conference, 28 November-1 December 1943. Soviet dictator Stalin (at left) meets US President Roosevelt for the first time; Churchill (at right) is supported by Brooke (centre, back row) and Royal Navy commanders.

THE BRITISH ARMY MAKES A LIGH
Rommel is routed and driven from Eg
B.O.S. 45.

47 An 'over-the-top' British propaganda poster, looking back on the dénouement in 1943 of the Desert War, portrays the Allied victory as much swifter and easier than it actually proved. Inexperienced US troops received a bloody nose in February 1943 at the Kasserine Pass in Tunisia, while it took until late March for Eighth Army to break through the heavily defended Mareth Line in eastern Tunisia.

Exercise Spartan, 9 March 1943, the largest trial of troops ever conducted on British soil: *TOP* **48** Covenanter tanks and artillery pass through a village. *ABOVE* **49** Farmers' haystacks were commandeered for artillery positions, disrupting civilian life as recorded by Anne and also Violet Bradby in her diary.

Tuesday 9 November

Both David & myself have been elected members of the Double Crown Club, David by Dick (presumably Dick de la Mare, production director at Faber) & Berthold (Wolpe, designer of the typeface Albertus and jacket designer at Faber), myself by Barnett (Freedman, great lithographer and friend of A & VR) & Shand. (See Introduction.)

Wednesday 10 November

Wrote to Mother.

Received another parcel from Chris. He dared to call up on the RT at Takoradi, via Ikeja. Ikeja wouldn't pass on the message, but I heard his voice saying: 'Is Red Ridler on duty in the Tower at Kano?' (VR was not exactly a redhead, but retained a gingerish tinge from his childhood.) I called Ikeja & told them 'yes'.

Received 67 & 68 from Anne.

Thursday 11 November

Wrote to David.

Friday 12 November

Reading *Low Company* (1936, a burglar's autobiography) by Mark Benney (1910-73, 'a better writer than he was a criminal').

Sunday 14 November

Visited Mission for first time. Met David's friend Miss Miller.

Monday 15 November

Wrote to Anne 56.

The engine of a Vent. packed in on its way from here to Maiduguri. (The Lockheed B34 Ventura was a twin-engine light bomber; see Appendix 2.) The pilot brought her back on one engine, but couldn't keep height. He tried to land on the wrong runway, touched down at terrific speed, bounced about 20 feet into the air, then shouted 'bellylanding' over the R/T, touched down again & pulled his wheels up. They all got out without any trouble, & the plane isn't badly damaged, though the belly was knocked about a bit. All 3 looked red in the face from excitement when they reported to the Tower.

Wednesday 17 November

Reading *Conditions of Peace* (about the war's economic causes and potential resolution) by E.H. Carr (1892-1982); & the André Gide (1869-1951; *La Porte Étroite* 1909 perhaps, or *Si le Grain ne Meurt* 1926?).

Went to the Mission again. Enjoyed the food, but found the games very trying indeed. The fun is so VERY clean.

Thursday 18 November

Have now had new shelves fitted in the Library, a great improvement. I should like to do more in the way of magazines, but the room is not suitable for sitting about in, & I am afraid that papers would not be returned once they are removed.

Friday 19 November

Wrote to Mildred. Received letter from Turner.

Saturday 20 November

Received photos, *Horizon* Sept, & proofs of *Cain* & *The 9* (presumably *The Nine Bright Shiners*, that & *Cain* being a volume of poetry and a play by AR).

Took part in another Doubles Tournament and survived 2 rounds.

Sunday 21 November

Saw *Come Live with Me* (1941 romantic comedy starring James Stewart & Hedy Lamarr, about an immigrée from Nazi-annexed Austria who has to marry to stay in the US) for 2nd time.

Monday 22 November

Wrote Anne 57.

Victor Smith has sent me *Barchester Towers* (Trollope, 1857), as a Christmas present I suppose.

Tuesday 23 November

George Smith went this a.m. I am very sorry about this, but we may be able to meet after the war. I can't think why we didn't make acquaintance earlier.

Wednesday 24 November

Wrote to Turner.

Visited Miss Miller with Mitchell & Albiston. She lived in Archfield Road (in Cotham, Bristol, very near to Trelawney Rd where VR grew up), & was a member of St Matthews (also in Cotham). I like her & enjoyed our conversation, though she is so eccentric that it isn't easy to find out what her attitude to Africans really is. She told me that they & their chiefs should do more for their own improvement & not leave it all to us. Also that Govt strongly favours the Moslems.

Thursday 25 November

Wrote to M&F.

Reading Maupassant short stories (1881 & later).

Sent off parcel containing spoons about this date.

Friday 26 November

Received signal about broadcast next Saturday at 9.15 by Child Relative (ie AR), as it put it.

Reg Bellenger has landed up in the Congo, at Libreville.

Saturday 27 November

Received *Transformation,* & 69 & 70 from Anne.

Wrote to Anne 58.

Tuesday 30 November

Put in for remustering to Airfield Control with Walker.

December 1943

Wednesday 1 December

Dobson is leaving tomorrow.

Received another binding letter from Bushell. Also copies of *N.E.W.*

Derr, one of the Yanks in the Tower, came out with the curious tale today that Churchill, Roosevelt & Cordell Hull (US Secretary of State) were in Cairo to meet a high-ranking German officer who, according to some US airman in Cairo, landed in a big German transport escorted by P38's. (The Lockheed P38 Lightning was a twin-engine, long-range fighter and fighter-bomber used by the US airforce from mid-1941 onwards; see Appendix 2.) I should not have taken notice of this but for a paragraph I saw in *Newsweek* for Nov. 15 which said that 'High Circles' in Washington were certain that Germany was now putting out 'peace feelers'.

Thursday 2 December

Started reading *Manon Lescaut* (1731, Abbé Prévost).

Friday 3 December

Wrote to Victor Smith.

Saw *Hit Parade of 1941* (1940), a poor Republic film (Republic Pictures, LA film corporation 1935-67), but for a good act by Borrah Minevitch (a notable harmonica player who appeared in numerous Hollywood films between 1934 & 1943).

Saturday 4 December

Wrote to Church & Bushell. Sent off parcel of books. Received 71 from Anne.

Listened in at 10 tonight. Anne spoke alone (presumably reading her poetry on the BBC), but I didn't hear the first part owing to surging. Mr Lynn insisted on trying to switch to a better station, & of course lost them both. I got back to the original one myself.

Sunday 5 December

Wrote Anne 59.

Monday 6 December

Wrote David.

Saw some B25's fitted with 75 mm cannon. (The B25 Mitchell medium bomber and ground-attack aircraft remained in use worldwide even as late as 1979; see Appendix 2.) They look highly dangerous from any point of view. The shells are ejected down a shute behind the breech, & then fall out through a trap door into the air.

Tuesday 7 December

Wrote to Mother.

Reading *The Fall of Paris* (1942, novel depicting the decay of French society from 1934 to 1940) by Ilya Ehrenburg (1891-1967).

Wednesday 8 to Saturday 11 December

Visited the old city to see the Sallah celebrations (for the end of Ramadan) the Moslem Christmas Day. We went down in a lorry at 8 o'clock, ploughing our way through thousands of natives whose fez-covered heads stretched away like snow into the distance. As a contrast to the white robes of the natives, the Emir & his chiefs, all on horseback, were clothed in rich colours. Prayers were being held in the field outside the main gate. Then with pistols firing the crowd moved in an amazingly orderly way towards the Emir's Palace. We followed in our truck, & found that a small stand with chairs on it had been put up for Europeans. Our C.O. was there with other officers, the D.O. & his wife. Also an obnoxious Yank who chewed gum & took moving pictures.

The crowd gathered in a wide space around us. While we waited for the Emir to appear in procession, we were entertained by trick cyclists dressed in football jerseys & sports caps. They went down well with the crowd, especially with the gaily dressed children. Then came a clown on stilts. He was followed by 3 witch doctors, 2 on horseback. One had a great wig of yellow goat hair which he shook violently as he approached. Another was dressed in bird feathers, while the third looked like an old clothes shop. Their idea of humour was to pretend to be amazed at the sight of us. They twisted their heads from side to side with short quick gestures, eyes staring, & chattered away at us. Then they gave place to the band. This was made up primarily of drummers & trumpeters with their long trumpets. They were supported by 3 camel drummers, who beat small drums slowly in 3/4 time.

At last the scurrying of horses announced the Emir's approach. The horses of himself & his cortège were buried under a mass of tinsel & brocade. His saddle pommel was of filigree silver. He wore a magnificent robe of cream silk. His slippers were covered with big feathers. All were dignified & solemn. The rest was anti-climax. Nothing particular happened.

Went down with Dave & Jock.

Received parcel from WMC (Working Men's Club? More likely than War Manpower Commission, which is US), also *Le Silence de la Mer* (1941 Paris-set novel by 'Vercors' aka Jean Bruller 1902-91, in which an old man & his niece resist by not speaking to their occupying Nazi officer), & other enclosures from Anne.

Sunday 12 December

Wrote Anne 60 (see below, with its variant on the description of the Sallah celebrations given above).
Wrote Mrs Franklin.

Letter No. 60 from Vivian to Anne, 12 December 1943
1212727 LAC Ridler RAF Kano, WAF
My dearest,
Your letter & enclosures of 10 October came today. I am very pleased to have Le Silence, *& will report on it in due course. Why I asked for it myself was a laudatory note in the* New Statesman. *I am wondering now whom I shall agree with. If you happen to be writing to Enrica, will you please tell her I have received it safely, & shall be writing by sea.*

When I read all those letters about the Wigmore Hall affair I feel more & more sorry that I could not have been there to hear & see you. You seem to have done so much better than the others, & to convey my pride in you is so ineffective at this distance. (AR records the event in her *Memoirs* (2004), p.141: in September 1943 she was one of the very few women poets – together with Kathleen Raine, Edith Sitwell & Lady Dorothy Wellesley – to be invited to give a public poetry reading, along with ten male poets, at the Wigmore Hall in aid of the National Council for Women & Aid to China. William Empson read a long, obscure poem, 'Bacchus', and danced on the spot 'like a satyr'. A Chinese poet participating criticized Britain's slowness in coming to the aid of China, which AR thought a bit rich. TS Eliot – whose assistant AR had been – gave her 'one of his delightfully ambiguous comments: "You couldn't have done better."') *I hope you will still think of reading for the BBC occasionally. It would be fun to hear you again in West Africa too, bless you.*

On Wednesday I went down to the old city early with a party of other fellows to see the Moslem equivalent of Christmas Day being celebrated. They call it the Sallah. It begins with the wholesale slaughtering of goats, but we were fortunately too late to see that. We got to the outskirts at about 8.15. The first sight of the crowd made a deep impression on me. They had assembled on a flat piece of ground just outside the main gate. I can't even guess how many there were – possibly 30,000 or more. Prayers were being held when we drew up in our lorry. The heads, each capped with a fez, stretched away into the distance like snow which transformed itself into a great sea each time they were bowed to the ground. All the men wore white clothes, and the children were decked out in bright coloured cottons, with powder on their faces. No women were allowed to attend.

The Emir & his chiefs were mounted on horses in the centre of the crowd, both species loaded down with splendid robes like crusaders. They looked appropriately sinister, keeping very still during the proceedings. When this part was over, a few blanks were fired by someone in a desultory way, and the crowd moved off – in an orderly way that amazed me, considering how many youths there were, rushing to & fro – to the centre of the city near the Emir's Palace, where he was to meet the Resident.

We pushed slowly through, bowing & smiling like dictators from our high lorry. A kind of dais had been put up, with chairs on it, for the White Man. We all sat down, waiting for the grand climax. At first the effect was rather damped by the appearance of three trick cyclists dressed in football jerseys. Then one of our corporals scurried in on a bicycle, much to our amusement. The crowd, looking marvellous and neatly packed around the street sides, remained patient & approving. Nothing happened for quite a time. At last a fiendish din announced the approach of the royal band, or its equivalent. It came into sight accompanied by jesters, one on high stilts, two on horses, and one on foot. They had wigs of goat hair, and their idea of amusing the crowd was to come very close to us and twitch their heads in amazement from side to side, as though wondering whether one could be white and sane at the same time. This delighted me more than anything else, because it was the first time I had seen satire in a Nigerian. They really were funny.

The actual climax, when it came, was really an anti-climax except for one small incident. This was when several horsemen dashed across the square with robes flying, pulling the horses back on their haunches when they reached the other side. The dust they raised, the yells & the mistiness of the morning, turned the scene into a Gary Cooper affair, and in fact I should have been more pleased to see him than the Emir, who appeared very slowly accompanied by various attendants, one of them carrying a large green & orange umbrella, & what seemed to be the rest of the orchestra mounted on three camels, tom-tomming away in 3-4 time.

I had a good look at the Emir when he came up. His dress was of the most lovely cream silk with little ornament. His slippers were covered with large ostrich feathers dyed blue, so that when he approached he seemed to be walking very neatly on two frying-pans. After the necessary salutations he remounted & rode slowly towards the Palace & his 200 wives. And that was that. Nothing exciting, but I would not have missed it.

These dramatic doings have quite squeezed out the poppets. But Janey must have her message. Darling Janey, Do you know what a hippopotamus is? I am asking you because the necklace in your parcel is made of hippo bone. Mummy can probably show you a picture of one. What big mouths they have! All the better to kiss you with, my honey. Here is another invisible kiss, but this time you must pass it on to Alison for me. Love from Daddy.

Blessings my dearest.
One month, two...?
Your Vivian

Monday 13 December

Received Income Tax Note & letter from Mrs Read.

Began *Barchester Towers*. Read *Le Silence de la Mer*.

Tuesday 14 December

Went to Mission for Tennis Tournament. They beat our team. Germaine is their best player; he has an unusually quick eye.

Several Nigerian children were playing on the swings & trapeze nearby. The missionaries' children speak Hausa & talk away with the local people.

Wednesday 15 December

Despatched the Tax Note. Wrote to Enrica. Saw *Lady Has Plans* (1942, she does indeed – secret ones, tattooed on her back). Fairly good.

Friday 17 December

Wrote to Anne 61.

Saturday 18 December

Received *Horizon* & oddments.

Saw *Arsenic & Old Lace* (1943, 'good macabre fun' directed by Frank Capra & starring Cary Grant, based on Joseph Kesselring's 1941 Broadway play) & *Let's Face It* (1943 musical comedy starring Bob Hope) at Yank camp.

No airmail. But more reliefs up, including w/ops (wireless operators).

Sunday 19 December

Saw *A Woman's Face* (1941 US melodrama in which the 'woman' Joan Crawford's facial disfigurement is healed), made by George Cukor. Very good indeed.

Monday 20 December

Wrote to David.

I have been feeling very cold at nights, though the temperature isn't much below 58 degrees. One man who has written from home says he just can't keep warm. He sleeps with all his clothes on, under 5 blankets, & remains ice-cold! What a prospect.

Tuesday 21 December

Went to Kano. Bought some material on the advice of a pleasant young blonde who happened to come in. I looked her in the eye without flinching while we talked of panties, petticoats & all the usual paraphernalia. She was very helpful in the end.

Wednesday 22 December

Went to Kano. Bought 2 fezzes & one aertex sports vest.

Received 72 & 73 from Anne. Also 1 from Mildred, Nellie & M&F.

Saw *Man of Conquest* (1939 western). Deadly.

Thursday 23 December

Reading *Brighton Rock* (1938, Graham Greene 1904-91).

The Gang Show arrived this morning by DC. They are playing tonight & I hope tomorrow night. Eric Christmas (1916-2000, British actor whose film & TV career took off in the 1970s) is not in this particular show, but may turn up in another one later. (Gang Shows were Scout-based revues created in 1932 by Ralph Reader, 1903-82, first performed in Britain & spreading worldwide; still extant today. Nazi Ambassador Joachim von Ribbentrop, 1893-1946, saw the 1938 London Gang Show and invited Reader to visit the Hitler Youth Movement! RAF Gang Shows were expanded versions touring to theatres of war from Iceland to Burma, travelling 100,000 miles and entertaining 3 ½ million servicemen; casts included future stars such as Peter Sellers, Tony Hancock, Harry Worth & Dick Emery. Reader was awarded an MBE (Military Division) in 1943 for services to the RAF; these included not only entertainment, but also intelligence work! He was deployed to report back from any stations he visited for signs of subversive propaganda, a matter of concern to RAF high command.)

Received letter & negs from Slim Williams. No news though.

Friday 24 December

Bought more stuff in Kano. Also had 3 pairs of pants stolen which Malone & I were unwise enough to leave in the bag outside UAC.

Went to Gang Show at night. Very good, though some members had a fit of the giggles & wrecked one sketch & a few small acts.

Saturday 25 December

Saw final of football competition. Then went to Service at 11. Dinner at 1400. Colossal feed, best I have had in the Service. Slept through until 6.30 in the evening.

Read Carter Dickson's *She Died A Lady* (1943 whodunnit featuring series detective Sir Henry Merrivale; Carter Dickson was US author John Dickson Carr, 1906-77).

Sunday 26 December

Wrote Anne 62.

Monday 27 December

Wrote Slim Williams. Received 75 & 76 from Anne, also 72. One from Mother, & one from Matt & Jan (Bradby).

Wednesday 29 December

Wrote to Mother. Received letters from Thea & Aunt Ada.

Thursday 30 December

Wrote to Jan & Matt.

Friday 31 December

Wrote to Thea.

A service was to be held at the Mission & I went along at 9 with Dave Bell. The chop was good, BUT it was followed by two solid hours of praying, singing awful hymns & testifying. We also had to endure a female soloist who tremoloed, slipped & slided from note to note. We got back at 1 & toasted each other with beer. Aussie had put a kitten in Fred's bed, & of course it messed it before morning, to my satisfaction.

Saturday 1 January 1944

Wrote Anne 63.

Started *The Yellow Mask* (1855) by Wilkie Collins. Surprisingly crude so far.

A new man, Cpl Laffey, tells me that the CMS now have some French books in. I shall go down on Monday to look round.

DIARY ENDS

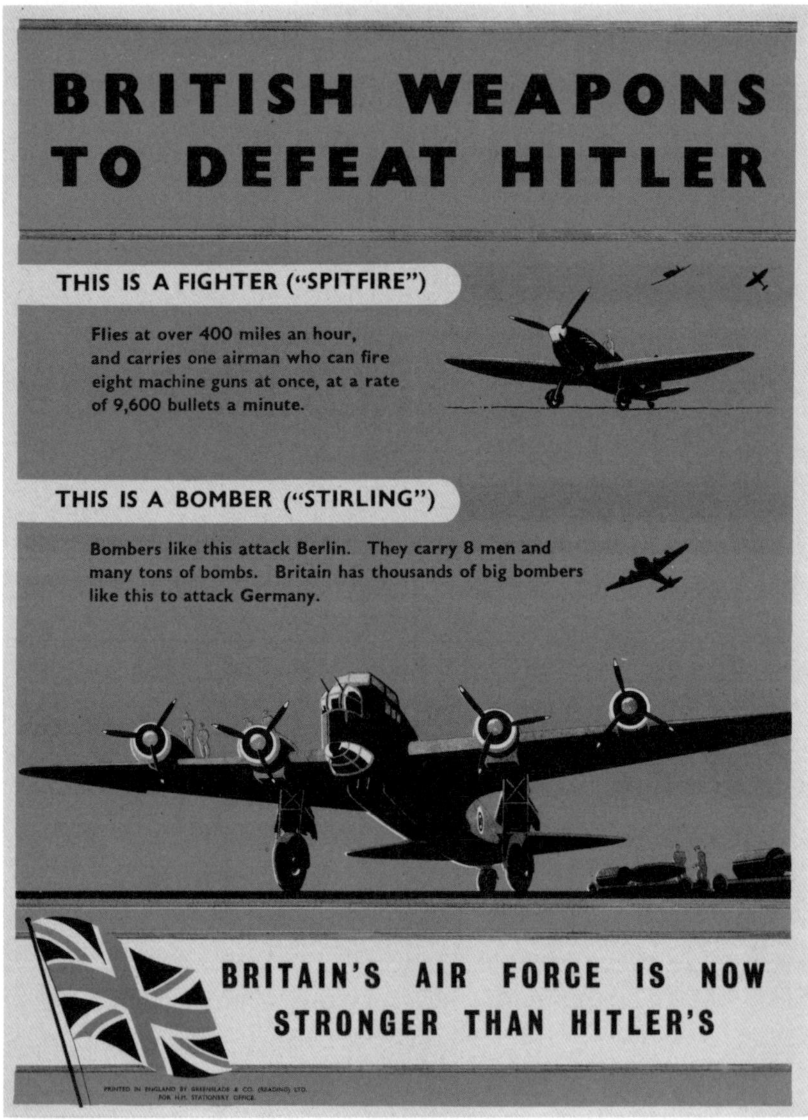

The Spitfire was the iconic British fighter in the war, able to compete effectively with the German Me109. The Stirling, Halifax and above all Lancaster heavy bombers were the backbone of the British air assault on Nazi Europe.

EPILOGUE

A Homecoming and New Postings

Vivian's war diary in Nigeria ends at the very beginning of January 1944. Whether or not he started another one is unknown: nothing has come to light at any rate. We have therefore to rely for what happens next primarily on the vivid weekly diary kept throughout the war by Anne's mother, Violet Bradby, experiencing the conflict from her and Kit Bradby's retirement home at Ringshall End on the edge of the village of Little Gaddesden, near Berkhamsted, just north of London. Violet's account is so colourful and rich in detail that it will be quoted here at length, though shortened slightly to focus on Vivian, his homecoming and subsequent postings, and on Anne and her wider family.

One relevant short letter from Anne to John Hayward for 12 August 1944 is included, which conveys her joy at Vivian's safe return. They had not seen each other for an agonizing 18 months, and Vivian had never met and held his now 14-month-old baby daughter Alison. And a single surviving letter of Vivian's in this period (to David Bland of 20 February 1946, conveying condolences at the death of David's brother Roger, a vicar) reveals that he is at the HQ of the British Air Forces Overseas where, as Violet's diary tells us, he is an intelligence officer now helping to edit the RAF magazine *Wing*.

WEEKLY WAR DIARY BY VIOLET BRADBY

Extracts June 1944–April 1946

➢

2 June 1944

Wire from Vivian on Thursday, safe in England such a relief.

Allies took Velletri & Valmontane (on the last line of German defence south of Rome) & have taken 20,000 prisoners.

➢

9 June 1944

On Tuesday June 6th in the hours between 6 & 8 am the long-expected invasion of France began. The points were on the Cherbourg Peninsula & the coast by Caen. The RAF & US had been pounding coast & batteries & so had the RN for the last days & in spite of what Rommel had done in coast defences the Allies managed to land without as many casualties as they had expected, tho' at one place esp. the resistance was bitter with fire from a post at point blank range. Churchill made two statements in the House, BBC gave 1st-hand broadcasts & we were all full of the thought of it all the time.

Rome was entered by the Allies on June 4th & the Germans are retreating all the way across Italy, with stiffer resistance in E side in the hills. Alexander's tactics swept the Germans aside so that Rome was hardly affected & the Germans hadn't time to do much demolishing, but they did some & some mining on the E side.

The (D-Day) invasion had to be put off for 24 hours owing to windy stormy weather.

Vivian came on Thursday evening from Blackpool, phoning up Berkhamsted (a postcard came in the morning saying he would probably be arriving) & Anne took Jane down in the Hiley's car to meet him. He was looking a bit yellow but in great form: he had come from Gib. in a ship containing 4,000 tho' meant only to hold 600. He had been away in W Africa since September 1942 (in fact having left the UK that October) & had never seen Alison. Jane v. excited & A took to him after a little shyness. His packs were crammed with presents for us all, mine were two jolly dress lengths, soap & Pond's coldcream.

Heard from Christopher from Southampton, v. busy & saying we are not to worry if we don't hear regularly. I wonder if he is going to France. (Christopher Bradby, Anne's elder brother, spent the war in the Royal Army Service Corps.)

➢

16 June 1944

Allies maintaining their footing in France & slowly extending it with the help of Naval bombardment & constant air bombing. Americans pushing up the Cherbourg Peninsula, Br. & Canadians along by Caen. BBC give war commentaries after the news each night, generally with a good deal of interesting stuff. Allies advancing rapidly up Italy & are past Orvieto on left wing. Churchill & the King both went over to France. US still will not recognize the French Committee of Nat. Liberation, & the difficulties with Gen. de Gaulle are great. It is said to be partly personal on Roosevelt's side & obviously de Gaulle is not at all easy to get on with.

Germans launch their 'secret weapon', a pilotless aeroplane. It seems to have a good deal of nuisance value but as they can't tell where it has crashed, not much military use.

Vivian & Anne very happy to be together & Jane loves having V at home.

➢

23 June 1944

Allies have got through Perugia. Weather very wet in Italy & uncomfortably windy for our landings in Normandy. Americans advancing up the Cherbourg Peninsula, Germans retiring into the town. Resistance stubborn E of Caen. Allies helped by the French underground forces. De Gaulle went over to Bayeux, & had a great reception. We saw pilotless aeroplanes, called by Americans 'Doodle Bugs', on two evenings going across the sky from S to N & heard they came down near Luton by a Hospital & at Leverstock Green. The Hosp. only had windows blasted. They cause much damage in London; they have now stopped firing at them over the city & fire or attack them with planes before they arrive over London. Westminster has had damage, one pier of Charing Cross bridge hit & Victoria Station. Aeroplanes constantly attacking their starting points in France. Germans excited over their new weapon.

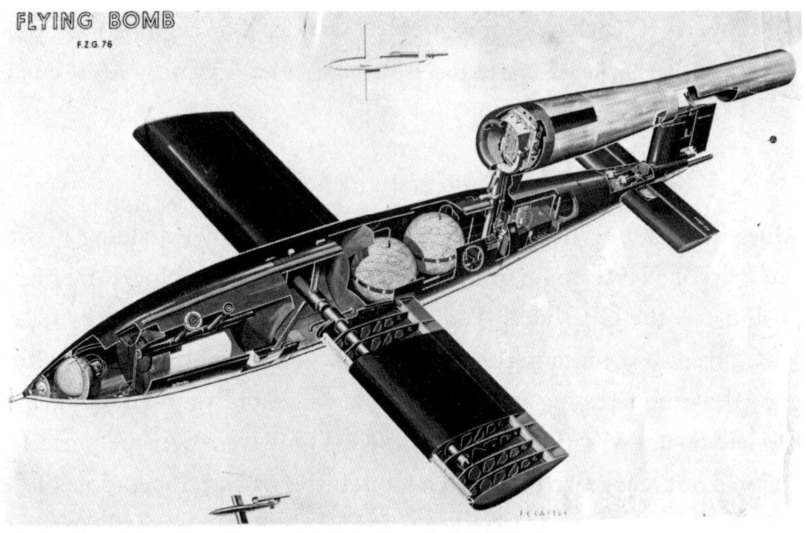

The Germans launched their 'secret weapons', the V1 (*ABOVE*) and V2 (*RIGHT*) rockets, against Britain on 13 June and 8 September 1944 respectively. As Violet Bradby notes in her diary, however, they were of little use militarily since they fell indiscriminately across southern Britain. In any case, they came too late in the conflict to affect its outcome.

Russians start a new offensive round Vitebsk, big breakthrough there & at Mogilev. Japs have had a heavy Naval blow & lost 350 planes. Tokyo bombed from carrier-borne planes.

Christopher is busy at S'hampton living in a bombed house. V went back to report at Blackpool on Friday.

➢

30 June 1944

Vivian has been posted to Westcott, RAF Camp near Aylesbury. Pilotless planes still causing much damage & alarm in London & S counties. Have alerts here but none of the bombs have fallen really near. Cherbourg taken by the Americans. Stiff fighting at our end of line round Villers Bocage. The Germans have much difficulty in bringing up men & munition owing to French sabotage & our bombing. Kit had a most vivid letter from GN Oliver now a Commodore written from HMS *Hilary* off coast of Normandy; he is enthusiastic about the efficiency of our sea operation in the landing & the spirit of the men.

Russians pushing rapidly through towards Minsk, taking numbers of prisoners & Germans thoroughly disorganized.

Alison has two teeth & two more nearly through. WI on Wednesday with Mime of Burghers of Calais in wh. Anne & I acted.

➢

7 July 1944

Vivian came home for weekend & again for the night on Wednesday. He rode back on Father's bike, 20 miles in the rain, & finds the bicycle very useful at the camp.... Letters from C still at S'hampton & expecting his turn to go over to 'the far shore' as the Army orders call it.

Flying bombs still being a great trouble in London & the South of England. Churchill made a statement about them in the House, & said they had known abt. them months ago & the RAF had been bombing the installations, & in one instance had killed a group of scientists who were working at the preparation of the bombs. Fatal casualties to date had been 2,750, almost the number of bombs which had come over, making one death per bomb, but there are about 8,000 casualties as well. Children are being evacuated from London, with their mothers, otherwise workers asked to stay at their jobs & seek shelter at night. . . . RAF managed to hit one deep cliff cave in France where they had stores of bombs. . . . US making another thrust in S of Cherbourg Peninsula. Our troops & Canadians E & W of Caen.

➢

14 July 1944

Flying bomb crashed in woods near Aldbury turn off Berkhamsted Common. Windows in the brick kiln cottage broken but no one hurt. Allies advancing slowly in Normandy. San Gemignano shelled by Germans & destroyed, 5th & 8th Armies advancing steadily on Leghorn & Ancona. Russians pushing on towards Brest Litovsk. Grodno taken & Dvinsk.

V came for a night on Wednesday. Wet & chilly.

➢

21 July 1944

Great sensation over attempted assassination of Hitler at Berchtesgaden (in fact at the so-called Wolf's Lair at the Berghof, Hitler's old HQ 4 miles from Rastenburg in East Prussia) by a group of Army officers. As all tel. communications cut between Germany & Sweden it is hard to know what is going on, but obviously Hitler & Goering are much alarmed & broadcast to the Germans between 12 & 1 the night after the morning's attempt (on 20 July). The officer who placed the bomb, Klaus von Stauffenberg, has been shot they say, & Himmler made C in C of the 'Heimathleer' (the Reserve Army; bizarrely and unbeknownst to Hitler, Himmler was also making secret peace overtures to the British & Americans). Col. Beck is said to have been the originator of the plot & to be 'no longer among the living'. As the summing up on the BBC said it may not be the end but the beginning of the end.

Ceaseless bombing from US & RAF & an immense Air bombing near Caen to prepare for infantry advance, but no large breakthrough by tanks as one hoped & of course rain came & helped the Germans. Leghorn & Ancona both taken, & on the Russian front Brest Litovsk &

Ostrov while Lvov is threatened & thousands of German prisoners were marched through Moscow, through silent crowds of Russians.

Letter from David Bland dated beginning of May.

➢

29 July 1944

Vivian came home on Sunday & again on Thursday. Also on Thursday Matt came for one night having been to a meeting at the Admiralty. He had not met V before! (Anne's brother Matt Bradby served in the Royal Navy during the war, first in Ceylon, then in charge of the Naval draft on board the battleship *Duke of York* on its voyage through the Atlantic to Britain in October 1942, and finally at Derby House in Liverpool, the Western Approaches Command Centre for the Royal Navy and RAF where integrated tactics against North Atlantic U-boats could be coordinated.)

Conflicting reports from Germany as to the Army plot against Hitler. Goebbels made a statement about it about 6 days late; he is to organize Germany for Total War! Russians continue to advance along their whole front, & have taken Lvov & Byelstock & thousands of Germans killed, 15,000 in one encirclement & 2,000 prisoners. US advancing in Normandy to Coutances. Flying bombs continue to be a menace ... Many are brought down & sites incessantly bombed by our planes. Hundreds of Londoners have been evacuated. Letter from Christopher saying his Company is on the move preparatory to going across to France. Weather bad in Normandy & poor on & off here.

I made up a petticoat for Anne from stuff V brought her from W Africa.

➢

4 August 1944

Americans are moving on fast into Brittany & find little opposition. They have taken Avranches, then Rennes & Brest. British troops having a stiffer time towards Vire south of Caen as it is the hinge of German line. Rommel was knocked out in an air raid, but is recovering. (He was hospitalized after two Canadian Spitfires strafed his staff car, which ended his military career; he survived till October 1944, when he was forced to commit suicide after being implicated – rightly or wrongly we do not know – in the July plot to assassinate Hitler; he had long wanted peace terms with the Allies.) Hitler has denounced a number of generals & senior officers & ordered that they are to be tried by the People's (Nazi) Court, wh. shows internal resistance movement much more widespread than they made out.

Russians sweeping on & are fighting in Warsaw & have taken Riga. Flying bombs continue to do damage. Churchill made a good speech on eve of H of C proroguing. Hopeful but serious as to effort still needed & evidently expecting the Germans will launch rocket bombs.

Raspberries nearly over. Vivian came over twice, & he drew out a Tablet inscription for Ella's grave, with the text They were lovely & pleasant in their lives, in beautiful lettering. (Ella David was one of Violet's elder sisters.)

➢

11 August 1944

Advance continuing – The sweep SE of the US troops kept secret so as to confuse the enemy. German attack on Avranches in force was repulsed, & they were encircled in a trap, with its exit at Falaise. Weather perfect & the RAF able to pound the retreating tanks & lorries. (The Allied victory was staggering: of 7 panzer (tank) divisions and 140,000 well-trained troops, only two dozen tanks and 1,300 men escaped.)

Letter from Christopher. He is near Caen, after a quiet voyage, camped in a field. He sounded cheerful. . . .

Germans evacuated Florence but blew up all the bridges exc. Ponte Vecchio which they blocked by blowing up houses at each end.

Letter from Anne to John Hayward
12 August 1944
Ringshall End

My dearest John,
It has been an indecently good summer for me. No flying bombs to speak of, tho' we watched two pass across the horizon; & no one dear to me killed. I have a brother in Normandy, but Vivian is safely in a camp only 20 miles off. He

can get over twice a week, & so for the first time the children can really get to know him. As soon as he arrived, the months of parting ceased to exist, & as far as family affairs go, all is happiness; but he is very much irked by the pointlessness of his job & his prolonged servitude in the RAF: he would like at least to get to France, but another trip to the tropics is more likely. I hope not: he came back on a ship carrying 6,000 whose normal complement was 650 (as we saw above, Violet gives the figures as 4,000 and 600 respectively: still a vast overcrowding!), *& kept on a table where he could not turn without touching the men on either side of him, or the man in a hammock just above. (Like Koestler's French camp in* Scum of the Earth.*)*

My red-headed Alison has changed from a mild, appealing baby into a termagant. Jane tells her long stories with a surrealist flavour, of which the best I've heard is:- 'D'you know how Dolly laid her eggs? First she sat on a rose, & then she sat on a gluclose tin & laid 'em. And she said to the chickens '<u>Don't</u> eat 'em. Don't, Don't, Don't. But they did!'

With all love, dear John, your tardy but still faithful

Anne

➢

18 August 1944

On August 15th a second landing made on the S coast of France on the Riviera. V. successful & Germans hardly made any resistance & our casualties v. light. Churchill who had been to Italy watched part of landing from a destroyer. Allies sweeping along in Normandy, & US troops have taken Orleans, Argentan & Tours etc. French Army now fighting in S of France under General de Tassigny. Russians having hard fighting round Warsaw & are on borders of E Prussia where Germans have been mobilizing everyone to dig trenches. Flying bombs go on but are many of them brought down by AA & fighters.

Battle of Normandy is now considered to be won, & Battle of France begun.

➢

25 August 1944

Enrica Garnier came for weekend & Vivian on leave for 10 days. Nellie (Violet & Kit's live-in cook-housekeeper) returned on Sunday night all the better for her fortnight's holiday. Wet & cold for some days. Nicholes corn was cut, poor crop.

After 4 days fighting Paris was freed by Free French & civilians, & everyone full of rejoicing but the Germans after asking for an Armistice to leave Paris, broke it & started fighting again. US troops were got in, armoured, but at the moment the town seems to contain many Germans still. Marseilles & Bordeaux both taken & troops have pushed up to Swiss border. Pétain has been taken off to Germany. Laval was being booed in streets of Bellegarde. Romanian town of Yassy taken by Russians, & Romanians gave in & accepted the terms offered earlier by Russians & began to fight against the Germans, great blow to them on account of Ploesti oil fields.

➢

1 September 1944

Humphrey (Violet's brother, the Publisher at Oxford University Press) came for 10 days. He was well though he gets tired easily. He & Kit had two games of golf.

Successes continue in France: Allies have now captured Le Havre & Dieppe & bomb sites for Doodle bugs so that by the end of the week, there was the longest lull from them that there has been since they began in June. Thousands of prisoners being taken & the Germans in full flight back presumably to the Siegfried Line. Dempsey the US General given equal command with Montgomery (who has been made Field Marshal) under Eisenhower. Rumours of slight jealousies over American troops being first in Paris etc. but Eisenhower seems to have smoothed things out with his usual tact.

Letter from Matt who had flown up to Scotland for a conference with the C in C & enjoyed his first Air journey. V's leave ended on Tuesday; he went down to Bristol to see his mother for two nights.

➢

8 September 1944

2nd Army made a rapid 50-mile advance & entered Brussels. Bulgarians & Finns both out of the War. Russians have been halted in Estonia temporarily but are advancing in the Carpathians. Heavy fighting round Rimini for the Gothic Line. Rundstedt appears to be the best German commander just now. (He was regarded by both Eisenhower and Montgomery as the outstanding German commander of the war.) Pas de Calais area has been cleared so flying bomb sites all taken & the few that come must be from Germany. Evacuees urged not to go back to London but they persist in doing so.

➢

15 September 1944

Allies enter Holland. Germans have flooded large areas. Brest & Boulogne still holding out. Bip wrote giving news of Christopher who seems well (Bip being his illustrator wife).

➢

22 September 1944

Thrilling airborne invasion of Holland to turn Siegfried Line. Operation v. successful but followed by desperate fighting for the bridge, & the troops were reduced to one sixth of their ration by the time the 2nd Army patrol got into touch & more reinforcements were dropped.

➢

29 September 1944

The paratroops at Arnhem had to be withdrawn after desperate fighting as a week of rain had prevented supplies & adequate air & tank support. Bridge at Nijmegen still held by one group & the two other groups remain also. (Montgomery's bold plan, endorsed by Eisenhower, was for Operation Market Garden to outflank the German defensive line by seizing 8 bridges across the lower Rhine near the Dutch town of Arnhem. Although the initial drop of 16,500 paratroops and 3,500 troops in gliders (1 British and 2 US divisions) was quite successful, the advance of the British 2nd Army's 30th Corps was so slow that by 25 September the British paratroops had to be withdrawn; the Germans took 6,000 prisoners.)

Busy with plum & apple & blackberry picking. Alison walks round her playpen but won't stand or walk alone. Jane & she have both had heavy colds. Finished navy blue sweater.

➢

6 October 1944

Letter from C from Belgium in a city (probably Brussels), v. busy in charge of 160 men but cannot tell us much because of censorship.

Fighting over Albert Canal & all along front. Aachen resisting. Dunkirk taken. Warsaw occupied by Germans who then ordered the entire population of 1,000,000 people to leave the city with no food or places to go to.

➢

13 October 1944

Calais taken. Canadians land at mouth of Scheldt behind Germans. Riga taken by Russians. Belgrade threatened. Fighting in Italy still heavy. Many Air successes against Japs, & 2 transports sunk.

➢

20 October 1944

Vivian was here for two nights. Melvilles to dinner on Thursday & we had music (Alan Melville would later become chorus master of the BBC Singers). Nellie out but we gave them soup, omelette & Cox apples.

Cheerful letters from C in Belgium & a parcel of chocolate & Lavender water. Churchill & Eden in Moscow for consultations with Stalin. Horthy the Hungarian Minister fled to Germany (in fact, after calling publicly for an armistice, he was removed by the Germans and imprisoned – hence he was not prosecuted at the later Nuremberg trials). Russians took Belgrade & are over the border in E Prussia. Slow advance by the Scheldt, weather bad.

➢

29 October 1944

Rain continues in Italy, holding up advance. Big triple battle at sea off the Philippines, in which casualties inflicted on Japs by aircraft; 1 battleship, 4 aircraft carriers, 10 destroyers etc. sunk & between 100 & 200 aircraft destroyed. (The Battle of Leyte Gulf, 24–25 October, was the biggest naval battle ever fought, in which the Japanese Combined Fleet, weaker than its US opponents, attempted to lure the Americans into a trap in order to prevent them landing at the island of Leyte in the Philippines. The ruse almost succeeded, but its ultimate failure meant the Japanese could never regain naval supremacy.)

WI talk on old history of L Gaddesden from Vicars Bell (the local schoolmaster and author). Coal rationing sounds as if it will be drastic & prob. this will be our 3rd winter without Central heating.

Hard fighting in E Prussia. Churchill back from Moscow after friendly talks with Stalin. Eden went on to Cairo & Athens.

Vivian had interview in London & has been accepted for a Commission tho' at present there is no vacancy in the Flying Control Dept.

➢

3 November 1944

V2 bomb fell on Commer Motor works near Luton killing 17 people. . . . Matt may be getting job as HM of Training School & has applied to the Admiralty for release.

➢

10 November 1944

Letter from Christopher; he had been to see *Richard III* in Flemish.

Churchill & Eden went to Paris & had grand reception. Lord Moyne assassinated in Cairo. Germans pushed back in Holland after hard fighting in flooded country. Eden went to Athens, where regular supplies are being organized to relieve the terrible shortage of everything. Italy & France in sad need too. Hitler made no speech on the Anniversary of the Beer Halle Putsch, various excuses given. Russians approaching Budapest.

➢

17 November 1944

Flying bombs (V2) continue to do damage in London & S England. Himmler has tried to make a convincing case for the non-appearance of Hitler, who is probably ill or mentally deranged.

➢

24 November 1944

Letter from C again, we think he is in Antwerp. Tokyo bombed by US, Strasbourg & Metz both freed by Free French forces. Allies continue to advance slowly.

➢

1 December 1944

Matt has been released from the Navy, & will take up his new post as Head of the Nautical Training School at Heswall on Deeside as soon as he has trained his relief at Derby House.

Finished knitted skirt for Jane. Alison still won't walk alone but is forward in saying words & understanding all we say. The Germans retreating in Hungary & Russians are approaching Budapest from two sides. Large forces against the Allies in the W, but we are slowly pushing them back. Antwerp is now in use, clear of mines and demolitions which will be a great advantage. (Although this port, crucial for the supply of fuel, had been captured by Montgomery on 4 September, his failure then to secure the estuary before his dash to the Rhine, enabled the Germans to prevent Antwerp's use till late November.) V2s continue to come over & cause casualties.

➢

8 December 1944

Vivian & Anne went over to Letchworth to see *Cain* performed by a quaker Co Ed School there; v. well done & great success. (*Cain* Anne's first play.)

Fighting in Athens between forces of the guerrilla troops & foot soldiers & police. Our forces have had to support the foot, & a good deal of shooting has been going on. Discussion in House with good speeches from Churchill & Eden. A large majority against the motion of censure. Allies pushing on in Holland. Russians closing in on Budapest. V2s still coming over & doing damage. Home Guard stand down & thanked by King in broadcast.

➢

18 December 1944

Fighting still going on in Athens: Gen. Alexander went to consult Gen. Scobie & Mr Harold Macmillan (1894-1988, Conservative politician and Alexander's political adviser, later British prime minister 1957-63). Russians still nearer Budapest. V2s came over most nights. Huge air attacks over Germany.

➢

22–25 December 1944

Humphrey came on Friday 22nd, bringing turkey etc. & we bought a couple of chickens. Aga began to get cold, Nellie in despair. SOS to Mr Hughes who came up & cleared a bit of pipe wh. caused more draught, it slowly went up & finally on Sunday was hot enough to cook properly & we had all the usual Xmas fare, mince pies, turkey, plum pudding, iced cake etc.

Rundstedt started offensive agst. the US 1st Army in the Ardennes & made dangerous progress of abt. 30 miles. The Americans had evidently not mined roads & had not found out that the Germans were massing for this attack. Depressing news for Xmas time. (Hitler – to the horror of his senior generals including von Rundstedt – dreamed of a repeat of his 1940 Blitzkrieg by a surprise assault with 500,000 men, 30 divisions and over 1,000 aircraft through the weakly defended Ardennes forest that would reach Antwerp and critically divide Allied forces. Faced by only 5 new or recuperating American divisions and aided by poor weather that hampered Allied air intelligence, the Germans attacked on 16 December and made quick gains. On 19 December Eisenhower, finally realizing the true gravity of the situation, ordered Patton's US 3rd Army to the south to attack northwards, while the US 1st Army in the north pivoted southwards. At last the skies cleared, and on Christmas Eve 2,000 Allied aircraft shattered German supply lines, turning the 'Battle of the Bulge' in the Allies' favour.)

Churchill & Eden flew to Athens on Xmas Day. Greek Archbp. is to be Regent, but fighting still goes on between Papandreou's forces & ELAS. P has now resigned. Budapest closely attacked. Germans shoot officers the Russians sent with a flag of truce. V2s continue & came over Manchester one night.

Carols in Church on Sunday after Xmas Eve. Anne went at 7 on Xmas Day the rest of us after Matins. Nellie persuaded to come in for dinner on Xmas Day. I gave Kit a Shetland pullover, he gave me woollen coat. Xmas tree decorated by V & A with home-made baubles – V biked over on Xmas Eve & stayed till Boxing Day.

➢

29 December 1944

We heard later that Montgomery has been put in command of N part of the forces opposing Rundstedt's armies & that there are US & British troops under him. The US regts. seem to have fought well & it must have been the staff work wh. was lacking. They held out well in Bastogne & refused to give in. The advance has now been stopped, though the Germans are taking the offensive further S.

Athens being cleared & the Piraeus of ELAS forces but they will probably continue to fight in the interior.

➢

6 January 1945

Still very cold. Had two soldiers in from the Monument camp for supper & games on New Year's Day. Nellie came in for games. Vivian here & very helpful.

Weather in Italy & on the continent very wintry, & fighting bitter. Churchill & Eden went to France. Admiral Sir B Ramsey who directed Naval ops. on D-Day was killed in a flying accident, so was Sir Trafford Leigh-Mallory & his wife (they died in a different air crash the previous November; he had been C-in-C of the Allied Expeditionary Airforce during the Normandy landings).

Went up to lunch with Bip at Hampstead, delighted with (her son)

Bonamy's growth & development. She is starting at the *Daily Mail* on Monday after 5 years of night work at the *D Express*. Took her 4 eggs & some apples.

➢

12 January 1945

Russians started big offensive on the Vistula with a heavy Artillery bombardment & advanced 25 miles, using white tanks. They have also taken most of Budapest in spite of desperate resistance.

Americans landed in force on Luzon with very little opposition. Convoy attacked off Norway & ships sunk. U-boats now have a new ventilating mast which enables them to remain at sea longer & makes them harder to detect.

V2 bombs continue to come over London & the S counties. Western Front has been hampered in the fighting by the weather wh. has been snowy & also in Italy.

➢

19 January 1945

Russians began a big push on the E front with much success as the weather now hard. Warm debate in H of C on Greece, Eden asked for vote of confidence which was passed with only 7 agst. Churchill defended Govt. policy, & the ELAS forces seem to have been very cruel & high handed, & made a reign of terror in the country. The Regent Archbp. Damaskinos seems anxious to do his best under v. difficult circumstances.

➢

26 January 1945

Very cold still with hoar frost on trees & hedges & sometimes 16 deg. of frost at night.

Russians are still making steady progress in Poland & Silesia, killing many Germans & taking some prisoners. They have taken Poznan, approached Breslau & reached the Baltic, so the Germans in that region are cut off except by sea.

On W front Germans pressing in Alsace but Rundstedt's salient by Bastogne has been pressed back to its starting point with heavy losses. (The Germans lost 100,000 men and nearly all their tanks and aircraft in the failed Ardennes campaign.) Letters from C who is in Holland, very busy & he apparently likes his new Company & Bip heard from a fellow officer on leave that they like having him.

➢

2 February 1945

Russians only abt. 50 miles from Berlin with refugees streaming in front of them. What a nemesis after all the miseries they have inflicted but of course it is not only the guilty who suffer unfortunately. In Greece ELAS have sent back hostages some of whom were v. cruelly treated & many murdered. They are having negotiations with the Regent & Greek Gov't but difficulties are immense.

➢

9 February 1945

Jane's 4th birthday on the 4th Sunday but she had her party on Monday. Mrs Gray, Dr Lund & Ann, Clarissa, Trixie Bell & Lionel Brooke. Nellie made a sponge cake & iced it, 4 candles from David Pennant's parcel from India, chocolettes, ginger bisc. & a plum cake. Vivian on leave for a week. He was in bed for a day & a half with a temp.; he & Anne went over to Hertford on Friday house hunting & to dinner one night with Melvilles.

Churchill, Stalin & Roosevelt in conference somewhere in the Black Sea. Plane carrying many of Churchill's staff crashed & 14 were killed. (Stalin, afraid of flying, insisted that the conference 4-11 February be held at Yalta in the Crimea, to which he could travel by train in his green Tsarist coach. Military strategy was discussed, but the main focus was the postwar world – the allocation of Allied areas of control in an occupied Germany; the boundaries and government of a postwar Poland; the return of prisoners of war; the new United Nations Organization; and the entry of the Soviets into the war against Japan. Roosevelt – frail and destined to die two months later – was so desperate to gain Stalin's backing for UNO that he eventually gave in on Poland, which the Soviets now controlled anyway. A skilful Stalin – aided by

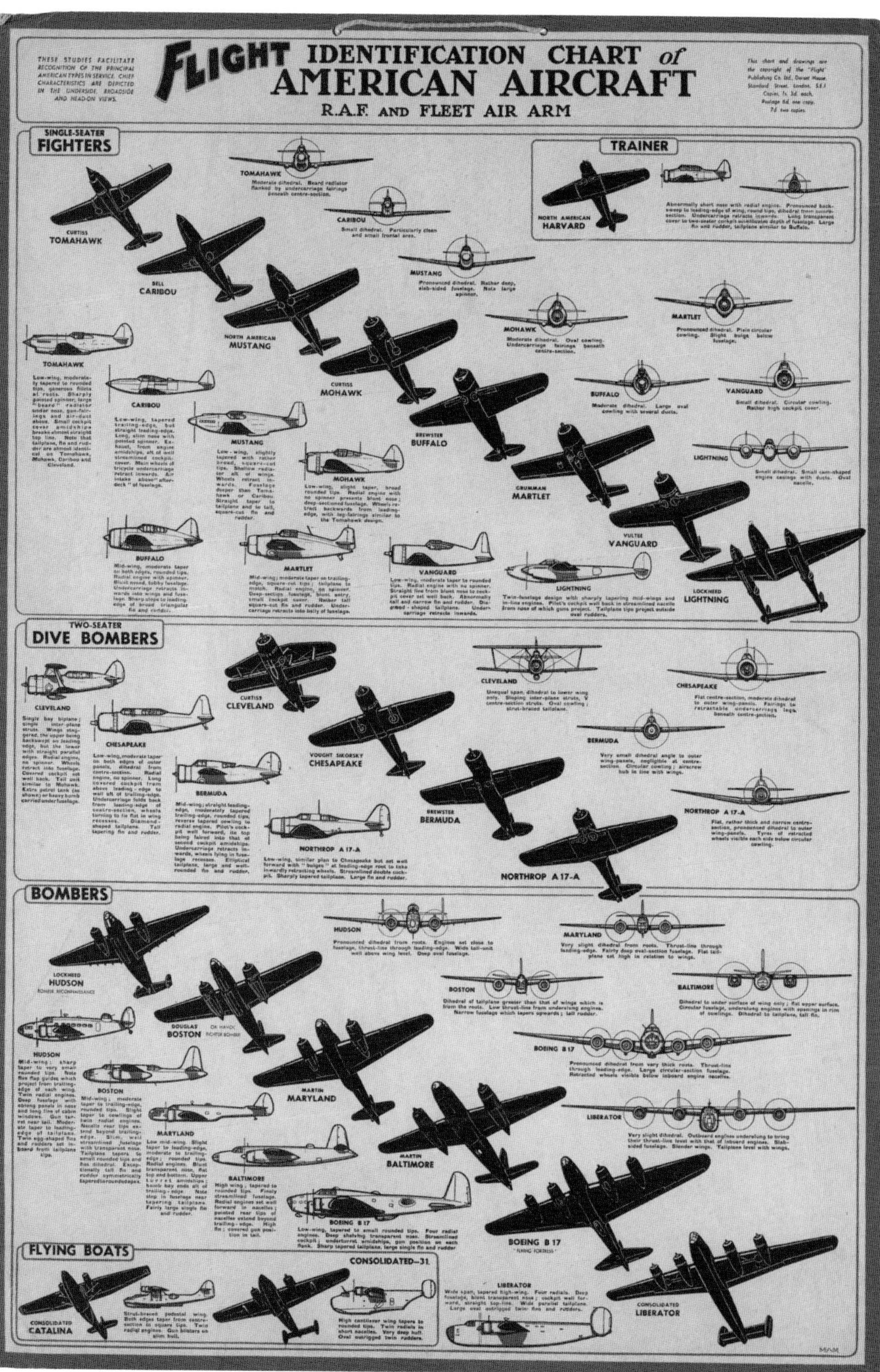

50 A *Flight* magazine chart on how to identify US aircraft used by British forces.

THE WAR FRONTS

MEDITERRANEAN: The Axis hold on North Africa was shrinking rapidly with the main scene of operations converging on the triangle bounded by the Axis-held ports of Bizerte, Tripoli and Bengasi.

American, British and French forces were closing in on the key cities in Tunisia from Algeria. A Fighting French unit using American-made equipment was reported moving up towards the main Axis base at Tripoli from the Lake Chad region, 1300 miles across the desert to the south, in French Equatorial Africa. Finally, on the Libyan front the British Eighth Army, moving in two main columns, continued its amazing gains. One column moved along the coast aimed at Bengasi and the other cut down past Mekili and drove toward the Gulf of Sirte and on to the pass at El Agheila. At this pass, bounded by salt marshes on one side and the Mediterranean on the other, Rommel was expected to make his first major stand. It was there that he had been able to stop British offensives in the past.

1 TUNISIA: Main Axis strength at the western end of the triangle was apparent at the naval and air bases at Bizerte and possibly Tunis. A growing force of German airborne infantry flown in from Sicily and Italian marines coming by ship from Sardinia was estimated at 10,000 troops.

The Germans and Italians were reportedly aided by Vichy French units but were by their own admission meeting with resistance from Frenchmen loyal to the Allied cause.

British and American ground forces, joined by North African French units, meanwhile, crossed the border of Tunisia. One column moving along the Mediterranean coast was reported within 70 miles of Bizerte. Another appeared to be cutting across Tunisia on a line from Bougie aimed at Rommel's main supply base at Tripoli.

Advance units of these Allied forces contacted Axis scouting parties sent into the Tunisian mountains by the enemy and the first main engagement of the war involving American and German ground forces seemed a matter of few days' distance.

British and American paratroops paved the way for the Allied forces moving in from French Morocco. Dropping from American transports and covered by American fighter planes British paratroops landed a[…] trol of key airports in Tunisia while Ameri[…] landed at points along the Tunisia-Morocco[…] by French units these forces moved into […]

2 LIBYA: The British Eighth Ar[…] press Rommel's forces […] and though the advance was slower […] this was caused far more by problems of s[…] munications than by German rear guard […]

The Allies still had overwhelming air […] were able to bomb and strafe the retreatin[…] harbor at Bengasi at will. U. S. Army […] tinued their leading role in the air action[…]

On the ground the British column adva[…] coastal road took Derna and pressed on […] about 150 miles to the southwest. Anothe[…] while, struck southwest from Derna and […]

Axis casualties, mostly Italians, were r[…] reached 75,000 including prisoners. The […] other hand, reported their losses at 13,0[…]

3 LAKE CHAD: The third pro[…] the Axis hold […] was reported from Lake Chad and dr[…] This force was said to be composed of so[…]

51 One of the weekly Newsmaps produced by the US War Department for distribution at home and overseas. For 23 November 1942 here key events worldwide are recorded, including the Allied advance in North Africa after the victory at El Alamein and Allied landings in Morocco and Algeria.

North Africa: The March Westward

Germans Report Russian Offensive 7

RAF Bombers Hit Northern Italy 4

Allied Forces Advance, Move Into Tunisia 1

2 British 8th Army Approaches Bengasi

3 Fighting French Reported Moving Towards Tripoli

Monday, November 23, 1942
Week of November 13 to November 20
Volume 1, No. 31

Rommel's road continued to be a hard one. His once proud Afrika Korps retreated deeper into Libya leaving behind tremendous supplies and prisoners. Symbol to show Allied hearts was this British flag again hoisted over Tobruk.

SALVAGE

Salvage is an important work following in the wake of the advancing Allied Forces. Special British squads collect parts of all kinds of equipment. These are then sent back to main bases and reconditioned for new action.

With damaged and sunk ships found in the harbor of Matruh British soldiers found this wreck left of a large German seaplane. Used as an Axis supply port, Matruh was often hammered by Allied planes before the main attack.

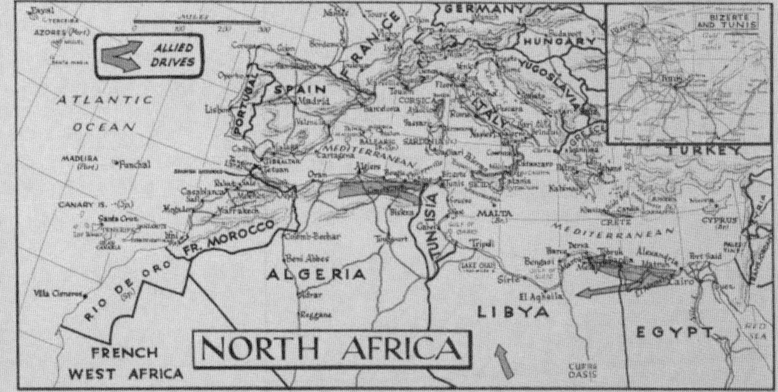

g French, who were equipped with Amer-
s and light tanks.

not be the first action involving Fighting from the Lake Chad region in Libya. Last French column took part in fighting 500 Tripoli where they raided Italian positions.

Fears of imminent invasion were rampant in the land of the Fascisti. As the oved into Tunisia they would be able to set omber bases to strike at Sicily, Sardinia and nainland. This, the Italians feared realisti- e followed by actual invasion.

f what such bombing might accomplish was orthern Italy just below the Alps. Big RAF ing the 1500-mile round trip jump from xth time this month, repeatedly hit the air- on center at Turin and the port of Genoa.

MONS: The U. S. Navy, in one of the greatest victories of the war, elmingly defeated a strong Japanese force the second major blow to recapture the a three-day running battle, in which U. S. ces from Australia and New Caledonia took art, our Navy sank 23 Jap ships and damaged seven others. Jap losses included at least one battleship, five cruisers, and five destroyers sunk and another battleship and six destroyers damaged. Our losses were two light cruisers and six destroyers sunk. Jap casualties were estimated at 30,000 men.

A later Navy report received from the Southwest Pacific, and which may have some duplication of the earlier, listed one Jap battleship, three cruisers and one destroyer sunk, and one battleship, one cruiser and one destroyer damaged.

Scene in Libya
Already well stocked with thousands of Italian prisoners a British officer takes a few more. These are Italian paratroops who were officered by Nazis. Their equipment poor and morale low. They said they were glad to be taken.

The enemy approached from two directions. One group of transports and protecting warships which had been observed gathering at Buin and Rabaul moved in from the northwest. At about the same time a strong Jap naval force moved down on the Guadalcanal area from the north.

As a preliminary to the landing attempt the Japs bombarded our positions on the island at night. Then as the enemy transports approached our air forces moved in and sank at least eight of twelve transports. Next day four transports were found beached at Tassanfaronga, about seven and one-half miles west of our positions on Guadalcanal. These were destroyed by air, artillery and naval gunfire.

The battle took place November 13-15 and on the last day the remnants of the Jap fleet were observed withdrawing to the north.

6 NEW GUINEA: Australian and American forces closed in on the Japanese base at Buna from two sides and supported by steady air superiority seriously threatened the Japanese at Buna and other bases on northern New Guinea. One force of American troops, flown across the Owen Stanley Mountains were southeast of Buna. The other force, composed mainly of Australians, continued to move over the mountains from Kokoda and were reported within 30 miles of Buna approaching from the southwest and were at Awala.

At Lae, northwest of Buna, Allied medium bombers destroyed 15 Jap bombers and fighters in a surprise attack on the airdrome there.

7 RUSSIA: Winter weather and the North African campaign were having their effects in Russia. Possibly because German planes were drawn off to Sicily, the Luftwaffe put only a fraction of its former strength over Stalingrad. The cold was constantly lamented in German communiques.

One strong German attack gained them two streets in the ruined Volga city but these were soon retaken. To top this, German dispatches began to speak of a Russian offensive action even as far north as Leningrad. The Nazis spoke of "violent new attacks" in the Nalchik area in the Caucasus and of Russian troop concentrations on the Don front.

THERE IS NO ALL-PURPOSE PLANE

HEA

FOR the United States, the requirements of this war are extremely varied. Our airplanes are in daily operation against the enemy on many fronts with variations in climate and battle stations that are the severest possible test of Military aircraft.

In the Aleutians they are operating over water and mountains in cold and forbidding weather, against Japanese establishments and aircraft. In the Solomons, operations are in stifling heat and drenching rains. In the desert a complicating factor is swirling sand. In Australia and New Guinea our aircraft in a single day may fly from subtropical temperatures to the chill of early spring. Operations continue in these areas and in Europe, India, China, the central Pacific, the Caribbean and the Atlantic.

It is proof of the soundness of United States design and the versatility of American crews that they carry on under conditions more varied and difficult than men and machines ever have met before. Some planes now in action have recognized deficiencies even within the purposes for which they were designed. Other American aircraft have proved excellent in every theatre in which they have been employed. No military aircraft is perfect, even for its designed specialty. The measure of excellence is the score of the showing against the enemy.

The goal toward which the United States and all the other warring powers are aiming is a balanced air force. To compare this with a balanced ground army is appropriate. No campaign in this specialized war has been won by tanks alone or by any other arm alone. Victory goes to the side with the best balance for a given situation.

No war in the air will be won with an air force concentrating on the fighter, the bomber or any other craft. It requires fighters of various types capable of operating with maximum effectiveness through all the levels of air operation, such as short-range fast-climbing interceptors for defense against enemy bombers or long-range heavily armed slugger types for the protection of one's own bombers.

The complete air force needs bombers to carry out each of the specialties of that class. It needs dive bombers for attack on enemy surface craft and for cooperation with ground forces. It requires torpedo planes for attacks on enemy shipping and warcraft. It calls for long-range reconnaissance craft, for light and medium bombers capable of a variety of work, especially low-altitude strafing. It needs transports for its service operations, aircraft for taking and developing pictures of enemy targets and planes for coastal patrol and offshore operation against enemy shipping.

No nation ever has attained a perfectly balanced air power. In their combined air squadrons the United Nations are close to the goal.

These photos show some of the leading American planes that have or are about to see major action.

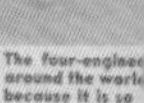

The four-engine[d] around the worl[d] because it is so to carry heavie[r]

The Navy's Vought-Sikorsky, F4U-1, is called the "Corsair." Its inverted gull-wing is a recognition factor and it has been called the "fastest fighter in the world."

The North American P-51, has been called the "Mustang" in Britain and has seen action over Western Europe. It is powered by the liquid-cooled Allison engine.

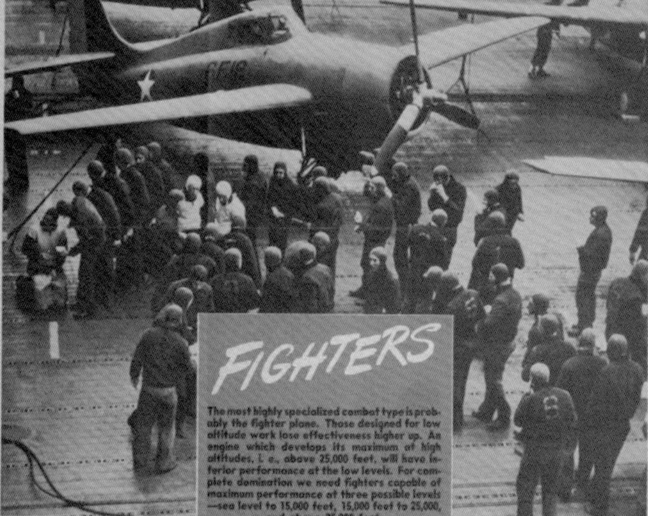

FIGHTERS

The most highly specialized combat type is probably the fighter plane. Those designed for low altitude work lose effectiveness higher up. An engine which develops its maximum at high altitudes, i. e., above 25,000 feet, will have inferior performance at the low levels. For complete domination we need fighters capable of maximum performance at three possible levels—sea level to 15,000 feet, 15,000 feet to 25,000, and above 25,000 feet.

The Grumman "Wildcat," F4F-3, is a Navy carrier-based fighter. It has also been used from land fields in the Southwest Pacific fighting. The same model is called the "Martlet" as used by the British Navy. Above shows the plane ready for action as plane handling crews on a carrier are served battle rations.

TORPEDO BOMBERS

The Douglas Devastator was the Navy's standard torpedo bomber when we entered the war. Development already under way soon caught up with it and it is being replaced by the Grumman Avenger which is bigger and more powerful.

TRANSPORTS

Just as other plane types have serv[ed] purposes so our heavy bombers have [op]erated as transports. A distinct trans[port] however, is the Douglas C-47 and C- which are modified versions of our civil air line commercial transport, Several other larger land and sea are in production and use

The Douglas "Devastator" TBD-1 is a torpedo bomber designed for aircraft carrier service. An identifying feature is its broad low wing that tapers back into the fuselage.

The new Grumman "Avenger" TBF saw first battle at Midway. It carries a torpedo inside the fuselage or 2000 pounds of bombs, has top speed of more than 270 m.p.h. and range of 1400 miles.

The Douglas C-47 or C-53 is the same plane as the Commercial DC-3. The C-47 is fitted inside for carrying cargo while the C-53 has seats for airborne troops.

The Curtiss "Commando" C-46 is designe[d] rying both troops and materiel, inclu[ding] artillery and reconnaissance cars. Noti[ce] whale-like nose.

52 The obverse side of one Newsmap provides a helpful guide to US aircraft.

…OMBERS

Our heavy Army bombers in their categories have proven superior in all theatres. They are high-altitude, long-range planes designed for precision destruction of restricted targets. They are not in the same category with the British four-motored Lancaster bomber which was designed for night bombing and which carries much heavier bomb loads at lower altitude and slower speeds. Each type has its specialties. The B-17 and B-24 have also served as transports.

…own "Flying Fortress." In action all …g missions often without fighter escort …-altitude day bombing it can convert …d shorter range for night bombing.

The Consolidated B-24 "Liberator" performs like the "Flying Fortress" at high altitudes and great range. Like the B-17 it has seen action in the Pacific, North Africa, Europe and the Aleutions. Recently both were used together over Western Europe and with their excellent armament knocked out many Nazi Focke-Wulf fighters.

…"Thunderbolt." Designed for high altitude work …lanes. While it has not yet been reported in action … It has a greater speed than the P-38 at extreme … radial air-cooled engine. With the P-38 it shows …e work but neither has been thoroughly tested in battle.

The Curtiss P-40 has gone through six major type changes from P-40A to P-40F. Types now in wide use are the "E" (Kittyhawk) and "F" (Warhawk). Powered with the Allison engine it has heavy hitting power, excellent armor and is a good medium-level fighter. It is a veteran having seen action on every fighting front and in North Africa has even been used as a light bomber. This is the plane used in China by the "Flying Tigers."

…8, is called the "Lightning." It is a high altitude …d great firepower. It has seen action in the Aleu…n engines. With the P-47 it is among the biggest fighter planes.

The Bell "Airacobra" P-39 has performance characteristics similar to the P-40. Its Allison engine is placed behind the pilot's cockpit and its heavy nose cannon make it excellent for strafing. Its tricycle landing gear is good on rough emergency airfields.

…VAL PATROL PLANES

The Navy's patrol bombers are the equals of any in the world and in range they are probably superior. Ships like the famed PBY are not built for speed but for ability to stay long hours in the air and to land on rough water for refueling and servicing. New heavy planes, notably the new Consolidated and Martin patrol planes are replacing it.

…lidated PBY-5 is known as the "Catalina." This was the …ane that spotted the German battleship "Bismarck" for the British Navy. It has tremendous range.

The Consolidated PB2Y-3 is called the "Coronado." With the "Catalina" and the twin-engined Martin "Mariner" PBM-1 it is carrying out long-range patrol work.

MEDIUM AND LIGHT BOMBERS

Our medium bombers are characterized by speed, long-range and good load characteristics. They have been used for patrol and in some cases as heavy fighters as well as for lightning bombing missions. Our dive bomber, the Douglas Dauntless used by the Navy from carriers and by the Army as the A-24, is the best in its category. It may find its equal or superior in the German latest Dornier and Junkers and will soon be supplemented by a newer design now in production.

The North American B-25 is nicknamed the "Mitchell." This is the plane type that made the raid on Tokyo. It has performed well on several fronts and is powered by two radial air-cooled motors.

The Martin B-26 is called the "Martian" and is powered by two air-cooled motors. An extremely fast medium bomber, it was used as a torpedo bomber at Midway and has a tricycle landing gear.

The Douglas A-20 is called the "Havoc" by the British and the "Boston" by our forces. It is a light two-engined bomber widely used over Europe and Egypt. Shown here on coastal patrol it has also been used as a heavy fighter.

The Douglas "Dauntless" is used by our Army, A-24, and Navy SBD-1, as a standard dive-bomber. It is shown here with its brakes down to retard the diving speed for better aim.

The Curtiss-Wright "Helldiver", Navy SB2C-1, is a new dive bomber for the Navy and described as the best in the world. It carries its bomb load inside the fuselage.

Prepared and Distributed by
ARMY ORIENTATION COURSE
Special Service Division, Services of Supply

Based on the report on performance of American Military and Naval aircraft prepared by the Office of War Information.

AIRCRAFT OF THE R.A.F.

Some Famous Types - I.

BLENHEIM

Constant scourge of enemy shipping, "Blenheims" also made the great daylight raid on the German power-stations near Cologne.

WELLINGTON

These long-range bombers have flown from England across the Alps to hit targets at Naples in Italy.

SPITFIRE II

Britain's most famous fighter. Now armed with two cannon and four machine guns, or eight machine guns.

HURRICANE II

"Hurricanes" played a leading part in the Battle of Britain. Now armed with twelve machine guns or four 20 m.m. cannon and used for low level bombing.

BEAUFIGHTER

Armed with four cannon and six machine guns, "Beaufighters" have scored great successes against German dive-bombers in Libya.

HAMPDEN

Medium bombers, continuously used in attacking objectives in Germany. "Hampdens" cut the Dortmund-Ems Canal.

HALIFAX

Among many raids carried out by these giant long-range bombers are attacks on the German harbours of Emden and Kiel, also Berlin.

FLYING FORTRESS

Emden, Rotterdam, Kiel and shipping in the Macassar Straits are among targets attacked by "Fortresses."

SUNDERLAND

"Sunderlands" have done brilliant work in guarding British convoys and bombing German submarines. A "Sunderland" weighs 20 tons.

STIRLING

Biggest bombers in the world, "Stirlings" have dropped their immense bomb-loads on Berlin among other targets.

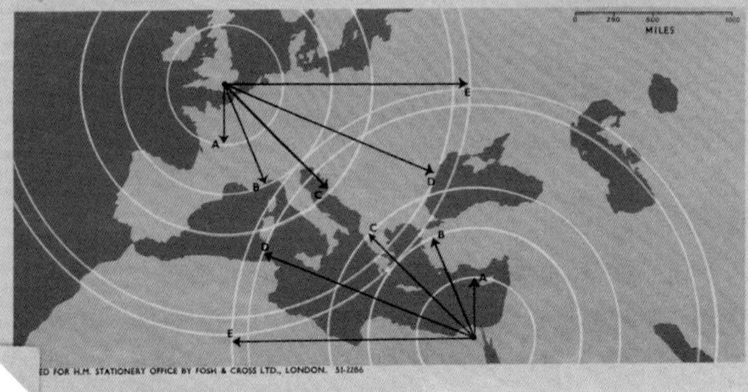

KEY TO MAP

- **A** Approximate range of British "Hurricane" and "Spitfire."
- **B** Approximate range of British "Beaufighter."
- **C** Approximate range of "Blenheim," "Hampden" and Boeing "Flying Fortress" bombers.
- **D** Approximate range of "Wellington" bomber, and Short "Sunderland" flying boat of R.A.F. Coastal Command.
- **E** Approximate range of "Stirling" bomber.

Arrows represent approximate operational range of each type of plane. (Total flying distance is double.)

ED FOR H.M. STATIONERY OFFICE BY FOSH & CROSS LTD., LONDON. 51-2286

ABOVE AND OPPOSITE **53, 54** Ministry of Information posters, *c.*1942, show the main aircraft – both British and American – used by the RAF.

AIRCRAFT OF THE R.A.F.

Some Famous Types – II.

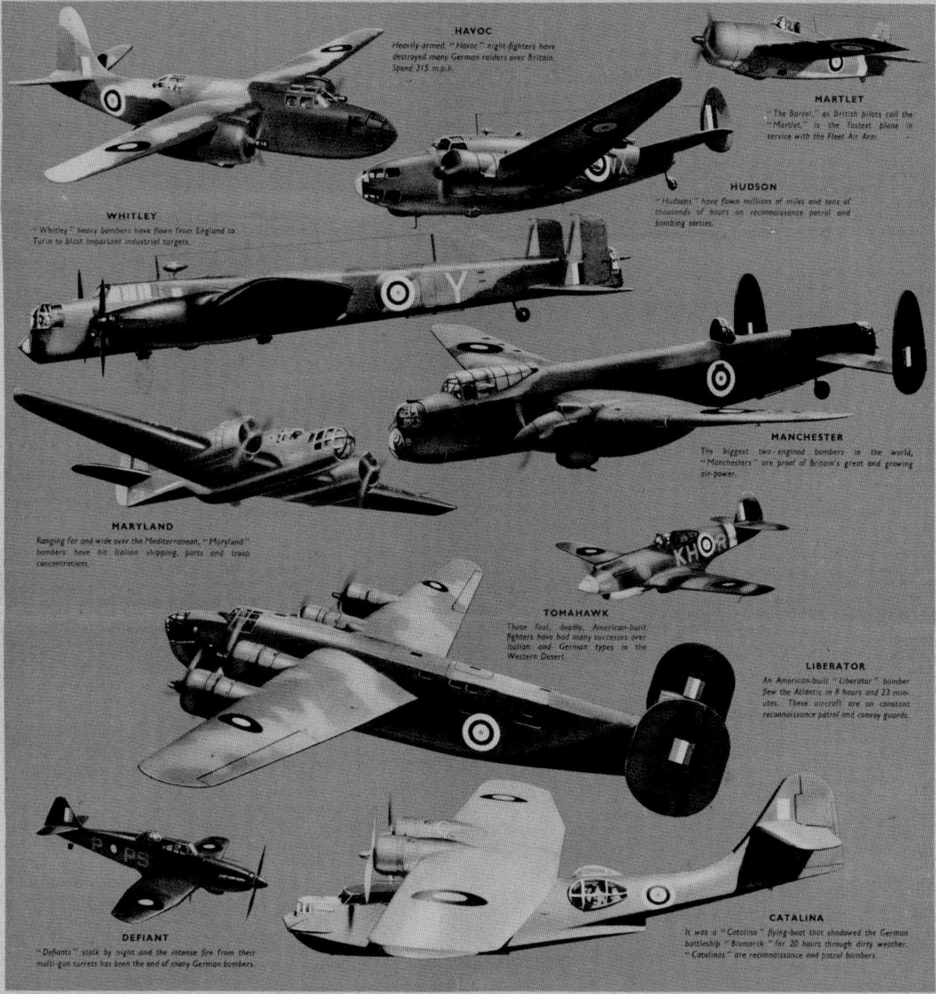

HAVOC

Heavily-armed, "Havoc" night-fighters have destroyed many German raiders over Britain. Spend 315 m.p.h.

MARTLET

"The Barrel," as British pilots call the "Martlet," is the fastest plane in service with the Fleet Air Arm.

HUDSON

"Hudsons" have flown millions of miles and tens of thousands of hours on reconnaissance patrol and bombing sorties.

WHITLEY

"Whitley" heavy bombers have flown from England to Turin to blast important industrial targets.

MANCHESTER

The biggest two-engined bombers in the world, "Manchesters" are proof of Britain's great and growing air-power.

MARYLAND

Ranging far and wide over the Mediterranean, "Maryland" bombers have hit Italian shipping, ports and troop concentrations.

TOMAHAWK

These fast, deadly, American-built fighters have had many successes over Italian and German types in the Western Desert.

LIBERATOR

An American-built "Liberator" bomber flew the Atlantic in 8 hours and 23 minutes. These aircraft are on constant reconnaissance patrol and convoy guards.

DEFIANT

"Defiants" stalk by night and the intense fire from their multi-gun turrets has been the end of many German bombers.

CATALINA

It was a "Catalina" flying-boat that shadowed the German battleship "Bismarck" for 20 hours through dirty weather. "Catalinas" are reconnaissance and patrol bombers.

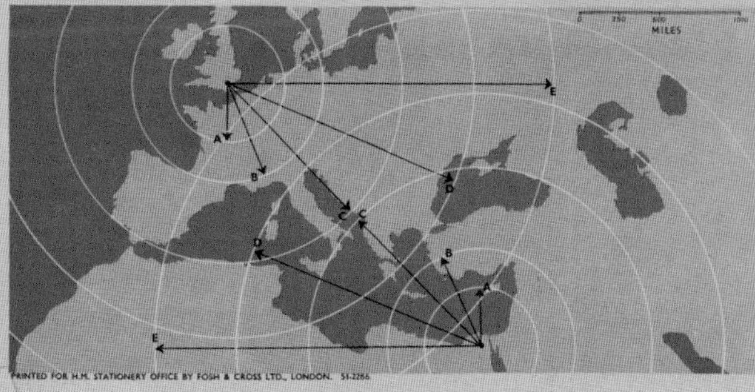

KEY TO MAP

- **A** Approximate range of "Tomahawk" fighter.
- **B** Approximate range of "Martlet," "Havoc," "Whitley" and "Maryland."
- **C** Approximate range of "Hudson" bomber.
- **D** Approximate range of "Liberator" bomber.
- **E** Approximate range of "Catalina" flying boat.

Arrows represent approximate operational range of each type of plane. (Total flying distance is double.)

PRINTED FOR H.M. STATIONERY OFFICE BY FOSH & CROSS LTD., LONDON. 51-2286

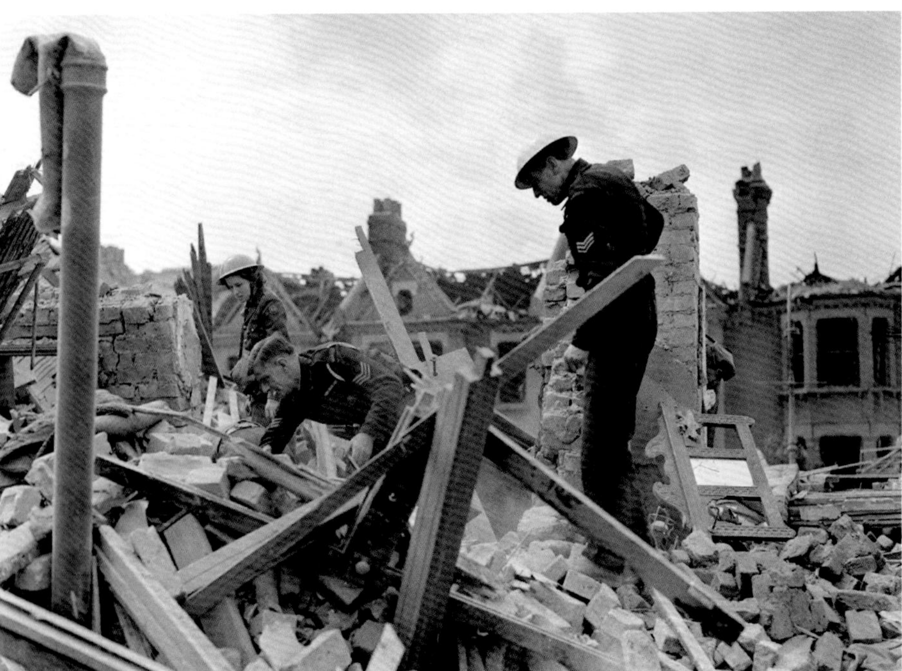

Menace of Hitler's 'secret weapons': *TOP* **55** A V2 rocket is launched from a base in Nazi Europe.
ABOVE **56** The aftermath of a rocket attack in London; the last rockets fell on England in March 1945.

his spies in his knowledge of British plans – outfoxed Churchill by reminding him of Soviet concessions to Britain over Greece, thus weakening the British case for free and fair elections in Poland.)

Russians still advancing on Berlin, have surrounded Konigsberg, taken Frankfurt-am-Oder. Montgomery's renewed offensive on Wcst by Nijmegen has begun well with 1st Canadian Army under under Gen. Crerar. Berlin constantly pounded by RAF & US Air force.

Bip is going out to Belgium for the *Daily Mail.*

➢

16 February 1945

Russians sweeping on towards Dresden & up to Stettin; Budapest has been taken at last, 16,000 prisoners & 49,000 killed. Dresden has been bombed 4 times running. (In the most controversial Allied bomb attacks of the war, 796 Lancasters and 9 Mosquitoes bombed Dresden the night of 13 February, causing a horrendous firestorm; next day 311 US B17 bombers also struck the city. Some 50,000 people lost their lives.) Refugees streaming hard from E front. David Bland's prison camp Stalag Luft III has been overrun by Russians, but we fear the prisoners are being marched back further into Germany.

Nellie's birthday, she is 59, gave her a lamp shade. Finished knitting a pullover for European children's relief parcels.

➢

25 February 1945

Lovely day on Sunday & we sat out on the terrace after lunch. A & V went up to London on Monday to see Donald Wolfit in *King Lear*; he was very fine they said.

Planes go over in flocks at night, & in the early morning to bomb Germany. New offensive begun on the W under Montgomery; it has started well. Poznan in Poland fell after holding out behind the Russians who left it in their rear.

➢

2 March 1945

The offensive in the W continues very successfully, München Gladbach & Krefeldt taken & Germans streaming back across the Rhine. Constant air attacks over the lines & 12 consecutive nights Mosquitoes attacked Berlin & 40,000 prisoners taken since the beginning of this offensive.

Letter from C dated February 27th; he had met Bip who was doing sketches of the battlefields for the *Daily Mail*, & is hoping to see him again before she returns next week. He was doing the Major's job & may get it permanently as he has been recommended for it.

Vivian comes over once or twice a week & is working at his drawings for *Flashy Fin* (Violet's story). Making a cardigan for Jane.

➢

9 March 1945

Melvilles to dinner on Thursday as Vivian was back then. Pleasant evening with paper games. The American 1st Army got over an undestroyed bridge over the Rhine at Remagen, & are enlarging the bridgehead; the Allies pressing them back all along the line, & have taken about 100,000 prisoners since the beginning of this push. Russians have cut off a number of Germans in the NE front by Danzig.

➢

16 March 1945

Perfect sunny weather, frost at night. Sat out on the terrace & Jane rocked on High Flyer (the rocking horse that Anne, and later Alison (now Kate), would inherit).

Allies taking thousands of prisoners & Germans retreating on the Rhine. Russians advancing to Danzig & have taken Kolberg on the Baltic. RAF began dropping the new 10-ton bomb. Berlin bombed by Mosquitoes every night for nearly a month. Starvation in Holland is terrible & French are very hard up for supplies & have a strong & flourishing black market unhappily. Wrangles abt. US & Gr. Britain's supplies of food stocks as to who should take most to the Continent; shipping v. short.

Vivian's illustrations for Violet Bradby's children's story *Flashy Fin* were imaginative and colourful, with striking blue and orange painted scenes. Sadly the story was never published.

➢

23 March 1945

1st Army under Montgomery began offensive after heavy bombardment & a cover of thick smoke. Very successful beginning with RN to help get troops across the Rhine in perfect fine weather to help us for once. Churchill out there to see the start! (He had always loved the thrill of frontline action, much to the alarm of his closest advisers.) Gen. Patton's armoured division also across the Rhine, so with the Remagen bridgehead there are now 3 crossings. . . . V2 fell in a ploughed field near Dagnal on Friday at about 7 am. Very loud crash which made us leap out of bed. The children slept through it! Windows broken in Dagnal & Well Farm ceilings came down but no casualties.

➢

30 March 1945

Armies advancing over Rhine, & taking numerous prisoners. Russians moving on to Vienna. Humphrey came on Maundy Thursday till Wednesday in Easter week. Weather not bad but cold all the time. V2s came over England on Good Friday & then ceased as Allies had overrun the sites. Jane & Alison continuing with whooping cough.

➢

6 April 1945

The push going very well. Japs being defeated at sea, Russians end their neutrality pact with Japan. Vienna besieged, Bratislava taken. Allies in Magdeburg, & the Ruhr is completely encircled. Some high up Germans assassinated in car going to Berlin, (inaccurately) said to be Goering.

C came down on Friday for one night, in good form – delightful to see him again. He had much to tell us of his time in France & Belgium & Holland. He couldn't bring Bip & Bonamy because of wh. cough. He took back 6 eggs, bottles of fruit, apples & cherry blossom. Disappointing that in spite of having been recommended by his Commander for taking over Company as Major, another man brought in from outside.

13 April 1945

The Ruhr pocket has been surrounded & 315,000 Germans taken prisoner. The Russians have begun the advance on Berlin & we are pushing on to Hamburg & Bremen. Letter from C who is back near the German border.

WI Festival down in Berkhamsted. Myra Hess soloist played finely. 25th Anniv. of the Festival so I had to make a short speech about K Talbot at the rehearsal, which she & Joy Heathcote both thought was a suitable one! Heavenly summer weather. Reg Snell (the schoolmaster who had put on a performance of Anne's play *Cain* at Letchworth – see 8 December 1944 above – and became a firm friend) came for the night to see about the Opera party they are giving for us some time in May. Vivian on 9 days leave.

20 April 1945

On the 16th Matt, Jan & the D's (their children Dan and Diana) came for a fortnight. Weather like summer & all the blossom rushing out, bluebells in the wood, daffs & cherry over.

Humphrey came to spend the Golden Wedding Day on the 17th with us. It was all perfect, & we sat out, talked & played croquet. We had betw. 20 & 30 telegrams, delightful letters & many presents. Br. set from H & his family. Garden seat from ours, towels fr. Nellie, £5 fr. Isabel Ashcroft, 10/– fr. Milly, Champagne fr. Christopher & Bip. Samples worked by Jan, pictures etc. fr. the children. Poems fr. Matt, Anne & Kit. He is giving me Glastonbury boots, I gave him pipes. Many lovely bunches of flowers & small presents. Moores, K Talbot & D Erhart, Bells, Wagers, Mrs Harmon etc. Robin (Milford, Humphrey's son) composed us a Trio.

JT Christie (Anne's godfather) came for the day on the 18th in v. good form. Jane frightened at Matt's puppy wh. tries to lick her knees.

Awful accounts of the camps at Buchenwald & Belsen. No news yet of David Bland, Russians shelling Berlin.

27 April 1945

Russians entering parts of Berlin. British take Bremen. Allies advancing well in Burma. Music Fest. in Berkhamsted. Matt & Anne both sang in Handel *The King Shall Rejoice*. V Williams Benedicite. Goossons played oboe solos. Jan & I went down to the Concert. Fine but very cold.

➢

4 May 1945

Heavy snowfall on Saturday 28th at night, which put our electric light out of order till Monday. Had to start dining room fires as well as drawing room at night.

Mussolini assassinated while trying to escape to Switzerland & his body hung head downwards in the square at Milan. After Alexander's vigorous push in N Italy wh. split the German forces, they laid down their arms. The partisans among the N Italians played a most useful part in the taking of towns. Alexander has done finely, as his troops had to be depleted to augment the armies in the West. Russians bombarding Berlin heavily.

➢

11 May 1945

Anxiously waiting for the final surrender of the German forces. Himmler who was taking over negotiations in Denmark with Count Bernadotte has now disappeared. Hitler announced to be dead in Berlin but how, if suicide or from bombs on Chancellery is not clear. (He had shot himself in his bunker on 30 April, while his newly wed wife Eva Braun swallowed a cyanide capsule; as per instructions, their bodies were set alight with petrol in the Reichschancellery garden.) Goebbels & his wife & family all found poisoned in an air raid shelter. Admiral Dönitz announced he had been nominated successor to Hitler. After delays, finally first the Germans surrendered to Montgomery's forces in the N part of Germany, then the Fleet & U-boats, then Norway & Channel Islands. The last part to give in was Prague, & there was fighting in Czechoslovakia up till May 8th VE Day. The news was announced in the 9 pm news on the 7th that the next day would be VE Day, &

arrangements already made were to go forward.

I went down to Holy Communion at 8 o'clock, & we all went to a special service at 11; Anne played the organ, & Kit wheeled Alison down in the pram & she & Jane sat with me as good as gold through the short, well-arranged service. Church full, hymns were 'Now Thank We All' & 'Praise to the Lord'. Nellie came down too. Vivian bicycled back from Wescott just too late.

Anne had a letter from David Bland, free (having escaped) & in Brussels! The only jar is the Russians evasiveness abt. Polish delegates in Warsaw who have apparently been imprisoned.

Awful accounts of the Camps at Dachau & other places; 4,000,000 persons murdered in one Camp alone in Poland. Himmler had given orders that no one in Dachau should be allowed to fall into hands of the Allies, but mercifully these orders had not been carried out.

Letter from C on a course of de-mining. Many PoWs arriving at Westcott. David Bland phoned from Bushey, & had long talks with V & A; he had escaped from his camp after being marched W from Stalag Luft III & had hidden under the floorboards of the hut for 3 days! He hopes to come here soon.

➢

18 May 1945

Anne goes up on Tuesdays to help at Ashridge as they are extra busy with P of War at the Hospital. Letter from C, he is in a small town on the edge of Holland. The SS men shot 20 of the men before Allies came & left the bodies in the street.

I went up to London for day on Thursday with Kit & Dorothy. I went to a René Clair film *Le Dernier Milliardaire* (1934, a satirical view of the problems of capitalism and the last film Clair made in France before moving to Britain and the US) & to shop but could get neither sandals, shoes for self nor white blouse for Jane. Colder again.

Tito claims Trieste for the Yugoslavs probably backed by Russia. Rations will probably be lowered. More horrifying accounts coming of the many concentration camp atrocities in Germany & Austria. The difficulties of our problems in Europe are immense. Big Thanksgiving Service on Sunday in St Paul's with King & Queen.

➢

25 May 1945

Weather cold again. Russians being difficult still over Poland. Montgomery appointed C-in-C of occupying British forces in Europe. Letter from C who has had 3 days leave in Brussels. Tokyo heavily bombed by US Liberators. P of War arriving at Westcott where V is stationed; 90,000 have arrived there by air (in fact a total of 34,587 during April and May). V had to go to Oakley as someone was ill & didn't come home for a week.

Labour Party want to leave Coalition, so Gen. Election to be in July. Great mistake not to keep Coalition on till Jap. War is over.

➢

1 June 1945

Chill, showers continue. Humphrey came on May 25th for the weekend. On Saturday morning Kit went down by bus to fetch 16/3 worth of buns & cakes. Meantime Vivian arrived & we all cleared the drawing room & arranged 23 folding chairs borrowed from the School Canteen & every small one in the house, the sofa at the back & the Golden Wedding garden seat. . . . Reg Snell came in time for lunch & fixed up lights & two reflectors for the stage wh. was in the alcove in front of the S window . . . Actors arrived about 2.15 . . . Visitors began to come at 3.30. Tea served in the dining room. Performance began soon after 4, & after it was over they just had time to change & have a cold meal before going off again.

The programme was Mozart's little opera *Bastien & Bastienne*, 3 sea songs by Dibdin & his opera *The Waterman* adapted. They were very good. Reg Snell sang & acted most amusingly & the soprano M Wigglesworth had a pretty voice & good movements. . . . Mr Tremlow was the tenor, also good & Mrs Snell did all the make up & designed the effective dresses. It was really a quite delightful show & the audience most enthusiastic in their praise, & some of them even wrote afterwards to say how much they had enjoyed it all. It was part of Humphrey's generous G Wedding present to us.

Disturbances in Lebanon where French & Arabs were at loggerheads. De Gaulle is touchy & on his dignity.

➢

8 June 1945

Anne went up to a poetry reading at the Empsons (the poet William Empson), bicycling back from Berkhamsted betw. 11 & 12. Enrica Garnier here for the weekend.

Vivian came on leave – he is to go to an OCTU for his training for a Commission in the Intelligence Branch of the RAF. Serenade party at K Talbots, the soloist Eve Maxwell Lyte sang songs in costume & acted them cleverly. . . . The WI choir sang 3 part songs behind the scenes. A & V went up to the first night of (Britten's opera) *Peter Grimes* with the Melvilles. They thought it very fine.

➢

15 June to 6 July 1945

Nellie went for her holiday, Anne coping with house & children after V left on the Sunday. Went to Matt & Jan at Heswall on 21st. Most interesting to see M at his new job. Then Cornwall. Voted at Ivinghoe day after our return. Bip & Bonamy came & Vivian for one night from his OCTU. Bip left Bonamy here.

➢

13 July 1945

Bonamy here for ten days. C & Bip came for the weekend, C on leave from Germany – looking v. well.

Had a picnic on Sunday with the Millers on Goose Hill. Having raspberries & Alpine strawberries most days, but not enough to do more than a couple of bottles & some lbs of jam. Constant bombardment of Japan going on. Nancy has turned v. queer with delayed shock after all the bombing of London, & Hugh having sad time. (Hugh Bradby, 1866-1947, was an elder brother of Kit's, married to Nancy.)

➢

27 July 1945

Election results came out on Thursday & Labour has swept the board. It is a surprise, & I feel sad for Churchill who has done so well for us in the War, but he set a wrong note during the Election. (Exhausted and increasingly irrational, Churchill had warned of a British Gestapo if Labour were to win. His failure during the war or election campaign to advocate for any kind of social reform after the war turned many, especially in the armed forces, against him.) Capt. Crawley, Labour, is in for Bucks. Div. in which we are. He is Bertha's sister-in-law's brother. Anne & the children went to stay with Robin & Kirstie for a week, house v. empty without them. Attlee PM, Bevin Foreign Sec., Dalton Chancellor of Exchequer. Sir Max Horton went to review the boys at Heswall & was v. encouraging. Anne's play (*The Shadow Factory*) is to be put on for a month at The Mercury (Theatre in London) in December & broadcast in January.

➢

3 August 1945

Anne & V & the children came back accompanied by Mrs Ridler till Wednesday. V has passed his Exam & is now an Officer in the RAF. Uncertain where he will be posted. I had £63 Royalties for last year, largest I have ever had.

C has at last got his Company & is a Major. He is down near Duisburg in a much devastated area, likes his officers. Edward has applied for passages (from Ceylon) for January 1946.

Kit & I went up to Lord's. Pleasant day seeing many friends . . .

The first two Atomic bombs dropped on Japan with devastating results. Russians declared War on Japs, on exact date we heard later from Churchill that they had promised.

Kit & I went down to tea at Oatfield, the Hammonds having come back from Manchester. (Lawrence Hammond had written leader columns for the *Manchester Guardian* throughout the war; Barbara Hammond was Kit's younger sister – see also Vivian's Diary for 25 February 1943.) Nancy in a Mental Home.

➢

10 August 1945

Car at last on the road again as batteries finally arrived. Lovely to be able to drive again. Anxiously awaiting surrender of Japan. Humphrey came on the 7th & stayed ten days, he is retiring at the end of September & has not found a house yet. Mrs Ridler left on Wednesday, going up to Euston with Vivian at the end of his leave. She is v. patient under her deafness.

➢

17 August 1945

Japan surrendered at midnight on August 14th, but we did not hear it till 8 o'clock on Wednesday 15th when Nellie called us with the news. Vivian had two days V-Day leave.

Long letters in *Times* about the Bomb & if it is legitimate to have used it. Japs have not yet been told that the Emperor has given in: hope they won't try & slip out of their agreement. Incredible to think War is over after nearly 6 years. The food & fuel situation on the Continent is desperate unless drastic measures are taken. Pétain trial ended in verdict of death penalty with rec. to mercy & he has been at once reprieved. Parliament opened by King on 15th in rain. He broadcast with hardly a stammer in the evening. Attlee made good opening speech in the House & Churchill a magnanimous one.

➢

24 August 1945

Vivian came on leave till he gets his posting, where to we don't know.

Arrangements continue for the surrender of Japan. Fears for winter shortage of food & fuel. Americans announce end of Lend Lease wh. seems to have taken our Gov't. by surprise & will increase difficulties.

Many plums & greengages. Bilberries poor this year.

➢

31 August 1945

Swans for weekend. (Sir Kenneth Swan, 1877-1973, was Anne's godfather.) Martin

Brownes came down for lunch & tea to talk over *The Shadow Factory.* (Martin Browne had previously directed T S Eliot's play *The Family Reunion.*) A & V & children went down on Thursday to Cornwall for nearly a fortnight to Penant Farm near Port Isaac.

➢

2 to 7 September 1945

Allies land in Japan, peace having been signed on US ship *Missouri* by Gen. MacArthur. Japs seem cooperative. Awful stories of their treatment of prisoners. Have not heard if John Milford still alive.

C very busy in Germany, says he dislikes Germans & hopes to be out of the Army in October.

➢

14 September 1945

Heard from Betty McKay that John Milford is safe and in Malta?

Humphrey came for a week. Anne & V & children came back from Cornwall. Went up to London with A & V for *The Old Man of the Mountain* (1933 American film presumably), enjoyed it but thought the end dragged. Took Tompion clock to be mended. Picked first of the apples.

➢

21 September 1945

Conference of Powers in London going stickily. Trial of the Belsen Germans going on. Heard from Edward, & from C who hopes to be back early in October.

➢

4 October 1945

Vivian, posted to Germany, came back for a week. Matt & J on leave at Harlech.

➢

12 October 1945

Sang in Church for Harvest Thanksgiving & Peace ditto. K Talbot conducted. Cold in church & I caught a cold & stayed in bed most of Monday & all Tuesday. Christopher came home on 12th & rang up v. glad to be out of the Army at last. He has been near Cologne.

Campbell & Kit Milford (Campbell was Violet's nephew) came on bikes for one night & camped on lawn, having meals with us. The Conference of the Powers in London has broken up without coming to any agreement, owing to the attitude of Russia. Grave fears for the coming winter in Europe owing to food & coal shortage. Humphrey has now left the OUP & gone for the present to Helen Wright at Winchester.

V & A went up to London to see *The Octopus* by Charles Williams & V was to go off next day to Dückeburg in Germany. Laval tried & his trial very much mismanaged.

➢

19 October 1945

Strikes, unofficial ones not approved by the men's leaders, in the docks. David Bland came for weekend. Sang in the Wesleyan Chapel on Sunday. Kit put children to bed as Anne, D Bland & I all went.

➢

26 October 1945

Christopher came down for weekend, demobbed & glad to be home. Lawrence & Barbara came up for tea on Saturday. My injections (for anaemia) given by Dr Phillips as Dr Skelton has been having an op. have given me a good deal of stiffness & discomfort. A & I went down to Berkhamsted in the car with the children in pouring rain for shopping.

➢

2 November 1945

Jane Cowling (Anne's friend and former colleague at Faber, where both had been secretaries to the head of production Dick de la Mare) came from Saturday to Monday. Trouble in Java, where the Indonesians, stirred up by the Japs are revolting against the Dutch. Edward & Bertha have a 2nd son born on November 6th, both well. Had my hair permed.

➢

9 November 1945

Handcraft Ex. in Canteen, I showed three bits of work. Anne went up to London to see the BBC man abt. her play, it will have to be cut down for broadcasting. Humphrey writes that he has bought a house at Drayton St Leonards, 11 miles from Oxford. It sounds very jolly.

➢

16 November 1945

Attlee flew to US to have talks with Truman over Atomic Bomb etc. Stalin seems to have disappeared from Russian politics at the moment: Molotov being spokesman on the Anniv. Day.

Weather raw & cold but can't have the central heating owing to coal economy. Wood fires in dining rm. in morning & drawing rm. in evening.

➢

23 November 1945

Anne's play is to be on December 19th, rehearsals begin on December 3rd. Edward & Bertha have settled on Edward Hugh for the baby's name.

Tea at Manor House on Saturday to meet 3 French women. Found my French not too rusty. One had hidden 5 US airmen. Several days of horrid fog.

➢

30 November 1945

Finished off jumper for Alison, Anne did back & front. A much delighted to wear it. Matt & Christopher came on Wednesday for two nights. V. good form.

➢

7 December 1945

Alice & David Pennant came for one night. Two concerts in Village Hall. Well attended, Choral Soc. sang V Williams *Carol Fantasia*. On Sunday went to the parish church at Tring & sang in Britten's *Ceremony of Carols*.

Anne went up to many rehearsals of *The Shadow Factory* at the Mercury.

➢

21 December 1945

Anne went up to the two last rehearsals of *The Shadow Factory*. On Wednesday 19th she & Kit & I went up for the 1st night. K & I stayed at the Chittys (close relatives). Most thrilling – It went v. well & the theatre had every seat taken. Robert Speaight in the part of the Manager was 1st rate & Alan Wheatley as the Artist was excellent. Everyone enthusiastic about the play. We had a large gathering of friends & relations. C & Bip, Humphrey, Olive Willis, Swans, Snells, Robin & Kirstie, Melvilles, Chittys, Kingsburys, Wilkinsons. Anne was called for & had to make a short speech from the stage. We went afterwards & had supper at a neighbouring restaurant with C & Bip. Anne with the Brownes.

Home next day with Humphrey. Nellie had looked after the children.

➢

28 December 1945

A pleasant quiet Xmas, & the children enjoyed it immensely & were v. good. . . .

➢

4 January 1946

I had a cold & cured it by staying in bed one day. Nellie went up to London for the night to see *The Shadow Factory*. Anne went up for Thursday night for ditto & supper with Martin Browne. Bonamy has chicken pox & Dan & Diana flu & then Jan. Weather cold & frosty. . . .

Vivian is moving to Dortmund, he is helping to edit the *Wing* weekly paper. E & B have not yet got their passage (from Ceylon).

➢

11 January 1946

Matt & Jan & the D's arrived on Sunday by car. All but Matt had had flu, & Jan breakfasted in bed for about a week. I treated them all to *National*

Velvet at Hemel Hempstead....

United Nations Organization (UNO) began their meetings in London. Great difficulties over Russian attitude in Persia & elsewhere & all the nations seem anxious & jumpy.

Diana is very good amusing Jane & Alison who tag about happily after.

➢

18 January 1946

Very cold. I had a temp on Saturday of 99.4, but after going to bed about 4, with two Aspirins I was all right next day. Thursday I treated M & J to *The Shadow Factory* wh. they enjoyed hugely & I did too, even more than the 1st time. Had a talk with Martin Browne in the interval & he introduced us to Robert Speaight.

➢

25 January 1946

M & J & Diana went home on Monday. Had a cable from E to say they were sailing on the 26th in a Polish ship. Dan went back to school, I dropped him at Tring station on my way to Drayton St Leonard to stay with Humphrey & help him move in. It is only 33 miles, & an easy drive, 9 miles beyond Thame. H & a nice daily woman busy arranging things when I arrived, & after lunch the Oxford removers came with a vanload of furniture, including luckily a bed for me to sleep on. The house is delightful, partly Tudor, & has central heating, fitted basins & electric light. A walled kitchen garden & three other bits of garden. Water from their own well pumped by an electric pump. Huge open brick fireplaces, & a fine store of logs in a barn. Very busy days, as I had to do the cooking.

Simon & Marion Nowell-Smith & John & their useful handyman came over on Thursday & fitted up electric plugs. I drove H in to Oxford for his injection (for pernicious anaemia) & shopping.

Saw Elsie (Milford, 1868-1959, Violet's sister-in-law and mother of Dick Milford, then Vicar of St Mary's in Oxford and co-founder of Oxfam). Sunday lunch with the Nowell-Smiths at Ewelme. (Simon Nowell-Smith, 1909-1996, was a celebrated bibliophile and bibliographer based in Oxford.)

➢

1 February 1946

Came home in the car on Monday 28th & had a warm welcome. Very tired, additionally so on account of missing my injection for a week. Anne went up to a lunch to meet the Archbishop.

UNO having important meetings in London. Russians being extremely difficult, & objecting to the presence of our troops in Greece. Bevin seems to be behaving with firmness.

➢

8 February 1946

Anne went up to London for the last night of *The Shadow Factory*, gave supper to Robert Speaight & Alan Wheatley (Martin Browne had been having flu). Stayed the night with C & Bip & came back with C on Sunday morning, & he stayed here for two nights.

Vivian came back on leave on Tuesday evening, having missed the Play by 3 days! Jane had her 5th birthday on February 4th & 5 children to tea. Nellie iced a sponge cake for her. She had a touch of flu & had to stay away from school.

Nuremberg trials still going on of German War Criminals.

➢

15 February 1946

We all went over on the Saturday to the White House to see Humphrey, taking our lunch of rabbit galantine & Swiss roll. Lovely day. We were able to use the car as Vivian had 13 gall. of coupons for his leave. Robin had come over to lunch too; v. jolly visit. David Bland came for the week-end. A & V went up to London on Tuesday & Wednesday. Cable from E & B from Port Said & an airmail letter. Went down to see a film on Thursday night, *The Rake's Progress* (1945 British comedy-drama about a modern upper-class cad played by Rex Harrison).

UNO having great difficulties over their discussions, owing to Vyshinsky the Russian delegate's obstructive tactics over every question which arises. Ben Smith (Minister of Food) announced the news of fearful world shortage of wheat & grave fears of famine. Cut in fat ration. Got blamed for not having taken steps sooner & for not having made farmers sow wheat earlier.

➢

22 February 1946

V found he had 48 hours extension so came back till Monday. Trouble in India & Egypt & great shortage in coal output in England. World altogether in a dreary state of dissatisfaction.

Letter from Vivian to David Bland
HQ 2001 Wing, BAFO c/o BAOR
20 February 1946

My Dear David,

When I reached London on Monday (I had 48 hours extension) I rang up Fabers, only to get the sad news from Berthold (Wolpe) *of Roger's death. Most dear David, I know my words can't comfort you, or Mary and her babies, but I will try to share the burden of grief which has come on you so suddenly. I wish that I could be with you now, even though neither of us wished to say anything, whereas here I can do next to nothing. But you will know that I am thinking and praying for you.*

I got back to camp at midday today to find nothing in particular changed. There are signs of heavy flooding in Holland, and it is still very stormy here, with rain and sleet coming in almost horizontally. A book from Anne awaited me, by none other than John C. Tarr, Printing Today.

It looks quite good and is v. well illustrated for 5/–. I think you should have a copy if you haven't already.

The Henry IV *was superb, both acting and décor. Laurence Olivier seems to have developed so much during the war, and of course Ralph Richardson is amazing. There is an article on the Vic company in that* Future *book you told me of. I bought a copy at Euston bookstall. The photogravure & colour work is unusually good – more surprising, the articles are too, & I think the whole enterprise should be a success. It is certainly cheap at 5/–.* (*Future* was a rival book-magazine to George Weidenfeld's similarly short-lived postwar venture *Contact*, which Vivian went on briefly to design in 1947; see the Introduction.)

All my love & blessings, David

Yours,

Vivian

'Have you known
Of any love but ended in pain?
Or any birth did not wring tears
With secret pathos of its journey?'
'Or any pain that could not nourish
The seeds of joy?'

➢

24 February 1946

Yotes & the Woodalls (Bertha's parents) to await Edward & Bertha's arrival. It had turned very cold but on Sunday when they arrived we had a lovely day. C went to meet them at Southampton. E looking much the same. B much thinner but in good form. David v. jolly & just like his photographs & Baby Hugh placid & good. E just got over flu so stayed in bed on Monday.

Rations have had to be reduced in British Zone in Germany alas.

➢

28 February 1946

Edward came here on February 28th for a few days but on Sunday felt sick & had a temp. So he stayed in bed till Tuesday & did not go out owing to the cold snowy weather till Thursday, when he went back to Yotes. It was a recurrence of his flu I think. He played the piano & it was lovely having him.

➢

18 March 1946

Churchill made an important speech in US urging America & Britain to make a firm stand if USSR will continue to drop an iron curtain across Europe & refuse to cooperate. Doubtful question if he were wise to speak out openly, & may make UNO ineffective, though of course Russia has already by blocking motions there, done its best to be obstructive.

Anne & I went up on Saturday to see *Cain* acted by Univ. College Dramatic Society. Well staged, acting mediocre.

C came down from Saturday to Thursday. Worked hard splitting & dragging in a fallen larch tree from Ringshall Copse wh. will keep us in firing for some time.

➢

25 March 1946

C has got a job with a firm called Betro (a publisher??) & is to start on April 1st. Weather cold. E & B & the two children came on Friday.

➢

31 March 1946

A week of glorious weather. K, E & I went up to London to see *Henry IV Part I.* Lunch with C & Bip at La Coquille first. (K's share of the jaunt.) Fine performance with Laurence Olivier as Hotspur & Ralph Richardson as Falstaff. Christopher to start next day at Betro, instead of April 1st.

Bip now busy on a job for Hodder & Stoughton. WI on Wednesday, Victorian evening. I read a short thing on my recollections. Mrs Gray on events in Q Victoria's reign & she wrote a playlet wh. was acted by Mrs Meyer & others. Lancers & Polka rounded up a very successful evening. E going in for Whitgift & if possible St Paul's.

➢

5 April 1946

Lovely weather till Friday. E & B had two good rides. David (their son) went to Mrs Wager's class with Alison. Jane's Kindergarten class is unhappily coming to an end. She has got on well there.

Anne & the children went back with E & B & their two to Yotes for a week. Hugh is a model baby, David very jolly & the cousins played &

bickered happily.

Prospect of famine in Europe & India is very grave.

Shadow Factory came out.

➢

12 April 1946

Went to Rugby with Kit from Monday 8th to 12th. Godfrey (Bradby, 1863-1947, Kit's elder brother) increasingly blind, but enjoys being read to & liked hearing *Shadow Factory*. Cold but fine. Easy slow journey by train as only have 7 gall. of petrol a month still.

Russians still being difficult over Persia. Commission in India trying to find a settlement.

VAB DIARY ENDS

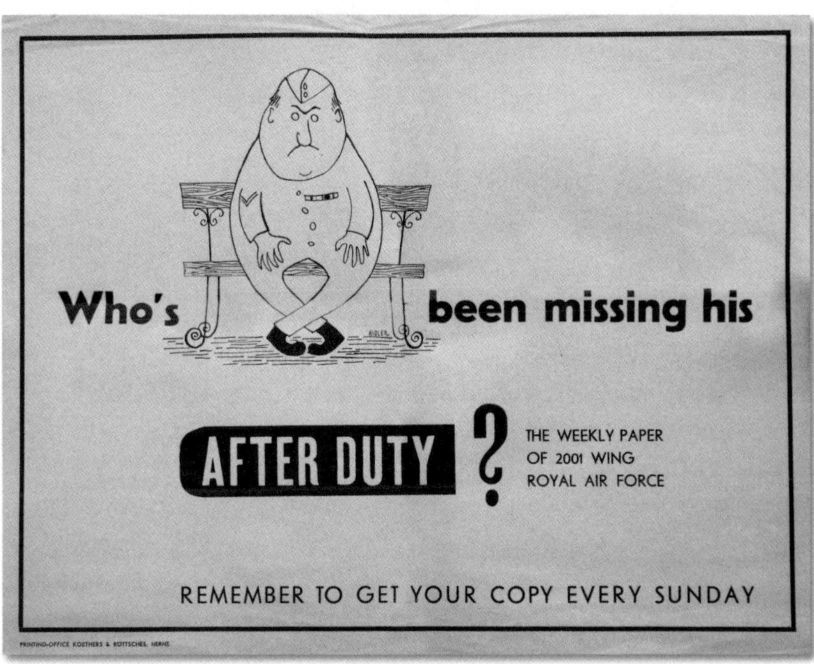

Vivian was 'Make Up' Manager for the RAF newspaper *After Duty* while in Germany in 1945-46, so will have designed this poster advertising the paper, as well as contributing the cartoon of a sad serviceman who has missed an issue.

Flight-Lieutenant David Bland with his wife Mary on their wedding day in 1947. Vivian acted as Best Man for his closest friend. David served as a navigator in a Halifax bomber before being shot down near Berlin on 23 August 1943 and incarcerated in Stalag Luft III.

Appendix 1

David Bland's War:
The Story of an RAF Bomber Navigator

Roger Bland writes: *These excerpts come from a bundle of letters that my father, David Bland, wrote between 1942 and 1945 to his sisters Margaret and Barbara, who were living together in Cornwall. They cover the time when he was sent to the USA to train as a pilot and subsequently a navigator in the RAF in 1941–42; his service in Bomber Command, flying Halifaxes, from 1942 until his plane was shot down over Germany in August 1943 and he became a PoW; and a sequence of letters from the PoW camp in 1943–44. There is a final letter from Brussels in May 1945 after he had been freed. The letters start with a series from Dallas, Texas and Pensacola, Florida between June 1941 and February 1942. David has been sent to the USA to train as a pilot. After an accident in June which sets back his training he transfers to becoming a navigator. I have included all the references I can find to Vivian and Anne and their children, together with a few excerpts that give an idea of the missions he flew on and his first card from a PoW camp, and the letter he wrote after he had been freed.*

4 January 1942 (Pensacola, Florida)

I had a long and interesting letter from Vivian yesterday. He's still at the same place & not getting on much. But he had some leave at the beginning of December & he's also made friends with a lot of people at Kirkwall including the local newspaper magnate who is called Twott! He printed some Christmas cards for Vivian. Anne's poems seem to have attracted a lot of attention & her picture appeared lately in *Lilliput* (a small-format British monthly magazine of humour, short stories, photographs and the arts, 1937-60; Anne had been photographed by Bill Brandt for the December 1941 issue, as the only female poet represented in an 8-page section including such male poets as Dylan Thomas, Stephen Spender and William Empson), as a result of which Vivian is known in camp as Mr Anne Ridler. It's a pity Faber didn't publish the poems because although the first edition has sold out the publishers for some reason won't reprint. (It was a 24-page pamphlet entitled *A Dream Observed and Other Poems,* issued in 1941 by Editions Poetry London, most of whose poems were subsequently reprinted in Anne's *The Nine Bright Shiners* published by Faber in 1943.)

There is a six-month gap in the sequence of letters as David completes his training in the USA and returns to England. David continues training at Hampstead Norris, Berks.

19 August 1942 (RAF Hampstead Norris, Newbury)

Anne is staying at Ringshall for the time being because there's a chance of Vivian being moved south. He's applied for a job in photographic intelligence, he tells me, but doesn't expect to hear anything for a long time. I have spent the weekend at Ringshall but don't want to make a habit of it because they've got a houseful now, with the family of her brother from Ceylon – the naval one (ie Matt Bradby), not the schoolmaster (Edward Bradby).

1 September 1942 (RAF Hampstead Norris, Newbury)

I spent Friday afternoon in London with Vivian who was on leave... I was in Faber's on Friday with Vivian and they are going to do the alphabets he designed for Jane. I don't think you've seen them but you probably soon will because they are printing a phenomenal number of them and selling them for only 6d. Vivian is also illustrating a book for them on Services slang (in the end illustrated by a different artist, and published by Faber in 1943 as *Service Slang* by JL Hunt & AG Pringle).

Robin Milford, Anne's cousin, lives only 2 or 3 miles from here at Hermitage & I'm going over to see him some time. He's a composer, as you probably know, and quite a good one, but he lost his little boy about a year ago & it rather unsettled his mind; however he seems to be getting better now.

30 September 1942 (RAF Hampstead Norris, Newbury)

Vivian has been refused a commission (presumably because he didn't know enough about the mating of birds) but still hopes for a photographic job of some sort.

David is transferred to RAF Elvington on completing his training.

17 December 1942 (RAF Elvington, Yorkshire)

I spent Friday night at Ringshall with the Bradbys & had a very nice time. Jane is beginning to talk & can walk a bit. They showed me one or two letters from Vivian & he doesn't seem to like Africa at all. His chief complaint seemed to be having to pay 6/- (or its equivalent in beads or shells) to a fat local woman for a bottle of Dettol.

15 March 1943 (RAF Elvington, York)

On Friday I was on the big Essen raid & the opposition was the hottest I've yet met with. Besides that, two rather important pieces of my equipment failed on the way so it wasn't really a very enjoyable trip. But I've just seen a special message from the A.O.C. Bomber Command in which he says that when all the facts are known, that the preceding raid will count as the greatest single victory on any front to date, so it looks as though the results were good. There's no doubt that Krupps was very badly damaged and the Pathfinders were certainly on the spot this time. I've never seen anything like the searchlights & flak there before but then it's the first time I've been to Happy Valley as they call the Ruhr. The first raid of course had very little opposition but they strengthened it up for us & considering that our losses were very light.... I've been made one of the senior navigation officers which means that when I'm not flying I help with the organisation of the raids & I find it very interesting.

I'm sending Vivian's photograph. I had a letter from him the other day & he seems a little happier in the new place.... Anne's baby is due to arrive in about 4 weeks and I want if possible to be at the christening.

David joins the Pathfinders' Force and is transferred to RAF Graveley. Pathfinders were an elite of 20,000 airmen who from August 1942 flew at the head of a bombing raid, dropping flares to light up a target area for the following main bomber force, as well as themselves releasing bombs. This innovation greatly increased the accuracy of such raids, but it was a perilous undertaking – some 3,600 Pathfinder crew would lose their lives by war's end.

8 April 1943 (RAF Graveley, Huntingdon)

Tuesday I had the whole day practically & went over to Ringshall – which isn't really far from here – to see Anne. Her baby's due in 2 or 3 days now & she seems very well. I'm supposed to be one godfather, & the Bishop of St Andrews the other!

16 April 1943 (RAF Graveley, Huntingdon)

Anne's baby (another girl) arrived safely on Saturday last. She was in a Berkhamsted nursing home and seems to be getting on all right. The Bishop of St Andrews is an old friend of their family & was rector of Little Gaddesden, I believe. I've only met him once and can't remember very much about him except for his beard.

19 May 1943 (RAF Graveley, Huntingdon)

I'm sending a photo I just had from Anne of her & Jane which is rather nice. She's had flu so the christening has been postponed which is rather a nuisance because I think I shall get the next week-end off & could have got over to Ringshall.

3 June 1943 (RAF Graveley, Huntingdon)

I was in London yesterday & got a christening present for Alison Ridler

– a rather nice old silver egg-cup which I'm getting Berthold Wolpe (who among other things is a silversmith) to engrave for me. I think it's rather an act of faith giving an eggcup especially as the eggs they had in those days seem to have been much bigger than ours. The christening is Saturday next but I'm not yet sure whether I shall be able to get over for it. . . . (He *is* able to go – see under entry for 7 June in Vivian's Diary.)

I had a letter from Vivian about 2 days ago & he's just being moved to Kano in Nigeria which is apparently healthier. He's already had 'a touch of malaria' to go 'with my old wound' but its only significance for him was he went to hospital and got more TEA.

Undated

PS Vivian seems quite to like Kano. He says it's kept clean by vultures!

15 August 1943 (RAF Graveley, Huntingdon)

This week has been the busiest since I came here with 3 trips so far: last night was what I've been looking forward to for so long – Italy – and it was a perfect moonlight night. The Alps looked superb & we crossed them about 20 miles south of Mont Blanc which looked very near and terrifyingly high (though we should have cleared it at the height we were flying). All the little hamlets had their lights on and at Turin itself the flak & searchlights were laughable. We could see Milan being bombed 80 miles away. I hope this helps the Italians make up their minds. . . .

On 23 August David's Halifax II HR865 bomber is shot down over Germany. It had taken off at 20.02 hours from Graveley as one of 23 Pathfinder bombers of 35 Squadron detailed to attack Berlin at the head of an armada of 710 bombers, in the first of a relentless series of air raids on the city that would last for 7 months. However, soon after midnight and some 125 miles short of the target the Halifax was hit by a night-fighter. The pilot, Lawrence Lahey – who like all 7 of the crew survived the crash and was interned as a PoW – on repatriation at the end of the war filed the following report: 'Hit by JU88 at 17,000 ft causing breakdown in hydraulics and fire in starboard wing and starboard inner motor. After applying the fire extinguishers to starboard inner to no avail, the order to bale out was given and acknowledged by each member of the crew who jumped in turn. The mid-upper gunner was slightly wounded in the legs and pilot [Lahey] had slight wound in the head. Aircraft crashed about 20 miles from Brandenburg.'

Three other Pathfinder Halifaxes were shot down that night as they confronted the most fortified capital in the world. Some 150 night-fighters and 700 heavy flak guns assailed the attackers, who could be pinpointed as targets by 200 searchlights. The main bomber force lost 56 aircraft, or 7.9% of those that set out, the greatest single-night loss of bombers in 4 years of war.

16 September 1943 (Stalag Luft III, Germany)

I hope you will have heard from Bristol by now that I am all right. This isn't a bad place & I've met lots of people that I know. When you next write to Bristol will you ask them to include a small comb in their parcel. I am becoming an expert laundryman & cook & the weather has been gorgeous lately. Do write soon – there should be a lot of news & you can write air-mail as often as you like but we are strictly limited. Much love to everyone – David.

20 December 1943 (Stalag Luft III)

I had a long and interesting letter from Anne with a description of her poetry-reading (in company with a lot of other modern poets) at the Wigmore Hall. It must have been very funny (see under entry for 12 December in Vivian's Diary) . . .

13 August 1944 (Stalag Luft III)

I had a letter from Anne in wh. she said that Jane when asked what V would say to her on his return said 'He will snort like a swine' – and she may not be far wrong. . . . Anne told me Thea's husband is missing, as you may have heard. . . .

8 October 1944 (Stalag Luft III)

Vivian is writing me cheerful letters from England – he is able to see Anne quite a lot.

4 May 1945 (Brussels)

I've now been freed – or rather I escaped – & am being flown home, very excited! Our camp (Marlag near Bremen) (Marlag was a PoW camp for captured seamen) was reached by the Guards last Friday & I was there disguised as a merchant seaman having left the RAF temporarily! I'll have quite a lot to tell you when I see you. I'm pretty well & they're looking after us marvellously, forcing food & everything else on us. We hope to fly on to England tomorrow but I won't see you for a day or two because there's lots of medical stuff to undergo first – to make sure we haven't gone nuts, I believe – & the worst of it is I very nearly have with excitement! Brussels is a marvellous city & is quite on a peacetime basis. I'll try & ring or wire you when I get back – expect to be at Gosford near Wolverhampton for a day or two. Please tell Roger (his brother). I'm writing to Bristol.

All my love, David.

THE HAN

(Fo

This is what YOU are making • • •

AILERON MASS BALANCE
TWO FUEL TANKS, BREATHERS & FILLERS
THREE FUEL TANKS & COMMON BREATHER including LEADING-EDGE TANK
AILERON TRIM TAB
WING FIX (INTERMEDIATE TO OUTER PLANE)
EXHAUST GLARE SHIELD
ROLLS ROYCE MERLIN XX MOTORS & ROTOL CONSTANT SPEED AIRSCREWS
CABIN-AIR INLET
AIR HEATER
TWO BROWNING M/C GUNS
LONGERON
HINGED (SIDE) BOMBDOOR, SWINGDOWN (UNDER) DOOR WITH HYDRAULIC OP. JACKS 34
TRAILING AERIAL
NAVIGATOR
DI-POLE AERIAL (LORENZ BEAM BLIND APPROACH)
RADIO OPERATOR

Maximum Speed.....300 m.p.h.
" Range....3000 miles.
FOUR GUN TURRETS
10 BROWNING ·303 S.

Drawing by J. H. Clark,
Copyright THE AEROPLANE

1—Navigation light
2—Bomb aimer's flat window
3—Bomb sight and arm rests
4—Turret balance flap
5—Bomb aimer's cushion
6—Hot-air hoses in spent cartridge tray
7—Navigator's folding seat
8—Navigator's table, lamp and chart
9—Camera stand
10—Parachute stowage
11—Gyro azimuth stand
12—Repeater compass
13—HT and LT units (radio)
14—Transmitting and receiving sets (radio)
15—Main electrical panel
16—Step-up to pilot's cockpit (parachute stowage underneath)
17—Main instrument panel, engine controls
18—Folding seats (second pilot and engineer)
19—Fuel cock controls
20—Motor starter buttons
21—Emergency flare releases
22—Sextant rest
23—Astro-dome
24—Engineer's instrument panel
25—Engineer's platform
26—Hot air to wireless operator (oxygen bottles nearby)
27—Boxed-in engine control runs
28—Accummulators
29—Rudder and elevator controls
30—Motor controls (out of 27)
31—Emergency hydraulic hand pumps and hydraulic accumulators
32—Hot air trunks from heater on inboard motors
33—Lower spar boom
34—Bomb door hinges and op. jacks
34a—Rear hinge, no jack
35—Doors to wing bomb cells
36—Wing bomb door operating rods and jack
37—Leading edge section
38—Rest bunk each side
39—Jointing frames
40—Step up to turret
41—Flame floats and sea markers
42—Ammunition tracks
43—Flare chutes
44—Emergency axe stowage
45—Elsan lavatory
46—D/R compass
47—Bulkhead and door to tail gunner
48—Tailplane fixings
49—Elevator hinge lever
50—Elevator control lever

A MIGHTY MACHINE of

Cutaway drawing of a Handley Page Halifax bomber. For David Bland's position in the plane see the key, nos. 7 and 8.

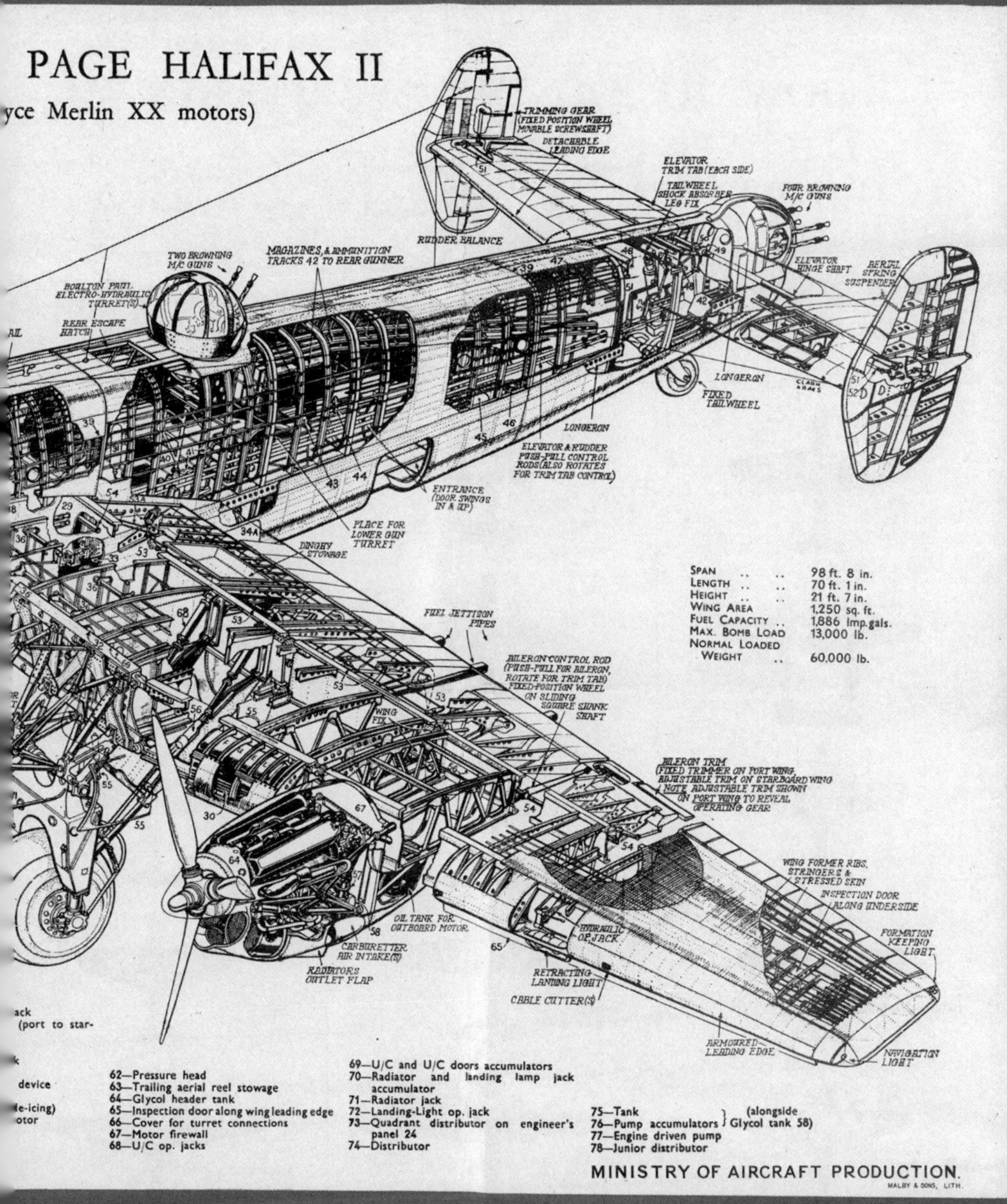
PAGE HALIFAX II
yce Merlin XX motors)
TRIMMING GEAR (FIXED POSITION WHEEL MOVABLE SCREWSHAFT)
DETACHABLE LEADING EDGE
ELEVATOR TRIM TAB (EACH SIDE)
TAILWHEEL SHOCK ABSORBER LEG FIX
FOUR BROWNING M/C GUNS
RUDDER BALANCE
ELEVATOR HINGE SHAFT
AERIAL SPRING SUSPENDER
TWO BROWNING M/C GUNS
MAGAZINES, & AMMUNITION TRACKS 42 TO REAR GUNNER
BOULTON PAUL ELECTRO-HYDRAULIC TURRET(S)
REAR ESCAPE HATCH
LONGERON
FIXED TAILWHEEL
LONGERON
ELEVATOR & RUDDER PUSH-PULL CONTROL RODS (ALSO ROTATES FOR TRIM TAB CONTROL)
ENTRANCE (DOOR SWINGS IN & UP)
PLACE FOR LOWER GUN TURRET
DINGHY STOWAGE
SPAN .. .. 98 ft. 8 in.
LENGTH .. .. 70 ft. 1 in.
HEIGHT .. .. 21 ft. 7 in.
WING AREA 1,250 sq. ft.
FUEL CAPACITY .. 1,886 Imp. gals.
MAX. BOMB LOAD 13,000 lb.
NORMAL LOADED WEIGHT .. 60,000 lb.
FUEL JETTISON PIPES
AILERON CONTROL ROD (PUSH-PULL FOR AILERON, ROTATE FOR TRIM TAB) FIXED-POSITION WHEEL ON SLIDING SQUARE SHANK SHAFT
WING FIX
AILERON TRIM (FIXED TRIMMER ON PORT WING, ADJUSTABLE TRIM ON STARBOARD WING NOTE ADJUSTABLE TRIM SHOWN ON PORT WING TO REVEAL OPERATING GEAR
WING FORMER RIBS, STRINGERS & STRESSED SKIN
INSPECTION DOOR ALONG UNDERSIDE
FORMATION KEEPING LIGHT
OIL TANK FOR OUTBOARD MOTOR
HYDRAULIC OP. JACK
CARBURETTER AIR INTAKE(S)
RADIATORS OUTLET FLAP
RETRACTING LANDING LIGHT
CABLE CUTTER(S)
ARMOURED LEADING EDGE
NAVIGATION LIGHT
ack
(port to star-
device
le-icing)
otor
62—Pressure head
63—Trailing aerial reel stowage
64—Glycol header tank
65—Inspection door along wing leading edge
66—Cover for turret connections
67—Motor firewall
68—U/C op. jacks
69—U/C and U/C doors accumulators
70—Radiator and landing lamp jack accumulator
71—Radiator jack
72—Landing-Light op. jack
73—Quadrant distributor on engineer's panel 24
74—Distributor
75—Tank } (alongside
76—Pump accumulators } Glycol tank 58)
77—Engine driven pump
78—Junior distributor
MINISTRY OF AIRCRAFT PRODUCTION.
MALBY & SONS, LITH.

ITISH WORKMANSHIP

HOW TO IDENTIFY WARPLANES

UNITED STATES

White bar with white star on blue background, outlined in red.

Here are shown eighteen of the more prominent combat planes of the United States Air Force. Study their silhouettes in order to become familiar with the type of ships being used by our gallant air force in all parts of the world. (These silhouettes were made as large as possible rather than in relative size.)

ARMY FIGHTER PLANES

Bell P-39 "Airacobra"

Lockheed P-38 "Lightning"

Curtiss P-40 "Warhawk"

North American P-51 "Apache"

Republic P-47 "Thunderbolt"

Vultee A-31 "Vengeance"

ARMY BOMBERS

North American B-25 "Mitchell"

Martin B-26 "Marauder"

Lockheed A-29 "Hudson"

Boeing B-17 "Flying Fortress"

Consolidated B-24 "Liberator"

Curtiss C-46 "Commando" (Transport)

NAVAL PLANES

Grumman F4F-4 "Wildcat"

Brewster SB2A-1 "Buccaneer"

Vought-Sikorsky F4U-1 "Corsair"

Curtiss SB2C-1 "Helldiver"

Martin PBM-3 "Mariner"

Consolidated PBY "Catalina"

44

Identification charts for US (*ABOVE*) and British (*OPPOSITE PAGE*) warplanes.

HOW TO IDENTIFY WARPLANES

GREAT BRITAIN — Red, white and blue bull's eye.

Shown below are a few of the more widely known British warplanes now being used by the Royal Force in protecting their country and in carrying out devastating raids into enemy territory. Each has a definite shape. Learn to identify them by their outline.

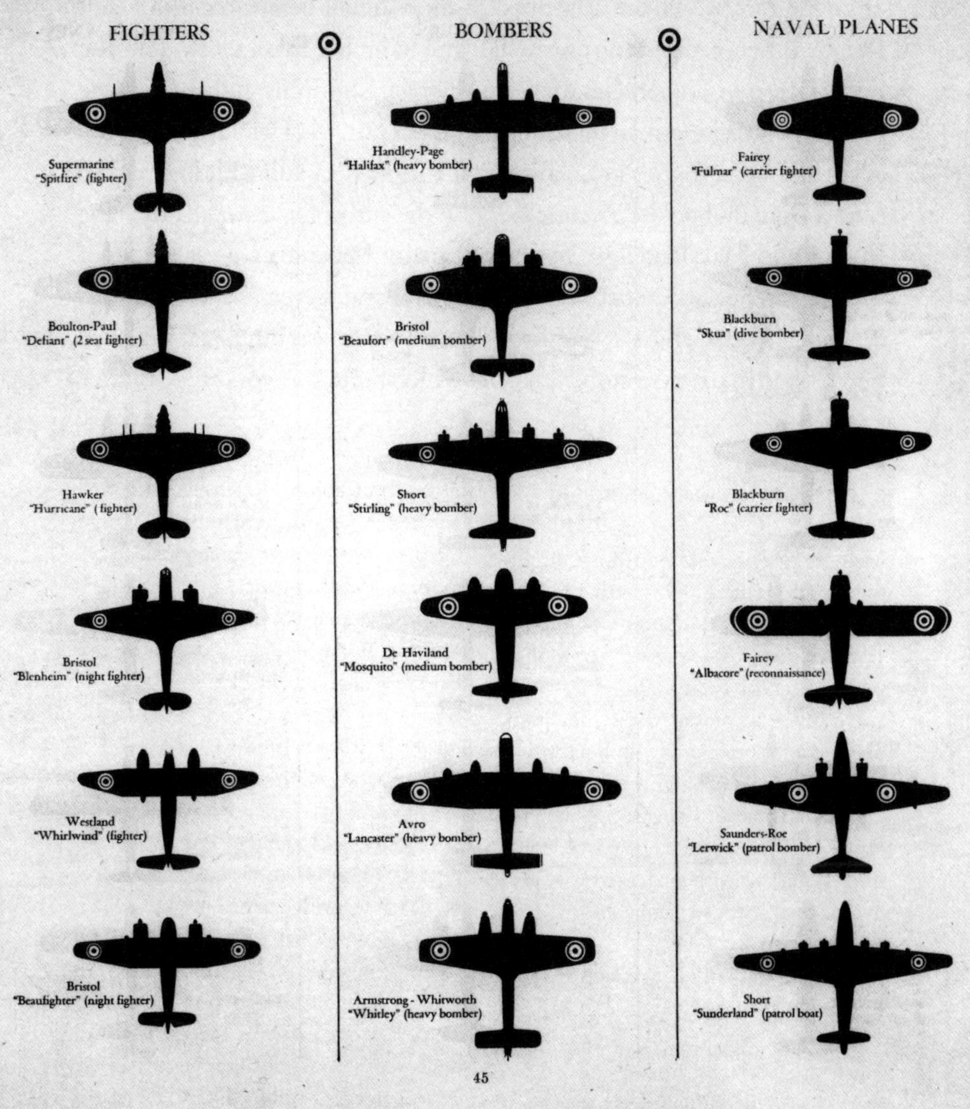

45

Appendix 2

Aircraft on the Takoradi Route Recorded by LAC Ridler

In his Diary Vivian records the presence at either Ikeja or Kano airfields of 16 aircraft, which are described in more detail below. He also heard about 4 other planes, none of which featured on the Takoradi Route – the Superfortress bomber, Catalina flying boat, Lightning fighter and the Condor, a lethal German maritime patrol aircraft, all of which are likewise described here. So too are 2 aircraft mentioned by John Pudney in the extract from his booklet *Atlantic Bridge* at the end of the Introduction – the Boston and Maryland light bombers. Finally Appendix 2 gives details of the Halifax heavy bomber in which David Bland served as a navigator, as discussed in Appendix 1; and lists all the aircraft assembled at Takoradi September 1940–31 October 1943, at which point the work there ceased.

FIGHTERS

Bristol Type 156 Beaufighter (British)

Diary 29 May 1943

Twin-engine, 2-seat, long-range night-fighter and anti-shipping strike fighter; over 5,500 built. Max speed 300 mph at 1,300 ft, max cruising speed 250 mph at 5,000 ft, service ceiling 15,000 ft, range 1,470 miles; 4 cannon, 6 machine guns, plus 1 torpedo and 2 250-lb bombs or 8 rocket projectiles. A highly effective, reliable aircraft crucial as a night-fighter in the Battle of Britain, attacking Axis shipping from Malta, and with the Desert Air Force in the North African campaign.

Curtiss P40 Warhawk (US) (aka RAF Kittyhawk)

Diary 7 April 1943

Single-engine, 1-seat ground-attack fighter-bomber; 14,000 built. Max speed 343 mph, service ceiling 31,000 ft, max range *c.*1,000 miles; 6 machine-guns plus up to 1,500 lb of bombs. Relatively undistinguished American fighter, built in large numbers, with numerous upgrades to try to improve performance, and used by 28 nations; Vivian's No. 349 (Belgian) squadron had an early version known by the British as the **Tomahawk**.

Hawker Hurricane (British)

Diary 13 July, 17 September 1943

Single-engine, 1-seat fighter/fighter-bomber; 14,500 built. Max speed 342 mph at 22,000 ft, service ceiling 36,500 ft, max range with external fuel tanks, 985 miles (internal fuel only, 480 miles); 12 machine-guns plus 2 250-lb bombs or single 500-lb bomb. Essential to the RAF's victory in the Battle of Britain when it destroyed more German aircraft than all other defences combined, the Hurricane nevertheless required superior Spitfires to deal with the Luftwaffe's Me 109s. The Hurricane later caused havoc attacking Axis columns in the Western Desert.

Supermarine Spitfire (British)

Diary 12 April, 17 September 1943

Single-engine, 1-seat fighter/fighter-bomber; c.23,000 built of all Mark I-XIX types. Max speed of Battle of Britain Mark II 357 mph, range 405 miles, service ceiling 33,800 ft, Mark XIV 448 mph at 26,000 ft, service ceiling 43,000 ft; 6 machine-guns plus 500 lb of bombs. Probably the most famous aircraft of World War II, the Spitfire was light, agile and aerodynamic with its elliptical wing design, but more costly and difficult to build than the Hurricane. Some 24 Middle East squadrons were equipped with the Mark V.

LIGHT BOMBERS

Bristol Bisley/Blenheim V (British)

Diary 12 May, 14 June, 15 June 1943

Twin-engine, 3-seat, light bomber; *c.* 1,000 built (cf Blenheim IV, *c.*3,300 built). Max speed 266 mph at 11,800 ft, service ceiling 27,000 ft, max range 1,460 miles; up to 1,300 lb of bombs. The last of the Bristol Blenheim designs, known briefly as the Bisley, it equipped 6 squadrons in the Middle East as a high-altitude bomber, but was withdrawn during the subsequent Italian campaign after suffering heavy losses to advanced German fighters.

Lockheed B34 Ventura (US)

Diary 15 November 1943

Twin-engine, 4- or 5-seat, light bomber; *c.*3,000 built. Max speed 315 mph at 15,500 ft, service ceiling 24,000 ft, range 950 miles; up to 2,500 lb of bombs. Largely used in coastal patrol and advanced training, some 400 were supplied to the RAF.

Martin 187 Baltimore (US)

Diary 29 May, 11 July, 19 July 1943

Twin-engine, 4-seat, light bomber; 1,575 built. Max speed 305 mph at 11,500 ft, service ceiling 23,000 ft, range *c.* 1,000 miles with 1,000 lb of bombs; max up to 2,000 lb of bombs. Liked for its structural strength, but its narrow fuselage meant crew could scarcely change position in flight.

MEDIUM BOMBERS

Martin B26 Marauder (US)

Diary 25 September 1943

Twin-engine, 7-seat, medium bomber; over 5,000 built. Max speed 283 mph at 5,000 ft, service ceiling 19,500 ft, range 1,100 miles; up to 4,000 lb of bombs. Initially called the widow-maker for its high accident rate, modifications vastly improved its handling and safety record. By the end of World War II the Marauder had the lowest loss rate of any US Army Airforce bomber. The RAF received 522 of the aircraft and it equipped 12 squadrons deployed in the North African and later campaigns from November 1942 onwards.

North American B25 Mitchell (US)

Diary 29 May, 1 June, 6 December 1943

Twin-engine, 5-seat, medium bomber and ground-attack aircraft; *c.* 10,000 built. Max speed 272 mph at 13,000 ft, service ceiling 24,000 ft, range 1,350 miles; 12-18 machine-guns, plus 8 rocket projectiles and up to 3,000 lb of bombs; later models could carry torpedoes. Introduced from 1941, the B25 remained in service across 4 decades. It saw action in the Allied victory at El Alamein in November 1942 and during the rest of the campaign in North Africa, as well as the invasion of Sicily and advance through Italy.

HEAVY BOMBERS

Boeing B17 Flying Fortress (US)

Diary 6 November 1943

4-engine, 10-seat, long-range, heavy bomber; *c.* 12,700 built. Max speed 287 mph at 25,000 ft, service ceiling 35,800 ft, range with 6,000-lb bomb load 2,000 miles, up to 17,600 lb of bombs. An iconic World War II American aircraft, renowned for its robustness and bristling with defensive armaments (13 machine-guns). The B17 *All American* made it home in February 1943 despite being nearly sliced in half. Though easy to fly, the Flying Fortress created conditions inside that were cramped and uncomfortable. The cabin was not pressurized and the crew suffered from altitude sickness and frostbite, despite wearing heated flying suits. Compare the pressurized Boeing Superfortess, below.

Consolidated B24 Liberator (US)

Diary 29 May, 8 July, 6 November 1943

4-engine, 8- or 10-seat, long-range, heavy bomber/reconnaissance aircraft; 18,475 built. Max speed 290 mph at 25,000 ft, service ceiling 28,000 ft, range 2,100 miles; 10 machine-guns plus up to 12,800 lb of bombs, but more usually 5,000 lb. Although somewhat overshadowed by the more famous B17 Flying Fortress and harder to fly, the Liberator was produced in greater numbers than any other US aircraft in World War II. RAF Squadrons 159 and 160 began operations with their Liberators in the Middle East in June 1942; one of this batch became the personal transport of Winston Churchill under the name *Commando.* Some 177 more advanced Liberators were sent from Benghazi on 13 August 1943 to bomb the crucial Axis oilfields at Ploesti in Romania, but although successfully causing damage, 55 aircraft and 440 crew were lost.

TRAINING AIRCRAFT

North American Texan (US) (aka RAF Harvard)

Diary 16 February, 18 February, 1 March, 23 March 1943

Single-engine, 2-seat trainer/close air support; 17,000 built of all variants. Max speed 205 mph, service ceiling 21,500 ft, range 750 miles. Presumably the numerous references in Vivian's Diary to crashes involving Texans at Ikeja reflect its role as a training aircraft.

MILITARY TRANSPORT

Consolidated C87 Liberator Express (US)

Diary 10 July 1943

4-engine, military transport; 287 built. Max speed 300 mph at 25,000 ft, service ceiling 28,000 ft, ferry range 3,300 miles at 215 mph at 10,000 ft, max load 12,000-lb of cargo or 20-25 passengers. A hastily designed derivative of the B24 Liberator bomber, introduced from late 1942 to fulfil the need for a transport with longer range than the ubiquitous Douglas C47 Skytrain (Dakota), for which see below. The C87's origins as a bomber caused many weaknesses, such as instability in flight with incorrectly loaded cargo, or a nosegear liable to collapse on rough airstrip landings when fully loaded. As a result, it was not popular with crews.

Curtiss C46 Commando (US)

Diary 29 June 1943

Twin-engine, 54-seat troop carrier and cargo transport; 3,180 built. Max speed 269 mph at 15,000 ft, service ceiling 27,000 ft, range 1,200 miles. With twice the cabin volume of the more widespread Douglas C27 Skytrain/Dakota, the Commando proved extremely useful when introduced from February 1943 on the South Atlantic ferry route from the US to Accra on the Gold Coast (Ghana) via Ascension Island, during the build-up of men and equipment in the North African campaign.

Douglas C27 Skytrain (aka RAF Dakota) (US)

Diary 29 May 1943: at Kano Vivian records seeing 'DCs' lined up with other aircraft. This presumably refers to the military version of the Douglas DC3 civilian airliner and transport known as the Skytrain by the US Airforce, and the Dakota by the RAF (possibly an acronym for Douglas Aircraft Company Transport Aircraft).

Twin-engine transport for cargo, personnel deployment and casualty evacuation; *c.*11,000 built to 1945. Max speed 229 mph at 7,500 ft, service ceiling 23,200 ft, range 1,500 miles; max load 6,000 lb or 25 paratroops or 18 stretchers for wounded. The most common, dependable and successful World War II military transport, produced in greater numbers than any other type. Its first major use as a carrier of airborne troops came with the invasion of Sicily in July 1943 (only a matter of weeks after Vivian spotted the plane at Kano), when C27s dropped some 4,000 paratroops.

OTHER AIRCRAFT

Armstrong-Whitworth AW27 Ensign (British)

Diary 1 June 1943

4-engine civilian airliner for up to 40 passengers, flown in support of the military in World War II; only 14 ever built (1938-40). Max speed 210 mph at 6,700 ft, service ceiling 24,000 ft, max range 1,370 miles at 5,000 ft. The Ensign was 114 ft long with a huge 123-ft wingspan, but was underpowered and unreliable. Engine trouble caused one on the Takoradi Route to make a belly landing on 3 February 1942 in Vichy-controlled French West Africa, eventually falling into the hands of the Germans after being flown to France. They pronounced the aircraft obsolescent and destroyed it except for the engines, which were fitted into captured Douglas DC3s.

MENTIONED BUT NOT SEEN BY LAC RIDLER

Boeing B29 Superfortress (US)

Diary 6 November 1943

4-engine, 10-seat, long-range heavy bomber/ reconnaissance aircraft; *c.*3,970 built. Max speed 358 mph at 25,000 ft, service ceiling 31,850 ft, range 3,250 miles; up to 20,000 lb of bombs. The largest and technically most advanced bomber of the war, with a pressurized cabin unlike the B27 Flying Fortress. In 1944-45 the Superfortress was crucial to the devastating bombing campaign against Japan, which culminated in the dropping of the atomic bomb on Hiroshima by B29 *Enola Gay* on 6 August 1945, followed three days later by a second on Nagasaki; together these brought World War II to an end.

Consolidated Catalina (US)

Diary 16 August 1943

Twin-engine, 7- or 8-seat, long-range maritime patrol bomber, and search-and-rescue flying boat; *c.*3,300 built. Max speed 179 mph at 7,000 ft, long range 117 mph, service ceiling 14,700 ft, max range 2,545 miles; 5 machine-guns plus up to 4,000 lb of bombs or depth charges. Slow but reliable and with a very long range, the Catalina proved invaluable in the successful prosecution of the Allied naval war in all theatres – Atlantic, Mediterranean, Indian Ocean and Pacific. On 26 May 1941 an RAF Catalina located the German battleship *Bismarck* as it attempted to evade

Royal Navy forces in the Atlantic; after a protracted chase and series of engagements the British finally sank the battleship on 27 May. By war's end Catalinas had rescued hundreds of Allied aircrew downed in the water, and sunk 40 U-boats.

Focke-Wulf Fw 200 Condor (German)

Diary 16 August 1943

4-engine, long-range maritime patrol and transport aircraft; possibly 280 built. Max speed 224 mph, service ceiling 19,685 ft, range 2,212 miles, endurance 14 hours; 5 machine-guns and 550-lb bomb load. The scourge of Allied shipping in the Atlantic, the Condor could carry anti-ship missiles. One early Condor became Hitler's personal transport, while a later version was allocated to Himmler.

Lockheed P38 Lightning (US)

Diary 1 December 1943

Twin-engine, 1-seat, long-range escort fighter and fighter-bomber; almost 10,000 built. Max speed 414 mph at 25,000 ft, service ceiling 44,000 ft, range 475 miles; 1 cannon and 4 machine-guns plus up to 3,200 lb of bombs. Fully operational in combat from November 1942, this remarkable and unusual twin-engine high-altitude fighter-bomber played a significant part in the North African campaign, effecting the wholesale destruction of German cargo and transport aircraft over the Mediterranean. However, if forced to fight at lower altitudes between 10,000 and 15,000 ft, the Lightning proved vulnerable to more manoeuvrable Luftwaffe fighters. In the Pacific theatre, Lightnings destroyed more Japanese aircraft than any other US Airforce type.

MENTIONED IN THE INTRODUCTION

Douglas A20 Havoc (RAF Boston) (US)

Twin-engine, 3-seat, light bomber; 7,478 built. Max speed 317 mph at 10,000 ft, service ceiling 25,000 ft, range 1,025 miles; 6 machine-guns plus up to 2,000 lb of bombs. One of the most extensively built light bombers of World War II, the Boston in its Mark III version served with 5 RAF squadrons in North Africa from early 1942, replacing Bristol Blenheims.

Martin 167 Maryland (US)

Twin-engine, 3-seat light bomber and reconnaissance aircraft; 450 built. Max speed 304 mph at 13,000 ft, service ceiling 29,500 ft, range 1,300 miles; 4 machine-guns plus up to 2,000 lb of bombs. Operational with the RAF from September 1940 and in the Western Desert from May 1941, the Maryland, though useful as a light bomber, found its real niche as a medium-range high-speed reconnaissance aircraft. The Baltimore largely replaced it from 1942.

DAVID BLAND'S WAR

Handley Page Halifax (British)

Appendix 1

4-engine, 7-seat, long-range heavy bomber; 6,200 built. Max speed 282 mph at 13,500 ft, service ceiling 24,000 ft, range with max bomb load 1,030 miles; 9 machine-guns plus up to 13,000 lb of bombs. Together with the comparable and even more famous Avro Lancaster (7,377 built, max speed 287 mph, up to 14,000 lb of bombs), the Halifax formed the backbone of the RAF's night-bombing campaign against Germany, equipping 34 squadrons and flying 75,500 sorties between 1941 and 1945 in the European theatre; 4 more squadrons in the Middle East acquired the aircraft. As well as being involved in the Pathfinder operations over Germany (experienced by David Bland as a navigator), the Halifax also proved useful for towing large gliders during the invasion of Sicily in 1943, when paratroops were deployed. It complemented use of the Dakota transport plane. Although suffering significant losses through a lack of defensive firepower, its punishment-absorbing durability enabled many a damaged plane to limp back to base.

AIRCRAFT ASSEMBLED AT TAKORADI, SEPTEMBER 1940–31 OCTOBER 1943

Source: RAF Narrative: West African Reinforcement Route, formerly secret account produced by the Air Historical Branch of the Air Ministry 'downgraded to restricted 11.12.73' and available online

Blenheim	1,149
Hurricane	2,306
Maryland	66
Tomahawk	232
Fulmar	36
Mohawk	18
Kittyhawk	262
Boston	341
Spitfire	740
Beaufort	42
Anson	14
Gladiator	6
Defiant	6
Miscellaneous	6
	5,262

In addition to the above, 156 Hurricanes were assembled at Apapa, Lagos, during October 1942–January 1943.

Poster portraying a Halifax returning from a bombing raid. Over 6,000 of this long-range heavy bomber were built, and it equipped 34 squadrons on European operations for which it made 75,500 sorties.

Chronology of the War Years and Takoradi Route

'The climate at Takoradi and the local malaria harassed the men erecting the crated aircraft. . . . The heavy wear on engines in their flight over vast sandy spaces reduced their fighting life. None of this aircraft supply was effective in 1940. But if we had not begun in good time the Army of the Nile and all its ventures could not have lived through the tragic events of 1941.'

WINSTON S CHURCHILL, *THE SECOND WORLD WAR* (CASSELL, 1950), VOL. II, PP 401-402

Bold: Events connected with Vivian and his family
Italics: Developments on the Takoradi Route
Roman: Other events

1938

2 July **Wedding of Vivian Ridler and Anne Bradby at Little Gaddesden in Hertfordshire.**

1939

7 April Italy invades Albania.

26 April Conscription introduced in Britain.

23 August Nazi-Soviet non-aggression pact.

1 September Germany invades Poland.

3 September Britain and France declare war on Germany.

Winston Churchill returns to government as first lord of the Admiralty at the invitation of the Prime Minister, Neville Chamberlain. A message goes out to the Fleet: 'Winston is back'.

Vivian and David Bland join the Auxiliary Fire Service.

11 October **Wedding of Anne's brother Edward Bradby to Bertha Woodall.**

21 October **Edward and Bertha embark by sea for Ceylon (Sri Lanka) on board the SS *Orion* which, as an unaccompanied vessel, zigzags through the Channel and Mediterranean to avoid any torpedoes. On 12 November they arrive safely in Ceylon, where Edward will become headmaster of the Royal College, Colombo for the duration of the war. Matt Bradby, Anne and Edward's elder brother, is already serving on the island as a naval officer.**

13 December Battle of the River Plate in South America, in which the German pocket-battleship *Admiral Graf Spee* – one of the few capital ships of the Kriegsmarine – is damaged in an engagement with the outgunned Royal Navy heavy cruiser *Exeter* and light cruisers *Ajax* and *Achilles*. Putting in to the neutral port of Montevideo, the *Graf*

Spee is only allowed 72 hours for repairs. Believing (incorrectly) that Royal Navy reinforcements are nearby, the captain decides to scuttle his ship on 17 December, giving Britain a morale-boosting victory.

1940

9 April German forces capture Denmark and invade Norway.
14 April Allies land in Norway.
10 May Germany launches Blitzkrieg to conquer Belgium, Luxembourg and the Netherlands and attack France.
10 May By extraordinary coincidence, the same day as the German attack a crisis in British politics forces Prime Minister Neville Chamberlain to resign. Winston Churchill replaces him in a new government of national unity with the Labour party under Clement Attlee. Lord Halifax becomes Foreign Secretary, Anthony Eden War Minister, and former trade union leader Ernest Bevin Minister of Labour.
2 June Allies withdraw from Norway.
4 June Allies evacuate 330,000 soldiers from Dunkirk which falls to the Germans.
10 June Italy declares war on Britain and France.
14 June Nazi occupation of Paris.
20 June *British Air Ministry decides to develop the West African Reinforcement (Takoradi) Route.*
21 June Italy attacks France.
22 June France surrenders, leading to a German-occupied north of the country and a German-dependent south administered from Vichy by Marshal Pétain.
28 June General de Gaulle, having evacuated to Britain, is recognized by UK as leader of the Free French.
3 July After France's surrender, the British are highly concerned that the powerful French fleet will fall into German hands. They seize all French ships in British ports, and endeavour to negotiate with the admiral commanding the key French naval base at Mers-el-Kébir in Algeria. The confused exchanges lead ultimately to a British squadron reluctantly opening fire, sinking the battleship *Brétagne* and seriously damaging other ships. The incident leads Vichy France to break off diplomatic relations with Britain.
10 July **Anne moves from the flat at 15 Taviton Street in London to live with her parents, Violet and Kit Bradby, at Ringshall End near Little Gaddesden.**
4 August Italian troops in Ethiopia invade British Somaliland.
13 August Luftwaffe launches full-scale assault on RAF and its airfields in Britain. Britain decides to send tanks to the Middle East.
18 August **David Bland's elder brother Pilot Officer John Bland, attempting to gain height in his plane along with other Hurricanes of 501 Squadron during a lunchtime Luftwaffe attack over Kent, is jumped by German air ace Gerhard Schöpfel in his Me 109 fighter, shot down and killed.**
21 August *Arrival of main RAF party at Takoradi, where a base for the reassembly of crated aircraft shipped by sea from Britain is being established; the planes will then be flown in small convoys via staging posts to the Middle East, a journey of about 3,697 miles that takes some 4 days (there is no night flying).*
25 August *Initial Reinforcement Route staging posts established.* First RAF Bomber Command night raid on Berlin.

5 September *Arrival of first crated aircraft – Hurricanes and Blenheims – at Takoradi, even as precious Hurricanes are also needed back home in the ongoing Battle of Britain.*
6 September *30 Hurricanes are landed at Takoradi from the carrier Argus.*
7 September Luftwaffe switches to bombing London and other cities.
11 September Italian invasion of British-held Egypt, gateway to the Middle East and Britain's crucial supply of oil.
15 September RAF inflicts heavy losses on Luftwaffe in decisive Battle of Britain Day, leading Hitler two days later to postpone indefinitely his planned Operation Sea Lion, the invasion of Britain.
19 September *Despatch of first convoy of erected aircraft from Takoradi to the Middle East (1 Blenheim guiding 6 Hurricanes).*
Mid-September **After a land mine drops near their Taviton Street flat Vivian and David Bland move to live at Ringshall End, commuting to work in London from there.**
27 September Japan joins the Axis alliance, signing the Tripartite Pact with Germany and Italy.
25 October *Arrival of first US-built crated Glen Martin Maryland bombers and British Fairey Fulmar naval fighters at Takoradi.*
28 October Italians invade Greece.
5 November Roosevelt re-elected as US President for third term in office.
11-12 November Successful British attack on Italian fleet at Taranto.
Inauguration of the North Atlantic Ferry Route: arrival of 7 Lockheed Hudsons at RAF Aldergrave in Northern Ireland, having flown non-stop from Newfoundland in 10½ hours. By November 1944 the Route will have delivered from USA and Canada to Britain 4,321 aircraft for the RAF and 10,468 for the US Army Air Force.
20-24 November Hungary, Romania and Slovakia join Axis.
2 December *Air Marshal A W Tedder – on his way to Cairo as Deputy AOC-in-C Middle East – arrives at Takoradi. He is 'very impressed' by how improvisation in difficult circumstances has successfully established the base.*
Mid-December **Vivian sworn in by RAF.**
9 December British mount counteroffensive in Egypt.
17 December *Arrival of first US-built Curtiss P36 Mohawk fighters at Takoradi.*
18 December Hitler issues directive to his subordinates for invasion of Soviet Union in May 1941.
31 December *By now a total of 28 Blenheims, 68 Hurricanes and 12 Fulmars have been erected and despatched from Takoradi to Cairo.*

1941

8 January *Arrival at Takoradi of carrier HMS Furious with 40 Hurricanes and 9 Fulmars.*
19 January British launch offensive against Italian forces in East Africa.
22 January British and Australian forces under General Archibald Wavell capture the port of Tobruk and 25,000 Italian soldiers.
23 January **Vivian departs for Padgate in Cheshire, and later Cranwell in Lincolnshire, to begin his RAF training as a wireless operator.**
4 February **Birth of Anne and Vivian's first child, Jane.**
6 February Wavell's British forces capture Benghazi.

8 February *Arrival at Takoradi of first aircraft sent direct from USA aboard a chartered Norwegian ship: 100 Curtiss Tomahawks and 20 Glen Martin Marylands (all need to be erected before despatch to the North African front).*
12 February Major-General Erwin Rommel arrives in Tripoli, Libya, to take charge of the newly formed Afrikakorps, which consists of both German and Italian forces.
1 March Bulgaria joins Axis.
7 March British ground troops – withdrawn from Wavell's North African forces – arrive in Greece.
11 March Lend-Lease becomes law in USA, allowing still neutral America to step up its aid to Britain.
20 March *HMS Furious arrives at Takoradi with 40 Hurricanes, plus 12 Fulmars and 6 Swordfish for the Fleet Air Arm.*
27 March Battle of Cape Matapan, in which British Mediterranean fleet sinks three Italian cruisers, thus removing the serious threat of the Italian fleet for the rest of the war.
4 April Rommel takes Benghazi unopposed.
6 April Germany invades Yugoslavia and Greece, and delays its planned invasion of Soviet Russia by a month.
12 April Rommel encircles Tobruk, which holds out till it is relieved in December.
24 April British forces begin evacuating Greece.
24 April *Churchill to General Wavell: 'Ever since November I have tried every method and every route to pump aircraft into the Middle East. Great risks have been run and sacrifices made, especially when two-thirds of one whole fighter squadron were drowned in trying to fly to Malta, and when Furious was taken off her Atlantic duties to make three voyages to Takoradi.'*
27 April Germans enter Athens.
Early May **Vivian receives his first posting: the RAF camp in Orkney where he is to keep watch for enemy aircraft that might attack the Royal Navy base at Scapa Flow.**
May *Takoradi ceases to act as a receiving base for American aircraft despatched from USA.*
10 May Hitler's deputy, Rudolf Hess, lands by parachute in Scotland, deluded by an astrologer into believing that he can broker peace between Germany and Britain. Arrested and interrogated by the British, he is denounced by Hitler; Stalin is convinced that this is a British anti-Soviet plot.
11 May *Churchill to General 'Hap' Arnold, head of US Army Air Forces: 'I am much obliged for the information reported by your observer in Egypt. The Air Ministry tell me that we have recently sent out to Takoradi the best officers we can find, but they are necessarily less familiar with American than with British types of aircraft and engines and welcome your offer of American experts. . . . Assembly of aircraft is not sole bottleneck of deliveries from Takoradi. Any acceleration must be matched by corresponding increase in transport aircraft for ferry pilots. Can your promised deliveries of American transport aircraft to Africa be accelerated?'*
16 May Italians surrender to British forces in East Africa.
20 May German paratroops land in Crete, which is captured by 1 June despite British resistance. The Germans lose 7,000 out of a force of 17,500 paratroops, a scale of losses that dissuades Hitler from ever again mounting a major airborne assault, including against the crucial British island base of Malta which survives the war unconquered by Axis forces.
24 May German battleship *Bismarck* sinks the ageing British battleship *Hood* in the North Atlantic.

27 May The *Bismarck* is sunk by the British Home Fleet after a protracted chase.
June *Formation of Anti-Raider and Defence Flights at Takoradi, to protect against potential long-distance attacks by Italian or German aircraft. The Germans are by now aware of the Takoradi Route.*
22 June Operation Barbarossa launched, the German invasion of Soviet Russia. Almost 3.6 million men in 153 divisions, around 3,600 tanks and over 2,700 aircraft – the largest force in European military history – attack on a wide front between the Baltic and Black Seas. They swiftly overwhelm the 2.9 million men of the Red Army, with their often obsolescent 10,000 tanks and 8,000 aircraft. Stalin, repeatedly warned by his agents of such an assault, has simply failed to believe that Hitler would tear up his pact with the Soviets. By 16 July Smolensk, halfway on the route to Moscow, has been taken. Yet, thanks to their newly created industrial base in the far east, the Russians are able to make good their severe losses of personnel and equipment, and prevent the rapid conquest of Leningrad and Moscow.
5 July Wavell is replaced by General Claude Auchinleck as C-in-C Middle East.
12 July Britain and the Soviet Union sign a mutual assistance pact.
20 July *Formation of RAF Ferry Command.*
27 July Japanese troops start occupying French Indo-China.
9-12 August Churchill, having sailed to Newfoundland aboard the battleship *Prince of Wales*, meets Roosevelt (President of a still-neutral USA); they agree an eight-point Atlantic Charter that places the war on a moral footing. But more important in practical terms than the unenforceable Atlantic Charter is Roosevelt's subsequent announcement that Pan-American Airways (PAA) would soon be ferrying war planes and transporting war supplies to Egypt via the Takoradi Route. The US War Dept now signs a contract with PAA for it to ferry US bombers via Natal in Brazil across the South Atlantic to Accra on the Gold Coast.
25 August British and Soviet forces invade Iran, vital source of oil supplies, to prevent it from joining the Axis powers.
8 September Siege of Leningrad begins.
19 September Germans capture Kiev and four days later Crimea.
2 October Germans launch offensive to capture Moscow.
19 October Russians move government east from Moscow.
24 October Germans capture Kharkov and ten days later Kursk.
16 November Churchill appoints General Sir Alan Brooke Chief of the Imperial General Staff – strategic military head of Britain's armed forces – to replace General Sir John Dill (who after America's entry into the war crucially cements Anglo-US relations as Head of the Joint Staff Mission in Washington). Brooke is daunted by taking over at this low point in Britain's fortunes, and at the prospect of working closely with the brilliant but mercurial and erratic Prime Minister.
18 November British Eighth Army launches Operation Crusader counterattack in North Africa, catching Rommel offguard.
29 November Soviet counterattack on Rostov forces German withdrawal.
December The British magazine *Lilliput* publishes an article on eight leading young poets, all photographed by Bill Brandt. Anne is the only woman among them.
5 December German drive on Moscow is halted in harsh winter conditions.

7 December Japanese launch surprise air attack on Pearl Harbor in Hawaii, base of the US Pacific Fleet. All 8 battleships there and 11 other warships are sunk or badly damaged.
8 December Japanese invade Malaya. USA declares war on Japan.
10 December The battleship *Prince of Wales* and cruiser *Repulse*, sent without air cover from the British base at Singapore to intercept the Japanese, are bombed and both sink, with the loss of 840 men.
11 December Hitler declares war on USA, as does Mussolini.
14 December Japanese launch invasion of Burma.
19 December Italian raid on Alexandria harbour using three manned torpedoes severely damages two British battleships, *Valiant* and *Queen Elizabeth*, putting them out of action for some time.
20 December Japanese attack Dutch East Indies.
23 December Rommel continues his retreat, abandoning Benghazi.
25 December Hong Kong falls to the Japanese.

1942

20 January Wannsee conference: from the autumn of 1941 a 'final solution' for the extermination by the Nazis of all Jews in Europe has been developed; now, at a suburb in Berlin, 14 bureaucrats including Adolf Eichmann meet to coordinate plans for the deportation of Jews to secret camps where they will be murdered by gassing. Already killing squads or *Einsatzgruppen* following behind troops in the invasion of Russia have slaughtered a million Jews. Over the next 15 months two million more will die at four death camps.
21 January Rommel launches fresh offensive into Cyrenaica, but halts at the heavily defended Gazala Line on 4 February.
15 February Singapore falls to the Japanese; 16,000 British, 14,000 Australian and 32,000 Indian soldiers become prisoners of war.
27 February Japanese forces defeat the Americans in the Battle of the Java Sea.
8 March Japanese land in New Guinea.
11 March US general Douglas MacArthur is ordered to depart from the Philippines so as to take command from Australia of Allied forces in the western Pacific. Some 70,000 US and Filipino troops are left behind and captured.
1 April *New Takoradi Route staging-post airfield opened at Ikeja, just inland from Lagos in Nigeria.*
1 April **Vivian at Ringshall End on a fortnight's leave from Orkney.**
5 April **In the so-called Easter Sunday raid 91 bombers and 36 Zero fighters from 5 Japanese carriers attack Colombo harbour and Racecourse airbase. Out of 38 Hurricanes sent up to meet them, 16 are destroyed, while an old destroyer and 3 merchant ships and a tanker are sunk in the harbour. The principal target, however, the Royal Navy Eastern Fleet, has previously put to sea, alerted to the imminent Japanese threat by intelligence reports. But two cruisers from the Fleet, sent back towards Ceylon, are spotted and sunk. The Eastern Fleet itself subsequently relocates its main base to East Africa. Matt Bradby RN goes there too. Meantime Edward Bradby, headmaster of the Royal College, Colombo, has had to relocate nearby, allowing the RAF to take over his school buildings; nevertheless the Racecourse aerodrome that has come under attack is uncomfortably close. He now does one night-shift a week observing RAF personnel**

in the operations room plot aircraft movements on maps, in case he needs to alert the Civil Defence authorities about another attack. He and his wife Bertha have a young son, David, born on 27 February.

9 April **Japanese navy planes attack Trincomalee on the eastern seaboard of Ceylon, in the mistaken belief that the Eastern Fleet might be there; they sink the old carrier HMS *Hermes* and a destroyer for the loss of 5 bombers and 12 fighters; the RAF loses 5 Hurricanes. The Japanese navy retires eastwards, never to return. The British Eastern Fleet comes back to Ceylon on 4 September 1943.**

16 April **Anne and infant Jane join Vivian on the return journey to Orkney, travelling by train to Inverness then flying.**

8 May Battle of the Coral Sea, the first contest between opposing carriers and their planes, is a tactical victory for the Japanese, but they fail to press home their advantage.

10 May *The ultimate sacrifice: Polish Sergeant Mikolajrzak, ferrying an aircraft on the Takoradi Route, has been forced to land in the desert. Suffering terribly from thirst and the heat, he records his last messages, discovered beside his plane after his death: '09.00 hours . . . let nobody land in the desert where there are no people, as there is no way out. Just like me, it is better to be killed. 12.00 hours It is terribly hot, I drink, or rather lick my scanty sweat. 13.45 hours I hear an aircraft flying to the south . . . my last hope, I cannot get up to have a look. My last minutes. God have mercy on me.'*

27 May Rommel launches assault on the British fortified Gazala Line, breaking through with the Luftwaffe's support.

June *Record erection (231) and despatch (186) of aircraft at Takoradi.*

4-7 June US Pacific Fleet wins the pivotal Battle of Midway, ultimately sinking 4 Japanese aircraft carriers for the loss of 1 of their own.

20 June **Jan Bradby and her two young children, Dan and Diana, arrive at Ringshall End, having made the perilous six-and-a-half-week journey by sea from Ceylon; her husband Matt Bradby RN had been told by the British that Ceylon could no longer be defended from Japanese invasion, so had sent his family home in early May.**

21 June Tobruk falls to Rommel's forces, and nearly all the 35,000-strong British garrison is captured. The port becomes a crucial supply base for the German advance into Egypt. Rommel, promoted to Field Marshal by Hitler, writes to his wife: 'I would much rather he had given me one more division.'

30 June British Eighth Army retreats to the Alamein Line in Egypt.

July *Another record broken at Takoradi: 224 aircraft erected (mostly Hurricanes and Kittyhawks) and 249 despatched (mostly Hurricanes, Blenheims, Spitfires and Beaufighters).*

2 July **Vivian and Anne are told on their fourth wedding anniversary that he is to go overseas. They leave Orkney only to learn it was a 'preliminary warning' and that he must await instructions.**

3 August Churchill and Alan Brooke, his military chief, arrive in Cairo to assess British forces.

7 August Churchill sacks the now tired General Auchinleck as C-in-C Middle East, replacing him with the highly experienced General Sir Harold Alexander. Brooke's protégé, the abrasive and self-confident General Bernard Montgomery, will take over Eighth Army.

10 August Germans reach outskirts of Stalingrad.

11 August In Operation Pedestal, a British convoy from Gibraltar makes it through to

Malta, suffering many losses but bringing vital supplies for the beleaguered island.
13-16 August Churchill and Brooke meet Stalin in Moscow, having flown from Cairo in Liberators via Tehran, the oil wells at Baku, and keeping below 200 ft along the Caspian Sea to avoid any German fighters in the vicinity. Brooke is impressed with Stalin's 'astuteness' and 'crafty cleverness', but can imagine 'his sending off people to their doom without turning a hair'. He finds the late-night dinners with their endless toasts and 'oily, fishy' food a trial, and has little success explaining to the Soviets why their demands for an immediate Second Front in the west are impossible to meet. (Wavell, also on the trip, sums it up in a ballad: '. . . I'm feeling rather in a stew./ . . . No Second Front in 1942.') But Churchill eventually hits it off with Stalin, and boldly asks him the reasons for the 1939 Nazi-Soviet Pact, the explanation being the weakness of the French army and the advantage of gaining Polish territory to act as a buffer against the inevitable German invasion.
19 August Poorly conceived raid, organized by the ambitious but inexperienced Louis Mountbatten, on the German-occupied French port of Dieppe. About 237 warships and 4,900 Canadian troops as well as over 1,000 British personnel take part, but several thousand Canadians are captured and over 900 lose their lives. The assault fails miserably.
30 August Rommel's last offensive at Alam Halfa which grinds to a halt by 5 September.
c.8 September **Vivian goes to London for a test in order to qualify for the Photographic Section of the RAF, but is told it is only suitable for candidates already familiar with RAF cameras.**
23 September Rommel, suffering from ill-health, flies to Germany for treatment and to visit Hitler.
14 October *Churchill to Secretary of State for Air and Chief of Air Staff: 'No explanation can justify the congestion of 98 Hurricanes, 61 Beaufighters, 36 Spitfires and 37 Kittyhawks at Takoradi when every one of these machines is urgently needed in Egypt. I ask that an immediate remedy shall be applied.'*
23 October Montgomery launches offensive with Eighth Army at El Alamein. He has 195,000 men (Rommel 50,000 Germans plus 54,000 Italians), 1,029 tanks (vs 496), and 530 aircraft (vs 350+); moreover the Afrikakorps lacks fuel and transport. But a minefield hampers the attackers. War Artist Edward Ardizzone watches the struggle from the HQ truck, but finds that 'You can't draw shell-bursts . . . [or use] watercolours in a battle.'
24 October **Vivian sails from Blackpool in a troopship bound for somewhere in the tropics, having been inoculated against yellow fever and malaria.**
25 October Rommel returns, and averts immediate disaster at Alamein.
Early November **Matt Bradby arrives back in Britain, having sailed from East Africa aboard the battleship *Duke of York*, where he has been in charge of the naval draft. He will later in the month take up a position at Derby House in Liverpool, the Western Approaches Command Centre for the coordination of Royal Navy and RAF tactics against North Atlantic U-boats.**
2 November Final British breakthrough begins at Alamein; Rommel is forced to retreat two days later; by 11 November he has been pushed out of Egypt. As Ardizzone records, 'Every soldier was smiling.'
3 November Colonel Mortimer Wheeler, famed excavator of Maiden Castle, has taken part in the battle at El Alamein as commander of the 42nd Light-Anti-Aircraft Regiment

protecting Eighth Army from German bombers. The breakthrough in progress, he records the scene: 'Burnt-out tanks – many of them ours – stray anti-tank guns, rifles, a line of enemy dead, their faces as livid as their green uniforms.' By March 1943, during the final push into Tunisia, he has been promoted to brigadier commanding 10,000 men of Eighth Army's anti-aircraft brigade. En route, with characteristic drive, he has taken the initiative to establish protection for the remarkably well-preserved Roman cities of Lepcis Magna and Sabratha.

8 November Operation Torch, the Allied invasion of Vichy French northwest Africa, begins. US general Dwight Eisenhower is in overall charge as C-in-C; a Western Force under volatile but inspiring General George Patton lands around Casablanca, having sailed direct from the US; while a Central Force heads for Oran and an Eastern Force Algiers – both have come from Britain protected by some 650 warships. In total 65,000 Allied troops take part and meet only sporadic resistance.

10 November Admiral Darlan, C-in-C of the Vichy French armed forces, happens to be in Algiers and eventually agrees to a ceasefire that stops all fighting in French Morocco and Algeria.

11 November In retaliation the Nazis occupy southern (Vichy) France; subsequently 17,000 Axis troops are sent by Hitler into Tunisia, successfully hindering the Allied advance for months but depleting his forces elsewhere.

13-15 November US forces win the naval Battle of Guadalcanal (part of the Solomon Islands in the western Pacific).

19 November Russian counteroffensive at Stalingrad begins.

27 November French fleet scuttled at Toulon to prevent it falling into German hands.

November **Vivian's troopship arrives at Freetown, Sierra Leone (a British colony); he is assigned at Hastings to RAF Belgian 349 Squadron which then sails round the southern coast of West Africa towards Takoradi on the Gold Coast (modern Ghana).**

December *Inauguration of the South Atlantic Bridge, whereby American bombers fly from USA to Accra on the Gold Coast via airfields in the Caribbean, Brazil and Ascension Island.*

1943

January *After the success of Anglo-American forces in North Africa, British Air Ministry decides that twin-engined planes are now safe to fly to the Middle East via the Mediterranean. Work at Takoradi is therefore scaled back. It will now focus on erection of single-engined Hurricanes and Spitfires, and handling and inspection of Baltimores and other US bombers flown across the South Atlantic for the RAF.*

4 January **Vivian's troopship arrives at Takoradi.**

10 January **Vivian's ship reaches Lagos; the following day the men are taken by bus inland to Ikeja to help develop the Takoradi Route staging post airfield there. Vivian subsequently unpacks wireless equipment, helps create the Signals Hut, and letters trucks and signboards before finally being able to do what he is trained for: guide planes in and out as a wireless operator.**

10 January Final Soviet offensive at Stalingrad begins.

12 January **The Belgian Commanding Officer (Malengreau) of Vivian's RAF Belgian 349 Squadron addresses his men.**

14-24 January Allied conference at Casablanca where Churchill, Roosevelt and the

Combined Chiefs of Staff, together with generals Eisenhower and Alexander, agree future strategy and announce the policy of German unconditional surrender.
23 January Eighth Army enters Tripoli.
2 February German Field Marshal Friedrich Paulus surrenders at Stalingrad; some 91,000 German and Romanian soldiers are taken prisoner, only 6,000 of whom survive the war. Around 150,000 Axis soldiers have died in the months-long battle for the city, to add to the 480,000 Red Army dead.
8 February Russians retake Kursk and six days later Rostov.
14-22 February Battle of the Kasserine Pass in Tunisia: an unexpected twin-pronged counteroffensive by General Hans-Jürgen von Arnim's panzer army and Rommel's Afrikakorps gives inexperienced American troops under a disastrous commander and poorly led, disorganized British forces a bloody nose. The Americans alone lose 6,000 men, 183 tanks, over 200 field guns and 500 transport vehicles. Rommel however has to turn back to protect his rear against the advancing British Eighth Army.
9 March Rommel, ordered by Hitler not to retreat into Tunisia and a sick man, leaves North Africa for good.
4-12 March **Exercise Spartan, the largest military training operation ever held in Britain, involving a million men across the south, disrupts life at Ringshall End.**
12 March **After feeling ill for a month and turning yellow, Vivian and many others are finally sent to a hospital in Ibadan to be treated for malaria.**
23 March **Vivian leaves hospital and returns to Ikeja.**
20-27 March Eighth Army finally breaks through the Afrikakorps defensive position at the Mareth Line.
10 April **Birth of Anne and Vivian's second child, Alison Kate. Vivian hears the news almost a fortnight later.**
18 April Admiral Yamamoto, head of the Japanese navy, is killed when US fighter pilots target his plane in the Solomon Islands.
19 April Jewish uprising in the Warsaw ghetto: determined to die with dignity after 300,000 from the ghetto have already been transported to the Treblinka extermination camp, the remaining Jews rise up and hold off 2,600 SS until 16 May. Their bravery inspires similar revolts elsewhere.
21 April **Vivian's malaria returns and he is sent to a different hospital for a week.**
27 April As Eighth Army closes in on Tunis, war correspondent Alan Moorehead – by now famous for his despatches for Beaverbrook's *Daily Express* – witnesses the final assault on a mountain stronghold above the city: 'The last Germans were flung off Longstop Hill this morning and this I believe to be the turning-point of the campaign . . . A blinding hot sun blazes down on the scrub and there is a watery heat-haze on each succeeding height. As you tramp upward, you are half-choked with fine white dust from returning ambulances and tanks . . . the front-line infantry lie about, half in, half out of the trench. . . . Each time a shell comes over, they listen shrewdly to its whine, which gives the direction, and then relax . . .'
7 May Allies capture Tunis and Bizerta.
8 May **CO Malengreau tells 349 Squadron that it is to be broken up.**
13 May Final Axis surrender in Tunisia; some 240,000 troops are captured.
12-25 May Trident conference in Washington, where Americans finally agree to British plan

to invade Sicily and Italy before launching a cross-Channel assault on Nazi-held Europe.
16-17 May Dambusters raid in Operation Chastise breaches two dams in the Ruhr Valley, using special bouncing bombs dropped by 617 Squadron Lancaster bombers. Catastrophic flooding kills 1,600 civilians; 53 aircrew and 8 aircraft are lost.
26-28 May **Vivian travels by train to Kano for his new RAF posting.**
5-12 July Germans launch a huge assault on the Kursk salient with 700,000 troops, 2,400 tanks and 1,800 aircraft, opposing 1.3 million Soviet troops, 3,400 tanks and 2,100 aircraft. It becomes the biggest tank battle in history. Soviet losses are higher, but hereafter they hold the initiative on the Eastern Front.
10 July Allied invasion of Sicily at dawn with 160,000 troops and paratroops and 2,590 ships. Montgomery's Eighth Army lands on the east coast, soon taking Syracuse before getting bogged down advancing to Catania, which only falls on 5 August. Patton's US Seventh Army protects the left flank on the southwest coast, before Patton decides controversially to advance to Palermo in the northwest which he takes by 22 July.
13 July Hitler cancels the Kursk operation, taken by surprise by the Allied Sicilian landings and needing to withdraw a panzer corps to oppose a now likely Allied assault on Italy.
16 July War Artist Ardizzone, having landed in Sicily with Montgomery's forces, follows Eighth Army as it pushes up the east coast towards Catania. In his war diary he writes: 'Learn that we must have lunched yesterday in the midst of two hundred hidden German parachutists. Anxious moment with low enemy aircraft. We get a grandstand view of impending battle. The [Catania] plain spread before us, our shells bursting among the low trees on the other side of the river, machine-gun fire, burning scrub. . . . The straight road in front of us under machine-gun fire, anti-tank gunners beside us in a cactus hedge. I do some drawings and have a snooze. We drink a bottle of champagne. Heaven. Brought to earth by the smell of dead bodies hidden somewhere, a smell that haunts one everywhere. Head back for Syracuse, pass an open lorry of Italian prisoners in civilian dress, a dejected lot. The MP [military police] told us they were paratroops caught wearing civi dress, they will probably be shot. I think by the look of them they realised that too.'
19 July Hitler meets Mussolini at Feltre in northern Italy, believing his own rhetoric will persuade the Italian leader not to make a separate peace with the Allies. His generals think it is a wasted effort.
25 July Mussolini is overthrown; Marshal Badoglio becomes prime minister in a new Italian government.
27-28 July RAF bombers ignite a firestorm in Hamburg, Germany, where more than 40,000 people are killed.
30 July *Erection of 5,000th aircraft at Takoradi.*
30 July **Jack Benny and Larry Adler arrive at Kano to entertain the RAF men there.**
2 August German forces move through Brenner Pass initiating Nazi occupation of Italy, where Hitler sends seven divisions.
11 August Germans begin evacuation of Sicily.
15 August Eighth Army captures Taormina.
17 August Allies reach Messina, but Axis forces have escaped to mainland Italy across the Straits of Messina with 60,000 troops and 40,000 vehicles.
17-24 August Quebec conference: Churchill, Roosevelt and their advisers agree outline plans for Normandy landings in 1944 and use there of artificial Mulberry harbours to

enable essential supplies to be brought in. Brooke, British CIGS, fights hard for importance of invasion of Italy, countering US military chief General George Marshall's conviction that exclusive primacy should be given to the cross-Channel assault about which the Americans believe the British are too doubtful.

23 August **Flight-Lieutenant David Bland is shot down in his Halifax Pathfinder bomber HR865 near Berlin, one of 4 Pathfinders from a force of 23 lost that night as they lead an armada of 710 Lancasters, Halifaxes and Stirlings. This launches 7 months of air raids on Germany's most heavily defended city. Subsequently David is imprisoned as PoW 2353 at Stalag Luft III in Silesia, some 90 miles southeast of Berlin. See also Appendix 1.**

1 September Italian government signs document of unconditional surrender.

3 September Montgomery's Eighth Army lands with ease on the southern tip of Italy, initiating the Allied invasion of the peninsula; the Germans under Field Marshal Albert Kesselring have already withdrawn north to Salerno and ruthlessly disarm Italian forces.

9 September General Mark Clark's largely American Fifth Army lands at Salerno, but meets strong German resistance until it is relieved by the advancing Eighth Army.

12 September Mussolini is freed by German commandos and installed in northern Italy as a Fascist figurehead.

c.15 September **Anne takes part in a Poetry Reading at the Wigmore Hall in London: of the 14 poets who read, she is one of only 4 women – the others being Edith Sitwell, Kathleen Raine and Dorothy Wellesley. The male poets include T S Eliot, Cecil Day Lewis, William Empson and Stephen Spender. The Hall is packed.**

25 September Russians take Smolensk.

26 September In Naples German troops pour kerosene over the shelves of the university library, destroying 50,000 books and manuscripts; two days later they find another cache, hidden for safe keeping in Nola, and set alight 80,000 more.

30 September Fifth Army captures Naples with its crucial port facilities. It 'smells of charred wood, with ruins everywhere', writes the British officer Norman Lewis. A day later War Artist Ardizzone finds a room on the first floor of a hotel: 'Floor above, a brothel. Girls in kimonos on its balcony and American troops going up and coming down looking rather sheepish. Man with a blowpipe goes round my bed to kill bugs, a bad omen. People very hungry, any lengths to get food. Women will lie with you for a packet of biscuits.' He subsequently visits a local hospital to find a 'Goyaesque scene of men, women and children – headless, armless, clothesless . . . Appalling stench, many corpses blackening, no transport to take them away.'

2 October **Vivian hears that his closest friend David Bland has been shot down, only learning five days later that he has survived.**

13 October Italy declares war on Germany.

29 October At Stalag Luft III three PoWs, using a wooden horse to disguise the digging of a tunnel, successfully escape and eventually reach Britain. David Bland is not among them.

31 October *The RAF base at Takoradi ceases to erect aircraft, now that Allied planes can safely fly by a more direct route to the Mediterranean theatre.*

6 November Russians take Kiev.

17 November Treblinka extermination camp closes following the execution of more than 780,000 people there. Killings continue at Auschwitz and other Nazi camps.

20 November American forces land in the Gilbert Islands, the first steps in an advance

across the central Pacific.

28 November-1 December Tehran conference between western Allies and Soviets, at which Roosevelt meets Stalin for the first time (Churchill now realizes 'what a small nation we are'). Stalin – who has long demanded a second front in the west – is told that Normandy landings will take place in May 1944 (they are later postponed to June).

Late November **Anne's first volume of poetry for Faber, *The Nine Bright Shiners*, is published and soon has to be reprinted.**

8 December **Vivian witnesses vast crowds at the Moslem Sallah celebrations for the end of Ramadan in the old city of Kano; it culminates in the arrival of the magnificently robed Emir on horseback.**

23-24 December **The Gang Show flies in to Kano to entertain the RAF men there.**

26 December German battle-cruiser *Scharnhorst* sunk by British cruisers as she attempts to intercept an Arctic convoy off North Cape of Norway.

1944

15 January Rommel is made commander of German coastal defences in northern France and the Low Countries, thought to be the most likely areas for an Allied invasion.

22 January Allied troops land on the coast at Anzio, near Rome, circumventing the German defensive Gustav Line across Italy which includes the fortified heights of Monte Cassino. The cautious British commander however fails to capitalize on tactical surprise.

27 January German 900-day siege of Leningrad is finally relieved; a million or more Russians there have died of starvation, cold and disease.

26 January-29 February German assaults on the Anzio bridgehead eventually fail, but it is not until the spring that the now-reinforced Allied troops can break out and link up with Fifth Army on 25 May. Some 7,000 Allied troops have been killed and 36,000 wounded or missing in action; German losses are 40,000, including 5,000 killed and 4,500 captured.

19-26 February Heaviest air raids on London since May 1941.

6 March US bombers begin daylight attacks on Berlin.

15 March Allies launch third major assault on Monte Cassino, but it is only captured two months later on 18 May by Polish soldiers.

15 March Japanese Imphal offensive from Burma begins. In a four-month battle, British general William Slim's Fourteenth Army finally prevails after fierce fighting; in late July the Japanese retreat becomes a rout. In total they suffer 53,000 casualties, including 30,000 killed, out of a force of 85,000; British casualties are 17,000.

24 March Breakout from Stalag Luft III involving 600 tunnel-diggers, of whom 76 crawl to freedom but only 3 reach Britain; 50 recaptured officers are shot on Hitler's orders, which causes outrage among the western Allies. The published account by a survivor is made into the 1963 film *The Great Escape.*

2 April Russians enter Romania.

22-27 May Allies bomb marshalling yards at Orléans, Le Mans and Aachen, together with bridges along the Seine in preparation for D-Day.

30 May Rommel inspects the Normandy coastal defences, having worked tirelessly over the previous four months to reinforce the Atlantic Wall, though he knows it exists more as propaganda than in reality. Field Marshal Gerd von Rundstedt, in overall command in the west, regards it as 'just a bit of cheap bluff'. Rommel wants panzer divisions stationed

on the coast to thwart any landing, but is overruled by superiors who want them held inland, so as to mount a counterattack in what is believed to be the most likely main invasion point across the Strait of Dover (a mistaken belief reinforced by the stationing of dummy tanks and warplanes in Kent).

2 June **Vivian wires Anne to say he is safely back in England.**

3 June Troops for D-Day embark, but because of poor weather the planned 5 June invasion is delayed by a day.

4 June Rommel leaves France to visit his wife for her birthday, aware that the Kriegsmarine has ruled out the likelihood of an invasion between 5 and 7 June because of the poor weather. He later meets Hitler to try to persuade him to release more panzer divisions.

4 June Fifth Army under General Mark Clark enters Rome; he is determined to claim the glory ahead of Montgomery's forces – thus failing to encircle the German Tenth Army as instructed. Kesselring is able to withdraw his divisions to new defensive positions on the Gothic Line in the mountains north of Florence. Here the Allies become bogged down into the autumn and beyond. But with their 20 divisions they eventually tie down 25 German divisions (20 further German divisions are stationed in the Balkans), thus greatly weakening the Wehrmacht's ability to reinforce either of the critical Eastern or Western Fronts.

6 June D-Day: at dawn 23,400 Allied paratroops are landed on the flanks of the Normandy invasion beaches; then, from 0630, five assault divisions totalling 75,215 British and Canadian troops on Gold, Juno and Sword beaches, and 57,500 US troops on Utah and Omaha beaches wade ashore under fire during the day; the British and Canadians suffer about 4,300 casualties, the Americans 6,000. The Allies succeed in advancing a few miles inland despite a late-day counterattack by the only panzer division guarding the Normandy coast. Over 1,200 warships support the action, together with 11,590 aircraft. Rommel returns to Normandy that night, his worst fears realized.

7 June Bayeux liberated.

8 June Construction of the two Mulberry harbours begins.

8 June **Vivian arrives at Ringshall End from Blackpool, having sailed in an overcrowded troopship from Gibraltar on his long journey out of Africa. He meets his second daughter, Alison Kate, for the first time.**

12 June Churchill visits Normandy.

13 June First V1 'doodle bugs' fall on England.

14 June De Gaulle visits Normandy.

15 June Long-range air offensive against Japan begins.

19-21 June Great storm in Channel largely destroys one of the two Mulberry harbours.

23 June In Operation Bagratian the Soviets launch a huge assault in the central sector, having tricked the Germans into thinking it might come to the south in Ukraine. (Russian air supremacy prevents almost all German reconnaissance flights.) Some 1.7 million men supported by 6,000 tanks and self- propelled guns plus over 7,500 aircraft attack across a wide area. By the end of August they are close to Warsaw and into Latvia.

27 June Crucial port of Cherbourg captured by the Americans.

Rommel and von Rundstedt are summoned to see Hitler at his Berghof base in East Prussia.

Late June **Vivian is posted to the RAF camp at Westcott, not far from Ringshall End. Here he will continue as a wireless operator for incoming and outgoing aircraft.**

1 July Von Rundstedt sacked as C-in-C in the west.
10 July British and Canadian troops finally capture Caen.
17 July Two Canadian Spitfires strafe Rommel's staff car, wounding him and ending his military career.
20 July Klaus von Stauffenberg fails in his attempt to assassinate Hitler with a bomb at the Berghof; the plotters are hunted down, tortured and killed. Rightly or wrongly Rommel is implicated in the plot. On 14 October he is forced to take poison; Hitler then cynically sends a message of condolence to his widow, before giving him a state funeral with full military honours.
Early August **Christopher Bradby, Anne's brother, crosses to Normandy with the Royal Army Service Corps, to which he has been attached since the beginning of the war. He becomes a Major one year later.**
1 August Second Warsaw uprising: General Tadeusz Komorowski, commander of the Polish (non- Communist) Home Army, attacks the German occupiers with 36,500 poorly armed insurgents. Himmler organizes a counterattack, and by 25 August 21,000 well-equipped troops backed by aircraft relentlessly begin retaking the city street by street. The Red Army is on the outskirts but fails to assist. Stalin is probably content to leave the Germans to kill any potential Polish leaders. Komorowski surrenders on 1 October. Some 15,000 insurgents and 200,000-250,000 civilians have died in the city.
4 August Germans withdraw the bulk of their forces from Florence. For the Allies, however, penetrating the heavily defended Gothic Line – which runs down the Apennine Mountains from north of Lucca southeast to Pesaro on the Adriatic coast – proves no easy matter, especially after autumn rains turn the terrain into glutinous mud. Nor does the withdrawal of six divisions for the French Riviera landings help.
15 August Operation Dragoon (formerly Anvil), the Allied landings on the French Riviera, begins. The initial assault by 3 US divisions is followed up by 7 French divisions. Aircraft from 7 British and 2 US carriers harry the 3 German divisions near the landing beaches, while 5 battleships and 21 cruisers bombard them. The Allied advance is swift: the key ports of Toulon and Marseilles – essential for bringing in US supplies needed further north in France – fall on 26 and 28 August respectively; Lyons is taken by 3 September. Churchill has watched the landings from a destroyer but calls them 'irrelevant', since they have meant withdrawing divisions from his favoured Italian campaign – a source of discord with the Americans.
19 August US, Canadian and Polish troops meet across the neck of the Falaise Pocket, trapping seven panzer divisions with 140,000 men and 2,500 tanks, of which only 1,300 men and two dozen tanks escape – a staggering Allied victory that brings the Normandy campaign to an end. But the cost has been huge: some 209,000 casualties (125,000 American, including 37,000 killed) out of a force of 2 million brought across the Channel.
25 August Second French Armoured Division enters Paris and the next day de Gaulle walks down the Champs Elysées, acclaimed by a vast crowd.
4 September Montgomery's Twenty-First Army group reaches the key Belgian port of Antwerp, but in his desire to divert forces so as to launch an airborne attack at Arnhem on the lower Rhine, he neglects to clear the Scheldt Estuary at the approaches to Antwerp. It is therefore not until late November that it is safe to start bringing supply convoys into the Antwerp docks, which finally allows the Allies to obtain the vital armaments,

oil and food that will enable them to win the war in the west.
8 September First V2 rockets fall on England.
12-16 September Second Quebec conference: Churchill, Roosevelt and their advisers agree the postwar division of Germany into occupation zones; Lend-Lease will continue until Japan is defeated.
17-25 September Operation Market Garden, Montgomery's bold plan to establish a bridgehead across the Rhine near the Dutch town of Arnhem: the initial drop of 16,500 paratroops and 3,500 troops in gliders is quite successful, but the advance of the British Second Army's 30th Corps is so slow that by 25 September the paratroops have to be withdrawn; the Germans take 6,000 prisoners.
5 October Russians enter Hungary.
7 October Germans decide to evacuate Greece.
9-18 October Churchill, Eden (Foreign Secretary), Brooke and four others fly via Naples, Cairo and the Crimea to visit Stalin in Moscow. Brooke records that, despite exhausting dinners where vodka and champagne are drunk in vast amounts into the small hours, they succeed in having fruitful discussions with the Russians about military matters, including the likelihood that the Soviets will attack the Japanese in the Far East. He is highly impressed with Stalin's detailed technical knowledge.
14 October British Expedition to Greece enters Athens.
20 October Russians and Yugoslav partisans enter Belgrade.
21 October First German city captured when Aachen falls to US troops.
23 October Britain and USA recognize de Gaulle as head of French provisional government.
24-25 October Battle of Leyte Gulf in the Philippines: the biggest naval battle ever fought, in which the Japanese Combined Fleet, weaker than its US opponents, attempts to divert the powerful US Third Fleet while the smaller US Seventh Fleet guarding the American landings on the island of Leyte is attacked. The ruse almost works, but its ultimate failure means the Japanese can never regain naval supremacy.
12 November *Tirpitz*, sister ship to the 42,000-ton battleship *Bismarck* and stationed in Norway, is finally sunk by two direct hits by Tallboy bombs delivered by Dambuster bombers. A constant perceived threat to Arctic convoys taking supplies to the Russians, she has already been reduced to a hulk by 22 separate air attacks.
5 December Allies take Ravenna.
16 December-16 January German Ardennes offensive, or 'Battle of the Bulge': Hitler, to the horror of his senior generals including von Rundstedt, dreams of a repeat of his 1940 Blitzkrieg by launching a surprise assault through the weakly defended Ardennes forest with 500,000 men, 30 divisions and over 1,000 aircraft. Catching the Allies completely offguard, the Germans make quick gains before Eisenhower – realizing the gravity of the situation – orders Patton's US Third Army in the south to pivot northwards while parts of General Hodges' US First Army on the northern side of the 'bulge' turn to the south. Stout resistance by American troops at Bastogne suck in as many 9 German divisions. Finally, when the skies clear before Christmas, attacks by 2,000 Allied aircraft shatter German supply lines. But it is not until 16 January that the Patton-Hodges pincers meet, by which time the remnants of the German forces have escaped – losing however all their tanks and aircraft and suffering 100,000 casualties.

1945

17 January Russians take Warsaw.

27 January Russians liberate the three death camps at Auschwitz in southern Poland; it is later estimated that 1.2-1.5 million have been gassed there, including 800,000 Jews.

28 January **Ahead of the advancing Russians, the Nazis close Stalag Luft III and force 6,500 US Army Airforce PoWs and 3,500 RAF PoWs – including David Bland – to travel westwards, a good many of whom by 4 February reach the German PoW camp for merchant seamen at Marlag near Bremen. Here, disguised (he writes) 'as a merchant seaman', Bland is eventually freed when the British Guards Armoured Division liberates the camp on 27 April.**

4-11 February Allied conference at Yalta in the Crimea (Stalin, afraid of flying, insists on this location to which he can travel by train in his green Tsarist coach), involving the three Allied leaders and a retinue of 700 people: the main focus is the postwar world – the allocation of Allied areas of control in an occupied Germany; the return of prisoners of war; a secret agreement between Roosevelt and Stalin ceding territory to the Soviets in the Far East in exchange for their entry into the war against Japan; and the boundaries and government of a postwar Poland. In the end Roosevelt gives way to Stalin over Poland, so desperate is he to gain Stalin's backing for the new United Nations Organization; Churchill's case for free and fair Polish elections is weakened by his being reminded of the concessions over Greece given him by the Soviet leader.

13-14 February In the most controversial Allied bomb attacks of the war, 796 Lancasters and 9 Mosquitoes bomb Dresden, causing a horrendous firestorm; the next day 311 B17 bombers also strike the city; some 50,000 people die in the inferno.

19 February US general Curtis LeMay, in charge since January of US Twenty-first Bomber Command, intends to send his high-flying B29 Superfortress bombers with fighter escorts to attack Japanese cities. For this he needs airfields on the small Japanese-held island of Iwo Jima, within striking distance of Tokyo and other cities for the shorter-range fighters. Although US marines land successfully, it takes more than a month of gruelling fighting (and 30,000 casualties) for them fully to secure the island.

26 February US Ninth Army reaches the Rhine south of Dusseldorf.

7 March Patton's US Third Army crosses the Rhine at Remagen.

9-10 March US B29 Superfortresses firebomb Tokyo, killing 80,000 people.

20 March Mandalay, former capital of Burma, falls to Slim's Fourteenth Army after he has deceived the Japanese by first feinting in that direction, then swiftly cutting their vulnerable lines of communication to the south at Meiktila. This opens the way for the British to regain the capital at Rangoon at the mouth of the Irrawaddy River on 3 May.

28 March Last of 1,050 V2 rockets falls on England.

30 March Russians enter Austria.

1 April Battle for Okinawa, the island southwest of Japan, begins: the 100,000 defenders are concentrated in the south, where ridges laced with caves and tunnels offer cover; the US Tenth Army lands uncontested to the north and captures the bulk of the island by late April; meantime the protecting US Fifth Fleet suffers kamikaze attacks that sink 30 ships and kill or wound 10,000 sailors. It takes until 20 June for the tenacious defenders in the south to be defeated, at a cost of 50,000 US casualties and 150,000 Japanese and Okinawans dead.

9 April **First planes carrying former PoWs arrive at RAF Wescott, where Vivian is stationed as a wireless operator. This month 13,778 repatriated servicemen will be brought in aboard 302 Dakotas, 104 Stirlings, 61 C46 Commandos, 42 Lancasters and 7 Ansons. In May 20,809 more will land from 710 Lancasters, 70 Dakotas, 27 Liberators, 26 Halifaxes, 22 Stirlings, 7 Commandos, 9 Fortresses, 2 Mosquitoes, 1 Anson and 1 Hudson. As Anne records, Vivian is kept busy 'round the clock' helping to guide in this huge number of aircraft.**
12 April Roosevelt dies and is succeeded as President by Harry S Truman. As Vice-President for 83 days, he has had little contact with Roosevelt and never been informed of the programme to build an atomic bomb. In his first speech on 16 April he insists on unconditional surrender by Germany and Japan. Churchill later calls him 'emphatic and decisive' in his dealings with the demanding Soviets.
15 April Hitler returns to the Reich Chancellery in Berlin, but bombing forces him to move to an underground bunker.
16 April Three Soviet Marshals, Rokossovsky in the north, Zhukov in the centre, and Konev to the south, on the east bank of the Oder and with 2.5 million troops, 6,250 armoured vehicles and 7,500 aircraft, confront the Germans. Zhukov, tasked with taking Berlin, unleashes an artillery bombardment before dawn on 16 April so intense that it shakes buildings in the city 40 miles away. He has deployed searchlights to blind the enemy, but in the ensuing smoke and glare his own attack collapses. Neither does an assault the next day with six armies succeed. Stalin now orders him to pivot around Berlin on the north side while Konev attacks from the south. Finally three of Zhukov's armies reach the Berlin outer defensive ring on 21 April, and four days later Konev's armour closes the encirclement.
22 April Bologna, behind the Gothic Line in northern Italy, finally falls to the Allies. Their advance thereafter is swift, reaching both Venice and Milan by 29 April and Turin on 2 May, when a ceasefire is agreed with the Germans.
25 April Soviet and US troops meet at Torgau on the River Elbe.
26 April Half a million Soviet troops launch a furious assault on central Berlin which is defended by regular troops and recently enlisted old men and boys, many of whom fight to the bitter end.
28 April Mussolini is shot by partisans while attempting to flee into Switzerland; his body is exhibited in Milan, strung up from the gantry of a petrol station.
30 April While Soviet troops are storming the Reichstag nearby, Hitler shoots himself in his Berlin bunker; his newly wed wife Eva Braun swallows a cyanide capsule; later their bodies are taken up to the Reichschancellery garden and set alight with petrol according to Hitler's instructions. The day before, he has appointed Grand Admiral Dönitz president of the Reich. The following day Joseph Goebbels and his wife Magda likewise take cyanide, having already poisoned their six children.
2 May Berlin surrenders to the Russians.
4 May Germans in the Netherlands, northern Germany and Denmark surrender to Montgomery at Lüneberg Heath.
5 May Germans surrender in Norway.
7 May General Alfred Jodl makes final surrender of Germany to Eisenhower near Reims.
8 May VE (Victory in Europe) Day; before midnight Field Marshal Wilhelm Keitel

ratifies the Reims surrender in front of Zhukov in Berlin.
10 May Russians take Prague.
Mid June **Vivian at last trains for a Commission in RAF Intelligence, passes the exam and by August is an Officer. He is subsequently posted to the Ruhr, where he spends the winter inspecting German factories for armaments that Britain might wish to acquire, as well as guiding visiting officials around the area.**
15 June British Parliament prorogued for a general election campaign after Labour withdraws from the Coalition government.
16 July First nuclear explosion of an atomic bomb at Alamogordo in Texas.
17 July-2 August Conference at Potsdam in Germany: third, last and longest meeting of all three principal Allies, though with Truman instead of Roosevelt and with Attlee half way through replacing Churchill (who loses the general election). The boundaries and peace terms for Europe are discussed, and Poland's future frontiers, but it is the Potsdam Declaration for which the conference becomes known: Japan must surrender unconditionally, those 'who have deceived and misled the people of Japan into embarking on world conquest' must be eliminated, and Japan will be occupied until this is achieved. Truman tells Stalin that US has 'a new weapon of unusual destructive force'; Stalin, already aware of the bomb from his spies, replies that he is 'glad to hear it' and hopes America will 'make good use of it against the Japanese'.
26 July Labour wins British election in a landslide victory, gaining 412 seats to Conservative 213 and Liberal 12; Attlee becomes Prime Minister and Ernest Bevin Foreign Secretary.
6 August US B29 Superfortress bomber 'Enola Gay' drops atomic bomb on Hiroshima, killing at least 140,000 people and leaving others with long-term radiation sickness, genetic injury and mental trauma.
8 August Russians declare war on Japan and invade Manchuria.
9 August Another Superfortress drops a second, more powerful atomic bomb on Nagasaki, using plutonium 239 as opposed to the uranium 235 at Hiroshima. Some 74,000 are killed and a similar number injured.
14 August Emperor Hirohito announces the unconditional surrender of Japanese forces.
15 August Former head of the Vichy government, Marshal Pétain, sentenced to death at the end of his trial, which began on 23 July. The sentence is later commuted to life imprisonment.
28 August US forces land in Japan, where General Marshall will become supreme commander of the Allied occupation. (In January 1947 he is made US Secretary of State – ie foreign secretary – by President Truman, and develops the Marshall Plan that will substantially help pay for the rebuilding of Europe in succeeding years.)
2 September Japanese officers formally surrender in Tokyo Bay aboard the US battleship *Missouri*. World War II is finally over.
2 September Lend-Lease is ended, having cost the US $48.4 billion (roughly $820 billion in today's money), $31.4 billion having gone to Britain principally in food aid, military goods and oil, while Soviet Russia has received $11 billion. But the British, in 'Reverse Lend Lease', have supplied $6.8 billion in raw materials and technology to US forces.

NEWSMAPS

After America had entered the conflict, the US War Department published Newsmaps weekly from April 1942 to March 1946. They typically featured maps of the world and of local areas seeing fighting, brief summaries of military action during the week, and photographs and materiel. The earliest Newsmaps were printed on one side only. However, beginning with no. 6, most had a second side which provided recognition cues for tanks, ships and planes; information about enemy organization, equipment, and uniform insignia; strategies for defeating or evading enemy action; and so on. As hostilities drew to a close Newsmap content switched to revelations of enemy atrocities, and to information on the peace process and reconstruction efforts around the world. Side two content then focused on preparation for the return to civilian life.

Newsmaps were produced in a large domestic version, a smaller overseas version, and an industrial version which contained content similar to other Newsmaps, but with added information about war production efforts. The posters were distributed to military installations, government and civilian groups working on War Department projects, and certain depository libraries. Industrial Newsmaps were displayed in war production facilities around the country. Overseas Newsmaps were sent out to field units of both the US Army and US Navy.

All the world maps were printed in full colour, as indicated in one of the images in the plates showing 23 November 1942. On the following six pages we also reproduce in black & white the Newsmaps for the Sicily landings (19 July 1943), the Normandy campaign (3 July 1944), the noose tightening on Germany (7 May 1945), and the final assault on Japan (20 August 1945).

We are grateful to the University of North Texas, which holds a complete set of the Newsmaps, for making them available for use in this publication.

NEWSMAP

MONDAY, JULY 19, 1943
WEEK OF JULY 8 TO JULY 15
201st Week of the War—83rd Week of U. S. Participation
Volume II No. 13

THE WAR FRONTS

1 SICILY: The first stage in the liberation of the European continent began with the successful invasion of the Italian island of Sicily. It was the greatest display of coordinated air, land and sea power ever attempted.

For weeks preceding the invasion heavy Allied air attacks delivered the necessary "softening up" blows at the enemy's shipping facilities, internal communications lines and airfields. Immediately preceding the invasion Allied warships bombarded coastal defense positions and with coordinating air support provided the cover of fire for the successful landing. Finally, the integrated mass of more than three thousand boats delivered American, British, Canadian and some French troops ashore, together with great quantities of armor and equipment. Thus provided, our ground troops immediately consolidated their positions along the southeastern Sicilian shore and drove inland to the north and west.

Hours before the invasion from the ships, American and British airborne troops landed in Sicily by parachute and glider behind the enemy beach positions. Gliders were cut loose to land at the eastern sector of the invasion zone while the parachute troops bailed out over the west. High winds scattered the forces but despite this and the enemy's anti-aircraft fire these units achieved success with only small losses.

Axis reports admitted the enemy was caught by surprise by the southeast landings and as the action developed it was evident that the largest portion of the estimated 300,000 German and Italian troops were established at the western tip of the island. Thus the greatest pressure fell on the left flank of the American Seventh Army which landed in the area between Gela and Licata. The British Eighth Army, which was not entirely the same organization that fought in North Africa, landed on the eastern corner of the island and included Canadian units which successfully occupied the extreme southeastern tip of Cape Passero.

Supported by naval bombardment, the Eighth Army pushed northward toward Messina, gained the port of Syracuse and Augusta and made landings governing the approaches of the port of Catania.

In the southeast corner American, Canadian and British units converged at Ragusa. Farther west American forces pushed along the coast to Agrigento. With the exception of Ragusa and Palazzolo, to the northwest, all the action had taken place on the low coastal lands. In less than a week the Allies had gained a considerable beachhead that was bounded by an arc swinging southward between Catania and Licata.

As the fighting progressed, however, it would enter Sicily's mountainous terrain. In addition, the enemy, despite heavy dive-bombing and strafing attacks on his communications, would probably be able to shift from the western to the eastern side of the island. One of his biggest problems was to do so before the Eighth Army reached Messina and thus pinched off the most direct supply line with the mainland.

2 AIR OFFENSIVE: The most spectacular air action was over Sicily and the southern Italian mainland as our fighters and bombers concentrated on enemy airdromes. As the landings progressed British and American planes from England roared over Nazi fields in France and the lowlands thus diverting enemy planes that might attempt a shift to southern Europe.

RAF Lancasters from England bombed Turin, in northern Italy in a long-range raid even as the invasion fleet was unloading. Some of these planes returned by a roundabout route over the Atlantic to England as a result of bad weather, while others continued to undisclosed points, generally taken to mean they had continued to bases in North Africa.

3 RUSSIA: After nine days of what was reported as some of the greatest tank battles of the war, the Nazi offensive on the 165 mile central front appeared to be diminishing. Berlin played up "bad weather" as the reason for reducing the heavy attacks launched little more than a week ago in the Belgorod-Kursk-Orel sector.

Soviet reports set the enemy's losses at tremendous figures. They included a total of 2772 tanks, 1187 planes and tens of thousands of casualties. The heaviest fighting appeared to have taken place near Belgorod, at the southern end of the Kursk bulge. There the Nazis made slight gains but available information did not indicate that the small change in position was commensurate with the tremendous cost in men and equipment. During the past few days, Soviet troops succeeded in whittling the enemy gains somewhat.

One point generally noted was that Berlin did not speak of the action as an offensive until after Sicily was invaded, but referred to it only as a counterattack of a Russian thrust. This change of view may have been aimed at detracting German domestic attention from Allied successes along the Mediterranean.

4 NEW GEORGIA: The Jap air base at Munda was subjected to heavy air and artillery bombardment as our ground troops, following two new landings on New Georgia Island, advanced at one point to less than a mile from the Jap strongpoint.

New reports of the sea battle at Kula Gulf revealed that at least nine enemy cruisers and destroyers were sunk against the loss of one light cruiser for the U. S.

This was the engagement that took place July 5-6. In a second engagement early July 13 in the narrow waters between Kolombangara I. and New Georgia I. the enemy lost a cruiser and three destroyers. Two other Jap destroyers were probably sunk.

The Jap warships apparently were blocked in an attempt to reinforce Bairoko. One of our two new landings was made north of Bairoko at Rice Anchorage and from there our ground troops pushed south and destroyed the Bairoko garrison. Our forces were earlier revealed to have made another landing six miles east of Munda at Zanana. This unit crossed over from Rendova Island, apparently under cover of our artillery there. Driving inland they established a road block between Bairoko and Munda and held it against enemy attack. The force at Rice Anchorage took advantage of this to knock out Bairoko.

Recurring air action was marked by frequent dog fights but the heaviest blow was struck when more than 100 American bombers teamed with destroyers and artillery to pound Munda and its surroundings. They dropped 70 tons of bombs. In later attacks loads of 67 and 52 tons were dropped.

5 NEW GUINEA: Heaviest fighting in the drive toward the Jap base at Salamaua was before the enemy positions at Mubo where the enemy was putting up stiff resistance to American and Australian troops moving in from the Nassau Bay area.

Our bombers attacked the enemy base at Rabaul and positions at Salamaua, Lae and Malolo.

6 ALEUTIANS: Now flanked by our growing base at Attu the Jap-held base at Kiska was described by Adm. Nimitz at Pearl Harbor as isolated and neutralized.

Subjected to repeated bombardment by our surface forces and aircraft the enemy was struck an additional blow when four Jap cargo ships which were trying to supply Kiska were intercepted by Army and Navy fliers 280 miles southeast of Holtz Bay on Attu. Our fliers sank one vessel, left a second sinking and damaged the other two.

7 SUBMARINES: American submarines operating in Pacific and Far Eastern waters added substantially to their record, the Navy Dept. announced last week. At the same time a joint statement issued by the British and U. S. Governments confirmed the fact that the United Nations have been winning the war against the Nazi U-boats in the Atlantic.

Ten more Japanese vessels, including one large and one medium sized transport and a large cargo vessel were announced sunk by our subs operating against the enemy's greatly extended supply lines.

LANDING ON THE UNDERSIDE

Allied pilots on missions over the Sicilian Strait in the dawn of July 10 were treated to a sight they will long remember. Stretched along the sloping beaches of Southern Sicily they were witness to the greatest invasion armada ever assembled, a mass of more than three thousand vessels of all types discharging their military cargo on a 100-mile front. A portion of what they observed is drawn here, based on the report of an American reconnaissance pilot who flew his P-38 high over the Mediterranean swells.

Smoke and flame extended ten miles inland as Allied warships poured steel without interruption on the enemy shore positions. Some dashed in close to the beaches, fired their salvos, then swooped out again.

There were all kinds of ships. A few wreathed in the smoke rising from their turrets, looked big enough to be battleships. Sleek destroyers weaved among the cargo vessels which lay to discharging their loads. Landing barges looked like squirming black fish leaving frothy wakes as they dashed back and forth between the transports and shore. Barges, with their loads of troops, tanks and supplies seemed to be everywhere. So great was the concentration that lay on the heaving Mediterranean that the sea appeared "black with ships."

On shore, gun-flashes cutting through the heavy smoke revealed enemy defense positions. Allied warships promptly pounded each position out of action as it was spotted.

One A-36 pilot returning from a dive-bombing mission farther inland observed that the scene of our ground troops pouring ashore and taking over Axis territory was "a beautiful sight."

So it appeared to the rest of the civilized world, as well.

NEWSMAP Prepared and distributed by ARMY ORIENTATION COURSE, Special Service Division Army Service Forces, WAR DEPT., 2E580 Pentagon Bldg., Washington, D. C.

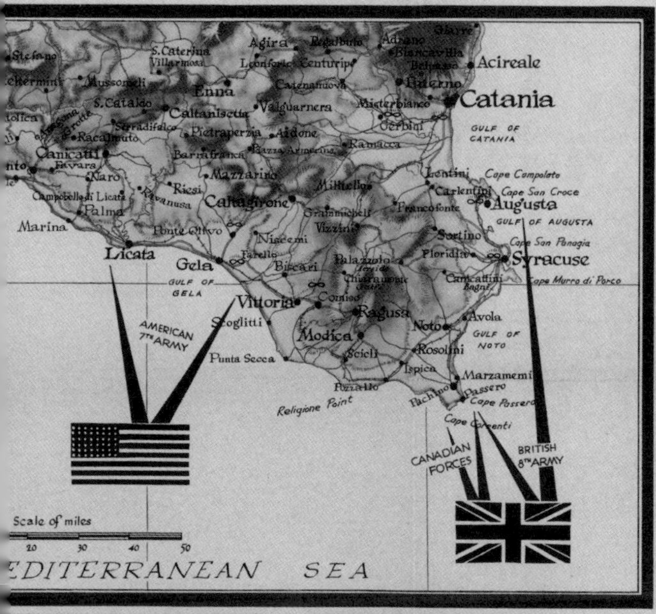

SENIOR COMMANDERS in the INVASION OF SICILY

GEN. DWIGHT D. EISENHOWER
Commander in Chief, Allied Forces in North Africa

★

ADM. SIR ANDREW BROWNE CUNNINGHAM
Commander in Chief, Allied Naval Forces in the Mediterranean

★

GEN. SIR HAROLD R. L. G. ALEXANDER
Deputy Commander, Allied Forces in North Africa
Commanding the 15th Army Group Invading Sicily

★

GEN. SIR BERNARD L. MONTGOMERY
Commander, British Eighth Army

★

AIR CHIEF MARSHAL SIR ARTHUR TEDDER
Commander in Chief, Allied Air Forces in the Mediterranean

★

ADMIRAL SIR BERTRAM RAMSAY
Naval Commander, the Eastern Task Force

★

VICE ADMIRAL HENRY K. HEWITT
Commander, American Naval Forces in the Mediterranean

★

LT. GEN. CARL A. SPAATZ
Commander, Northwest African Air Forces

★

LT. GEN. GEORGE S. PATTON, JR.
Commander, U. S. Seventh Army

★

AIR MARSHAL SIR ARTHUR CONINGHAM
Commander, Northwest African Tactical Air Force

★

MAJ. GEN. JAMES H. DOOLITTLE
Commander, Northwest African Strategic Air Force

★

AIR VICE MARSHAL HUGH P. LLOYD
Commander, Northwest African Coastal Air Force

The Newsmap for 19 July 1943 gives a dramatic depiction of the Allied assault on 10 July by sea and air on Sicily's southeast coast. A Lockheed P38 twin-engine fighter flies directly at the viewer.

NEWSMAP

FOR THE ARMED FORCES

251st Week of the War – 133rd Week of U. S. Participation

FROM CONGRESSMAN Ed Gossett 13TH TEXAS DISTRICT

THE WAR FRONTS

FRANCE: American troops gained the first main objective of the French campaign with the seizure of the major ocean port of Cherbourg. Our troops drove to the sea on both flanks of the city while a direct assault overcame stubborn enemy resistance at Ft. du Roule, on the southern side of the city. Resistance continued in the two peninsulas to the east and west of the port, but this was being overcome. The enemy captives, which unofficial observers expected to reach 30,000, included the German commander of the garrison, Lt. Gen. Von Schlieben and the Nazi sea defense commander of Normandy, Rear Adm. Hennecke, who surrendered to Maj. Gen. Joseph Collins, commander of the American Seventh Corps.

Cherbourg had hardly fallen, when U. S. Army Engineers and Navy repair units went to work repairing its facilities. Considerable time will be saved when troops and supplies from the U. S. can be moved directly to France without the stop-over in Britain.

As the Cherbourg campaign closed, British and Canadian troops on the southeast sector of the Allied position opened a strong drive southeast of Tilly-sur-Seulles, taking Colleville and cutting the rail line and main highway from Caen. They were meeting strong resistance from enemy infantry and armor.

The days preceding the fall of Cherbourg saw strong support offered by Allied air and naval units. All types of enemy installations were heavily attacked, including the robot bomb launching points from which the enemy continued to strike at England. In addition, American and British warships carried on tremendous bombardment duels with German long-range shore batteries. One correspondent reported that 14 Allied warships shelled Cherbourg at once in a three-hour bombardment shortly before the port was captured.

EASTERN FRONT: The Red Army opened its summer offensive on the main Eastern front in the 250-mile area extending north from the Pripet Marshes to Polotsk. The first big Nazi bastion to fall was Vitebsk, and others that followed within the week were Orsha, Zhlobin and Mogilev. The advance appeared to be in two main drives north and south of Mogilev, both aiming at the key rail junction at Minsk. Thousands of towns were being liberated and London observers estimated that the first week of the offensive would see 100,000 Germans killed or captured.

On the Finnish front the Red Army was advancing beyond Viipuri, while in the area between Lake Ladoga and Lake Onega the Finns were being cleared from the Leningrad-Murmansk rail line.

ITALY: Increased German resistance slowed the Allied advance northward, but American, British and French troops continued to make substantial gains. The battle line, now some 80 miles north of Rome, runs as directly east-west across the 170-mile width of the Italian peninsula as the terrain permits. Gains along the Tyrrhenian Sea coast represented an advance of more than 120 miles in the three weeks since the capture of Rome. American Fifth Army troops on the west coast took the port of Piombino and were moving steadily toward the port of Leghorn, where the enemy was observed destroying harbor facilities farther inland. With French troops on their right flank, U. S. troops were converging on Siena.

British troops, who have been driven from Chiusi which had been the scene of the bitterest fighting since the fall of Rome, regained the town and advanced on both sides of Lake Trasimeno.

AIR WAR: The pattern for three-way shuttle-bombing by means of which heavy Allied bombers can reach every corner of Nazi-dominated Europe, was completed last week.

Early in the Mediterranean campaign, Allied bombers made the round trip between England and Mediterranean bases, bombing German aircraft and the other production points inside the Reich and France. Last month the leg between Italy and the Soviet Union was established by the Eastern Command of the U. S. Strategic Air Forces with bases somewhere in Russia. Last week our heavy bombers hit Berlin from British bases, then proceeded to Russia. From there they struck a German-operated synthetic oil plant at Drogobych, in southwestern Poland, 75 miles from the Russian-German front, and then proceeded to Mediterranean bases.

From Italian bases, strong forces of Liberators and Fortresses hit Nazi oil refineries, rail yards and an aircraft plant in the Vienna area, running into the heaviest Luftwaffe opposition in recent weeks. Other heavy blows were struck at Budapest, Brod, in Yugoslavia, an oil plant at Trieste, and the oil and rail concentrations at Bucharest.

SOUTHEAST ASIA: The city of Mogaung, an objective considered as important as Myitkyina, fell to the Allies, following a three-day assault by British and Chinese ground troops striking from the north and the south of the Jap stronghold. The attack was supported by American fliers.

The city is the outlet from the valley of the same name, which connects the Ledo Road from northern India with the broad Irrawaddy River Valley. It holds the key to the western approach to Myitkyina, which has been partially occupied by besieging Chinese, American and British troops. The two towns are some 25 air miles apart.

On the Salween River front, 100 miles southeast of Myitkyina, Chinese troops cut the Burma Road ten miles southwest of Lungling, and continued pressure on that base and towards Tengyueh, the Japanese base to the northwest.

In India, mopping up operations proceeded east and west of the Imphal-Kohima Road, and progress was being made in the direction of Ukhrul.

CHINA: Japanese troops moving south along the rail line from Changsha were less than ten miles from Hengyang, the strategic Hunan Province rail junction. Even while this direct attack on Hengyang continued, another Japanese force appeared to be flanking the town and occupied positions 38 miles to the southeast. American and Chinese fliers killed hundreds of Japs in low-level sweeps between Lake Tung-Ting and Hengyang. They knocked out several bridges and destroyed many trucks. A press dispatch from Chungking stated, however, that the 14th USAAF had evacuated its base at Hengyang in the face of the Japanese advance.

SAIPAN: U. S. Army and Marine forces, who now occupy the lower half of 15-mile long Saipan Island, encountered stiffening resistance from Japanese infantry, following the capture of Mt. Tapotchau, a 1554-foot peak in the center of the island. The line last week ran from the lower portion of Garapan, the main Japanese town which is on the western shore, southeast to the captured peak, and then directly east to put the northern shore of Magicienne Bay in American hands. The island at this point is some five miles across.

While there have been no tank battles, our forces have captured 40 enemy tanks and destroyed 36 more. Southwest of Saipan, our carrier-based planes hit enemy installations at Guam and Rota.

PACIFIC: "Task Force 58," the newly revealed American unit which has the entire Pacific Ocean to the gates of Japan as its stamping ground, last week took the measure of a powerful enemy force between the Philippines and the Marianas and sent it scurrying back to its home waters between the Philippines and Formosa.

The principal actions fell into three phases—a Jap attack by carrier planes on our fleet units covering the Marianas landing operation on 18 June, our returning air attack on the strong enemy fleet on 19 June, when it was discovered between the Marianas and the Philippines, and an American fighter sweep over Iwo in the Volcano Islands to the north of the Marianas on 23 June.

In the 18 June attack the enemy lost 402 planes to our 27. U. S. planes that attacked the enemy fleet the next day sank one aircraft carrier, damaged four others, a battleship and three cruisers, and sank three auxiliary vessels. Also, 26 enemy planes were shot down and other vessels damaged. We lost 95 planes and 49 men. In the Volcano Islands our fighters shot down 116 enemy planes, with eleven probables, as against our loss of five planes.

Added to this toll was another big Jap carrier reported as probably sunk by a U. S. submarine, although it was not described as part of the fleet encountered off the Philippines. Other U. S. submarine action further reduced the Jap Navy by 16 vessels.

SOUTHWEST PACIFIC: Creation of a new air arm to be known as the Far Eastern Air Force, with headquarters in Australia and New Guinea, was announced by Gen MacArthur. The new organization combined the 5th AAF which operated in Australia and New Guinea and the 13th AAF which went through the Solomons campaign and the current regular attacks on Rabaul and the New Ireland area. Lt. Gen. Kenney heads the new force. The Australian and Dutch air forces in Australia and New Guinea will remain under the Southwest Pacific Allied Air Force.

Operations in the theater consisted mainly of the unceasing pattern of air bombardment. Supporting the Marianas invasion, heavy units from the Southwest Pacific neutralized Truk, Palau and Yap, and in addition, hit enemy shipping and installations in western New Guinea.

NEWSMAP Prepared and distributed by ARMY INFORMATION BRANCH ARMY SERVICE FORCES 205 E. 42nd Street, NEW YORK 17, N. Y. Navy distribution by EDUCATIONAL SERVICES SECTION BuPers, Navy Dept., Washington, D. C. MONDAY, JULY 3, 1944 • WEEK OF JUNE 22 TO JUNE 29 • Volume III No. 11 F

In this Newsmap for 3 July 1944 we can see how far the Allies have advanced in Normandy since D-Day on 6 June, as well as progress on other fronts.

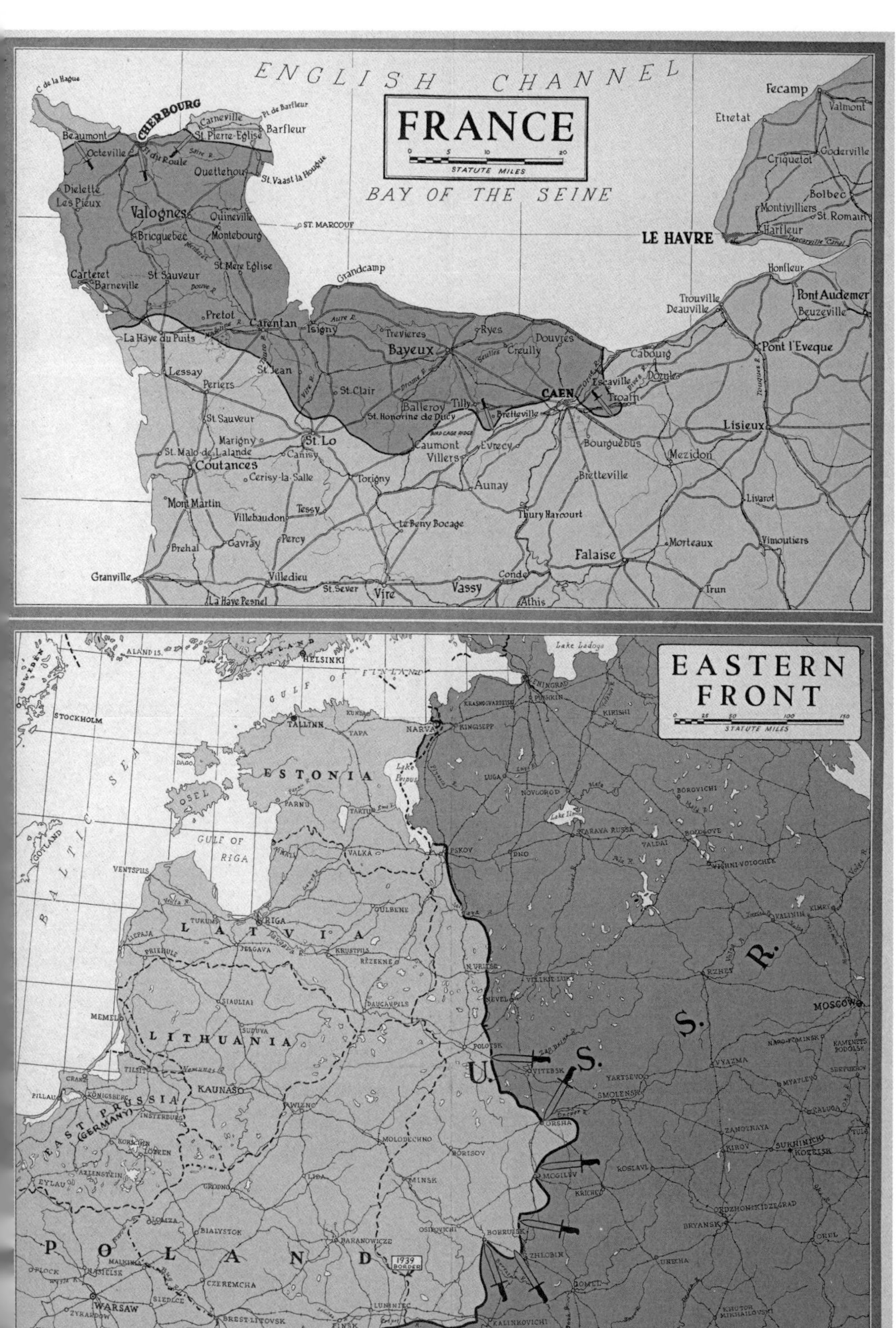

ENGLISH CHANNEL
FRANCE
STATUTE MILES
BAY OF THE SEINE
CHERBOURG
Barfleur
Valognes
Carentan
Isigny
Bayeux
CAEN
St. Lo
Coutances
LE HAVRE
Fecamp
Honfleur
Lisieux
Falaise
Granville
EASTERN FRONT
STATUTE MILES
ESTONIA
LATVIA
LITHUANIA
EAST PRUSSIA (GERMANY)
POLAND
U. S. S. R.
BALTIC SEA
GULF OF FINLAND
GULF OF RIGA
PRIPET MARSHES
MOSCOW
WARSAW
RIGA
TALLINN
HELSINKI
1939 BORDER
1941 BORDER

U. S.-SOVIET ARMIES JOIN
Driving fourteen hundred miles in two and one half years from the great and crucial battle of Stalingrad the Red Army met the U. S. First Army at Torgau, Germany, seven hundred miles from the June Sixth Nineteen Forty Four Dee Day assault on the Normandy Beachheads
6 JUNE 1944
28 APRIL 1945
16 JAN 1945
12 JAN 1944
CAEN
COLOGNE
TORGAU
RADOM
SARNY
KIEV
KHARKOV
STALIN
500 MILES
British Second Army and American Airborne troops deepened Elbe bridgehead threatening to cut off Denmark, while Russians push west from Berlin neared Allied lines.
Red Army victory banners flew over Reichstag May First as Russians crushed last resistance in the ruined Nazi capital. Whereabouts of Hitler and other Nazi leaders was unknown.
Americans and Russians joined at Torgau cutting Germany in two. After U. S. First Army made first juncture both it and U. S. Ninth met Soviets at other points.
U. S. Seventh Army took Munich and moved toward Innsbruck and Brenner Pass as Third Army crashed toward Berchtesgaden and national redoubt in Bavarian Mountains.
Italian front collapsed with Fifth and Eighth Armies taking Turin, Milan, Genoa and Venice and driving toward Brenner Pass. Mussolini was executed by Partisans.
NORTH SEA
BALTIC SEA
FRISIAN ISLANDS
DENMARK
HOLLAND
BELGIUM
GERMANY
POLAND
CZECHOSLOVAKIA
FRANCE
SWITZERLAND
AUSTRIA
ITALY
HUNGARY
YUGOSLAVIA
BATTLELINE 1 MAY
LONDON
PARIS
BERLIN
HAMBURG
Bremen
Hanover
Frankfurt
Cologne
LEIPZIG
DRESDEN
PRAHA
(PRAGUE)
MUNICH
VIENNA
Strasbourg
Stuttgart
Turin
MILAN
Genoa
Venice
Trieste
Bologna
ZURICH
Berne
Geneva
LYON
GULF OF GENOA
STATUTE MILES

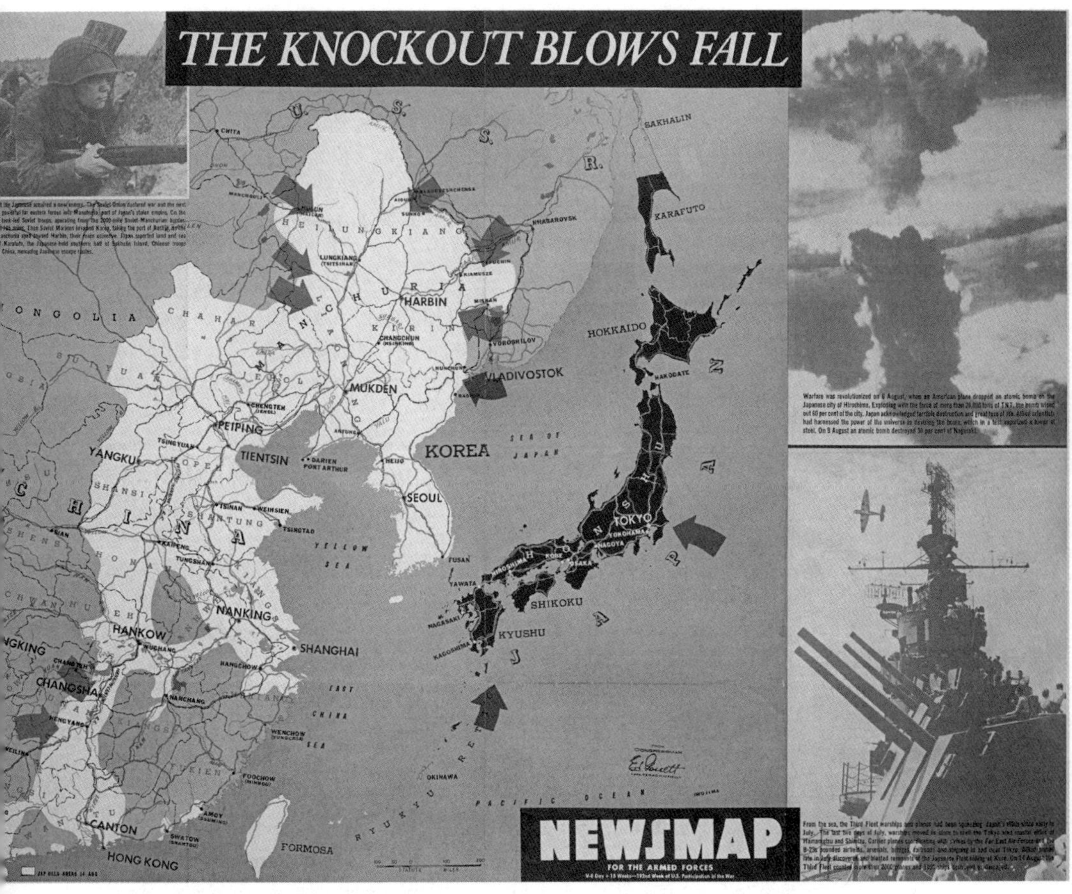

OPPOSITE In this Newsmap for 7 May 1945, covering events of 24 April to 1 May, Nazi Germany is shown almost entirely overrun from East and West. At the top infantrymen of the US 69th Division greet Red Army soldiers on the Elbe River bridge at Torgau. In Italy Mussolini has been shot by partisans on 28 April, while on 2 May German forces agree a ceasefire after Turin has fallen to the advancing Allies.

ABOVE Germany has already surrendered by the time this Newsmap of 20 August appears, depicting the final stages of the war against Japan. Heavy arrows indicate the main points of Allied attack. On 6 August US B29 Superfortress Enola Gay drops an atomic bomb on Hiroshima, creating the terrible mushroom cloud shown at right. On 8 August the Soviets declare war on Japan and invade Japanese-held Manchuria. While to the south Chinese Nationalist forces penetrate territories still occupied by the Japanese there.

Further Reading

MAIN SOURCES

Winston S Churchill, *The Second World War*, vols I-V (Cassell, 1950) Reveals how Britain's war leader quickly realized the urgent necessity of establishing the Takoradi Route, and monitored its progress.

Oliver Clutton-Brock, *Footprints on the Sand of Time: RAF Bomber Command Prisoners of War in Germany 1939-45* (Grub Street Publishing, 2003) In 528 pages, this vast compendium covers all the German PoW camps and lists all 10,995 airmen who were incarcerated in them – including David Bland, together with details of his aircraft and date shot down.

Alex Danchev and Daniel Todman (eds), *Field Marshal Lord Alanbrooke: War Diaries 1939-1945* (Weidenfeld & Nicolson, 2001) Gripping, compulsively readable diaries of this brilliant strategist and formidable Chief of the Imperial General Staff 1941-45, who worked so successfully as a foil to the mercurial, impulsive Churchill.

ICB Dear and MRD Foot (eds), *The Oxford Companion to the Second World War* (Oxford University Press, 1995; selectively updated online edition, 2011) A remarkably comprehensive and authoritative work of reference, with 1,750 entries on different aspects of the war; numerous photographs, maps, tables and chronology.

Will Iredale, *The Pathfinders* (WH Allen, 2021) A brilliantly told story of the brave Pathfinder force that spearheaded Bomber Command's assaults on Germany from 1942; gives a detailed account of David Bland's 35 Squadron mission on 23 August 1943 which resulted in his and 3 other Halifax bombers from the squadron being shot down (see Appendix 1).

Robin Oakley, *Treks & Palavers* (Seeley Service, 1938) Can hardly be bettered as an insight into the mindset – at once altruistic yet to the modern reader patronizing – of a British colonial administrator in Nigeria in the 1920s and 1930s; vivid portrayals in both text and photographs of Kano where Vivian was later stationed.

John Pudney, *Atlantic Bridge: The Official Account of RAF Transport Command's Ocean Ferry* (HMSO, 1945) Best and very readable description of how the Takoradi Route came into being.

RAF Narrative: The West African Reinforcement Route (Air Historical Branch, Air Ministry, n.d.) A formerly secret and substantial account now available in typescript online.

Deborah Wing Ray, 'The Takoradi Route: Roosevelt's Prewar Venture beyond the Western Hemisphere' *The Journal of American History*, vol. 62, no. 2 (1975), pp. 340-358 An eye-opening discussion of how the President circumvented the legal niceties of US neutrality before Pearl Harbor in order to begin supplying American aircraft to the British for the North African campaign.

Anne Ridler, *Collected Poems* (Carcanet Press, 1994) Includes her wartime poems.

—, *Memoirs* (The Perpetua Press, 2004) Includes an account of Vivian and Anne's lives and experiences during the war.

Humphrey Wynn, *Forged in War – A History of RAF Transport Command 1943-1961* (HMSO, 1996) A former Takoradi Route pilot recounts the establishment of Transport Command in the last year of the Route.

—, *Wings Without Weapons* (Woodfield Publishing, 2008) Enjoyable and first-hand account of flying the Takoradi Route by one of the ferry pilots.

THE NORTH AFRICAN, SICILIAN AND ITALIAN CAMPAIGNS

Corelli Barnett, *The Desert Generals*, 2nd edition (Allen & Unwin, 1983) A pioneering account that endeavours to restore the reputation of General Auchinleck, after Montgomery had claimed in his *Memoirs* of 1958 that all was defeat, retreat and confusion before he arrived on the scene.

Artemis Cooper, *Cairo in the War 1939-1945* (paperback reissue, John Murray, 2013) A skilful and entertaining evocation of life in the hothouse atmosphere of the Egyptian capital as the Desert War progressed.

Jonathan Dimbleby, *Destiny in the Desert: The Road to El Alamein* (Profile Books, 2012) Acclaimed analysis of the crucial British victory, setting the battle in its wider context.

James Holland, *Germany Ascendant 1939-1941* The War in the West vol 1 (Bantam Press, 2015) Includes the start of the North African campaign in a compelling narrative; good maps, tables and timeline.

—, *The Allies Fight Back 1941-1943*, The War in the West vol 2 (Bantam Press, 2017) The most recent and probably best account of the North African campaign during the struggle with Rommel, written from multiple points of view; highly readable with maps, tables and timeline.

—, *Sicily '43* (Bantam Press, 2020) Covers the next phase of the Allied fightback in the fullest narrative available.

—, *Italy's Sorrow: A Year of War 1944-45* (HarperPress, 2008) The best and most detailed as well as vivid account of the latter part of this gruelling campaign. See also Holland's *The Savage Storm: The Battle for Italy 1943* (Bantam Press, 2023).

Humphrey Wynn, *Desert Eagles* (Airlife, 1993) Story of two American Kittyhawk pilots in the Desert Airforce.

WORLD WAR II IN GENERAL

Antony Beevor, *The Second World War* (Weidenfeld & Nicolson, 2012) An unsurpassed full narrative treatment of the whole war, written by a preeminent military historian famous for his gripping bestseller *Stalingrad.*

Jonathan Dimbleby, *The Battle of the Atlantic* (Viking, 2015) A masterly account of how crucial to ultimate Allied success was victory in the Atlantic.

Richard J Evans, *The Third Reich at War* (Allen Lane, 2008) Recognized to be a 'terrifying masterpiece' on its publication, this is the most comprehensive and compelling account of Nazi Germany in the war. Insights and revelatory details include the deportation to the Reich of 650,000 Italian soldiers as prisoners of war after Italy had surrendered and their abominable treatment as slave labourers: 50,000 would die.

Victor Davis Hanson, *The Second World Wars* (Basic Books, 2017) Eschewing a strictly narrative approach, an eminent American historian takes different themes – alliances, air power, ships, soldiers, tanks, commanders etc – to paint a fresh picture of the 'first global conflict.'

Max Hastings, *All Hell Let Loose: The World at War 1939-45* (HarperPress, 2011) The brilliant, prolific historian of the 20th-century's wars here vies with Beevor as the author of the best narrative overview of the great conflict.

Neil Kagan and Stephen G Hyslop, *Atlas of World War II* (National Geographic, 2018) The best atlas of the war, combining wartime maps and new cartography with succinct descriptions and timelines of each phase. A cheaper paperback version containing new maps only is also available.

Richard Overy, *Blood and Ruins: The Great Imperial War 1931-1945* (Allen Lane, 2021) A great historian argues in this magisterial but demanding analysis that – seen properly as a conflict between old and aspiring empires for territorial control – World War II began long before 1939; comprises 4 broadly narrative chapters and 7 thematic ones.

Andrew Roberts, *Masters and Commanders: How Roosevelt, Churchill, Marshall and Alanbrooke Won the War in the West* (Allen Lane, 2008) Shrewd and engrossing discussion of the crucial decisions made by the key players among the Western Allies.

——, *The Storm of War: A New History of the Second World War* (Allen Lane, 2009) A fine account by this highly regarded and very readable historian.

Daniel Todman, *Britain's War: Into Battle, 1937–1941* (Allen Lane, 2016) and *Britain's War: A New World, 1942–1947* (Allen Lane, 2020) Two outstanding recent books by the co-editor of Alanbrooke's War Diaries which provide a highly readable chronological account of Britain's part in the war, from a social perspective as much as a military or political one.

BIOGRAPHIES, MEMOIRS & DIARIES

Lord Alexander of Tunis, *The Alexander Memoirs 1940–1945* (Cassell, 1962; reissued with Introduction by James Holland, Pen & Sword Books, 2020) Appointed by Churchill as Middle East C-in-C from 1942, Alexander proved crucial to subsequent Allied success in the Mediterranean, skilfully managing the inflated egos of Montgomery and Patton, and instilling confidence in the men under his command as they fought all the way from Egypt to Tunisia, Sicily and up through Italy.

Edward Ardizzone, *Diary of a War Artist* (The Bodley Head, 1974) Vivid and entertaining illustrated diary entries as this brave non-combatant sketched his way from Egypt to Sicily, Italy and Normandy in his capacity as an Official War Artist.

Christabel Bielenberg, *The Past is Myself* (Chatto & Windus, 1968) A gripping, totally involving memoir of the press baron Lord Northcliffe's niece, who married a German lawyer in 1934 and lived through the war in Germany. When her husband was arrested for his connections with the July 1944 plotters who attempted to assassinate Hitler, she herself had to endure encounters with the ruthless SS.

Charles de Gaulle, *The War Memoirs of Charles de Gaulle: Unity 1942–1944* (Simon & Schuster, 1959) The frank memoirs of the difficult Free French leader, giving his own side of the story in his fraught relationship with the British and Americans, Churchill and Roosevelt especially.

Douglas Fairbanks, Jr, *A Hell of a War* (Robson Books, 1993) The film star writes entertainingly of his time in the US Navy and at Scapa Flow in 1942.

Max Hastings, *Finest Years: Churchill as Warlord 1940–45* (HarperPress, 2009) Engrossing overview complete with the author's often thought-provoking judgments.

James Holland (ed), *An Englishman at War: The Wartime Diaries of Stanley Christopherson DSO MC 1939–45* (Bantam Press, 2014) Plunges one into the reality of war as Christopherson's Sherwood Rangers, a valiant armoured unit, fights its way via El Alamein, Tunis, Normandy, Arnhem and the Rhine to the ruins of Berlin.

Ian Kershaw, *Hitler* (Penguin Books, 2009) For the general reader, this one-volume version of Kershaw's superb biography is probably the best life of the tyrant among a plethora of rival titles.

Simon Sebag Montefiore, *Stalin: The Court of the Red Tsar* (Phoenix, 2004) This and the same author's *Young Stalin* are the two best and utterly compelling lives of the Soviet dictator for the general reader; Robert Service's *Stalin: The Biography* (Macmillan, 2004) is a more academic study by a noted scholar of Soviet Russia.

Alan Moorehead, *The End in Africa* (Hamish Hamilton, 1943) —, *Eclipse* (Hamish Hamilton, 1945).

Tom Pocock, *Alan Moorehead* (The Bodley Head, 1990) Moorehead was the most famous war correspondent of World War II: these three books convey the essence of his fearless frontline reporting. In *Eclipse* we follow him from Sicily to Rome, then Normandy to Arnhem and the 'Battle of the Bulge' and on, finally, to Germany.

Roland Penrose, *The Lives of Lee Miller* (Thames & Hudson, 1985; compact paperback, 2021) Penrose, the son of the great fashion and war photographer Lee Miller, creates a dramatic tale from the many extraordinary episodes in her life, not least in wartime London and later following US troops as they grindingly assault Germany – culminating with the horrors they find after liberating the death camp at Dachau; fully illustrated.

Andrew Roberts, *Churchill: Walking with Destiny* (Allen Lane, 2018) Definitive and masterly life, from cradle to grave.

Mortimer Wheeler, *Still Digging* (Pan Books, 1958) The famous and flamboyant field archaeologist, excavator of Maiden Castle and key sites in India during his tenure as Director-General of Archaeology there, vividly describes his life and how he raised a regiment at the beginning of the war which subsequently fought with distinction in North Africa. Jacquetta Hawkes's biography, *Mortimer Wheeler* (Weidenfeld & Nicolson, 1982), corrects aspects of that story in an admiring account.

Alan Whicker, *Whicker's War* (HarperCollins, 2005) The celebrated postwar television presenter here relives the 660 days he spent narrowly avoiding death as he followed Allied troops all the way from a Sicilian beachhead and up through Italy to the Alps. As Director of the Army Film Unit he recorded many dramatic scenes, not least the sight of Mussolini strung up beside his mistress outside a Milan garage. Riveting and laced with laconic humour.

AIRCRAFT AND THE AIR WAR

Patrick Bishop, *Fighter Boys: The Pilots Behind the Battle of Britain* (HarperCollins, 2003) ——, *Bomber Boys: Fighting Back 1940-1945* (HarperPress, 2007) Acclaimed and bestselling accounts of the airmen who risked their lives to lead the British fightback.

Geoffrey D M Block, *The Wings of Warfare* (Hutchinson, 1945) A useful contemporary account of the air war, with photographs and diagrams of key planes.

Jonathan Glancey, *Spitfire: The Biography* (Atlantic Books, 2020) Entertaining and meticulously researched story of the iconic fighter.

David Mondey, *The Concise Guide to British Aircraft of World War II* (Chancellor Press, 1994) Together with the same author's volumes on American and Axis aircraft in this series (both Chancellor Press, 1996), these are an invaluable source of information about the main fighters and bombers, illustrated in colour as well as with technical diagrams.

Thomas Newdick, *German Fighter Aircraft of World War II* (Amber Books, 2020) This and its companion volume on German bomber aircraft (also Amber Books, 2020) are like the Mondey titles extremely well illustrated in colour.

Richard Overy, *The Bombing War: Europe 1939-1945* (Allen Lane, 2013) The definitive account, dispelling many of the myths about this devastating mode of war.

Adrian Stewart, *Hurricane* (William Kimber, 1982; reissued in paperback Canelo, 2021) A good survey of the exploits of this vital fighter throughout the war; includes an excellent chapter on the plane's role in North Africa and the start of the Takoradi Route. Other well-illustrated accounts are two Osprey titles: *Hurricane Aces 1939-40* by Tony Holmes, and *Hurricane Aces 1941-45* by Andrew Thomas.

Philip Whiteman, *The Aircraft Book* (Dorling Kindersley, 2021) A visual treat in the best DK tradition, this major work of reference covers all the most important aircraft of the past century, notably of World War II.

THE HOME FRONT

Among a variety of titles, three may be mentioned here:

Angus Calder, *The People's War: Britain 1939-45* (Panther Books, 1971) No doubt somewhat out of date half a century after it was written, this 768-page panorama of Britain at war remains an astonishing achievement for its scope and narrative drive; packed with information it's hard to find elsewhere.

David Welch, *Persuading the People: British Propaganda in World War II* (The British Library, 2016) Drawing on the vast archive of the wartime Ministry of Information, which now resides in the British Library, this superbly well-illustrated large-format book shows how a stream of patriotic material encouraged Britons to maintain a stiff upper lip, eat healthily under rationing, and 'know your enemy'.

Jerry White, *The Battle of London 1939-45* (The Bodley Head, 2021) A distinguished professor of London's history, White here conveys through a mosaic of individual experiences what life was actually like in the city as it came under sustained attack during the war years.

Sources of Illustrations

IN-TEXT ILLUSTRATIONS

Half-title NARA
Frontispiece NARA
pages 6-7 Map drawn by Giles Darkes, adapted from John Pudney, *Atlantic Bridge* (HMSO, London, 1945)
p.8 NARA
p.14 Ridler Archive
p.30 NARA
p.34 Ridler Archive
p.142 NARA
p.146 above & below National Museum of the United States Air Force (U.S. Air Force photos)
p.163 Ridler Archive
pp.181-82 Ridler Archive
pp190-91 NARA
pp192-93 David Rumsey Historical Map Collection
p.199 NARA
pp222-23 World War II Newsmaps in UNT Digital Library. University of North Texas Libraries
p.224 World War II Newsmaps in UNT Digital Library. University of North Texas Libraries
p.225 World War II Newsmaps in UNT Digital Library. University of North Texas Libraries
pp.234-35 Ridler Archive

PLATES

1-16 Ridler Archive
17 IWM
18-32 Ridler Archive
33, 34 ETH-Bibliothek
35 Photo by Paul Almasy/Getty Images
36 NARA
37 Precise source unknown
38 NARA
39 IWM
40-42 IWM
43, 44 NARA
45 IWM
46 Library of Congress
47 NARA
48, 49 War Office Second World War Official Collection
50 Bancroft Library, University of California
51, 52 World War II Newsmaps in UNT Digital Library. University of North Texas Libraries
53, 54 NARA
55 NASM
56 Ministry of Information Second World War Official Collection

Acknowledgments

The Editor is much indebted to Roger Bland for providing extracts from his father David's letters that form Appendix 1. Grateful thanks are extended to Michael Schmidt and Carcanet Press for permission to publish two poems, and short quotations from others, taken from Anne Ridler, *Collected Poems* (1994). Hugh, James and Rachel Bradby, and Diana Marchant, spent much time helping to track down Bradby family photographs suitable for publication, as did Jane Scott, which is appreciated. Edward Wates has throughout provided invaluable support in ensuring publication data is made available to the book trade. Richard Deal of Dexter Premedia and Gareth Acreman of Gomer Press have been unfailingly helpful during the production process.

The full-size cover *(ABOVE)* and reduced-size spreads *(OPPOSITE)* for Vivian's colourful alphabet which Faber published in 1942 in a huge edition of 50,000 copies. See also page 34.

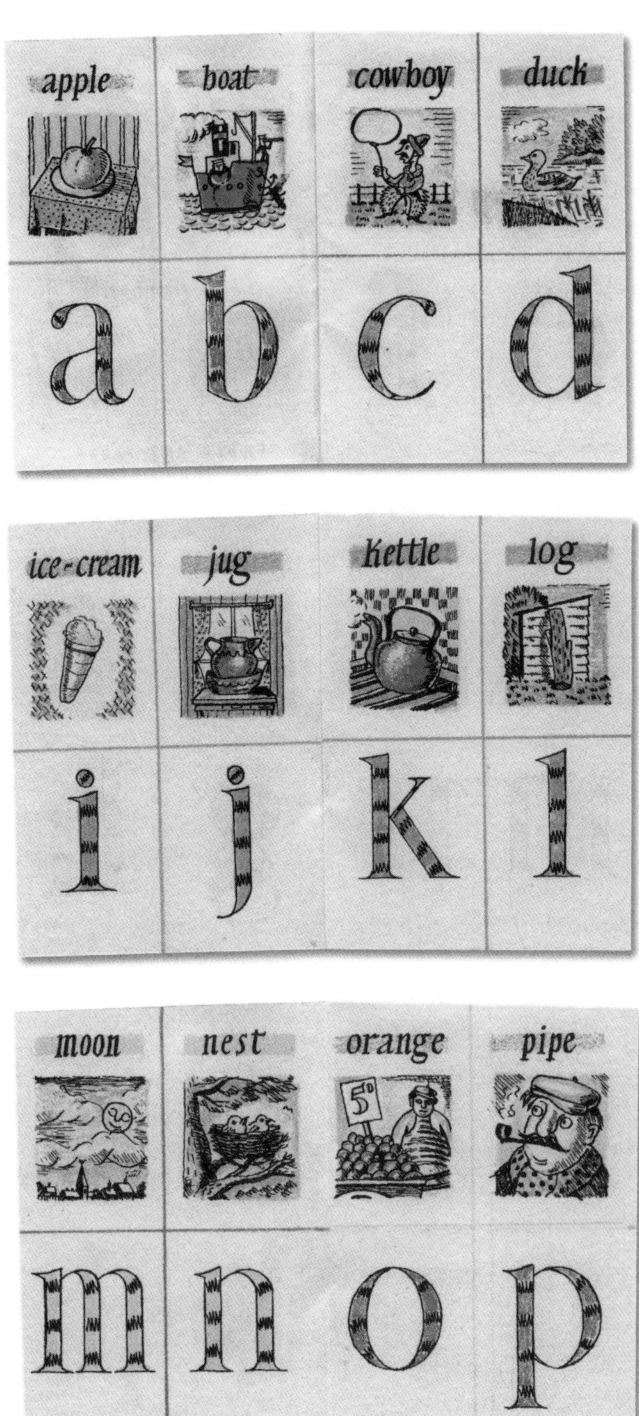
apple
boat
cowboy
duck
a
b
c
d
ice-cream
jug
kettle
log
i
j
k
l
moon
nest
orange
pipe
5D
m
n
o
p

Index

Page numbers in *italic* refer to the illustrations; plates are indicated by plate numbers (pl. 3 etc). All books read and films seen by Vivian Ridler while in Nigeria and recorded in his Diary are listed alphabetically within the main entry covering his life and career.